PROJECT MIND

About the Cover

The cover art, reproduced from a painting by the French mystic, Irene Jacob, depicts rays of Accelerated Thought generated through essence-desire, penetrating and unlocking the secrets of the obscure matter of a dark planet, infusing it with luminescence. Flaring granules emerge as conscious cells to circulate in the blood of the cosmos, vivifying it with love.

In man the microcosm, the matter of this "dark planet" represents opacity of spirit — our resignation to limitation and restriction — the acceptance of "death and taxes." Greed, addiction, envy, sloth, cynicism, pettiness and all kinds of excess are engendered by the culturally mediated, artificial and addictive needs that matter induces in us.

A new, holistic, breakthrough-oriented science with Project Mind as its model will create unlimited material abundance, eliminating physical lack and suffering. More important, it will disperse those acquired, nefarious effects crystallized in our presences, collectively known as materialism. Accelerated Thought, in transforming the abnormal conditions of our distracted existence, will release our minds to experience reality and reveal our true lacks as being essentially non-physical. Our present opacity of essence will give way to the coherent lucidity of divine intelligence as we discover that our "body" is, in reality, all Mind.

·   ·   ·

Project Mind is a utopian concept soliciting active participants for a unique kind of "think tank" whose result would be such material abundance and well-being that mankind would be free to fulfill its infinite potential.

Project Mind

The Conscious Conquest of Man & Matter
through Accelerated Thought

T. Kun

Unimedia Publishing

Indian Rocks Beach, Florida

Zinor imprint design by Richard Carlow.

A Zinor Book, Published by Unimedia, Indian Rocks Beach, Florida.
Printed in the United States of America on acid-free paper.
Copyright © 1993. All rights reserved, including the right to
reproduce this book or parts thereof in any form.

Text includes quotations from *A Feeling for the Organism*: *The Life
and Work of Barbara McClintock*, by Evelyn Fox Keller. Copyright
© 1983 by W. H. Freeman and Company. Reprinted by permission.

Library of Congress Cataloging in Publication Data

Kun, T., 1945-
    Project mind : the conscious conquest of man and matter through
accelerated thought / T. Kun.
          p.   cm.
    Includes bibliographical references and index.
    ISBN 1-880646-02-1
    1. Psychology and philosophy   2. Philosophy of mind.   3. Mind
and body.   I. Title.
BF41.K86 1993   92-41961
150'.1--dc20   CIP

TABLE of CONTENTS

ACKNOWLEDGEMENTS vii

INTRODUCTION ix

NOTE to the READER xii

OVERVIEW xvi

CHAPTER ONE 1
     Things Are Not What They Seem

CHAPTER TWO 7
     Lessons in Life

CHAPTER THREE 21
     A World in Danger — Matter, Greed & Separation • Matter —
     Perdition or Paradise? • Truth & Freedom

CHAPTER FOUR 31
     False Bases of Hope • New possibilities for a New Age • Mind
     over Matter — Misconceptions & Possibilities

CHAPTER FIVE 41
     Creativity & Breakthrough — Conventionality & Distraction •
     Creativity, Eureka & Accelerated Thought • Creative Individu-
     als as Subjects for Accelerated Thought • Existing Conditions
     Discourage Creativity • The Need for Self-Knowledge • Ab-
     straction & the Illusion of Freedom • Form as Intermediary
     Between Mind & Matter.

CHAPTER SIX 71
     Thought Transformation — the Search for Meaning & Purpose
     • Vision of Truth and Utopia, Fundamental to our Humanity

CHAPTER SEVEN 83

    Special Conditions Needed to Promote Accelerated Thought • Thought Compression — Focusing to Break out of Distraction • Meaning & Awareness — Knowledge & Reality • A Clear Direction • Energy Accumulation & Illumination

CHAPTER EIGHT 103

    Breakthrough, Time & Matter • Difficulty & Stagnation • Overcoming Deflection • The Worst of Subjectivity — Society & Transcendence

CHAPTER NINE 121

    Certainty — The Key to Objective Consciousness • Certainty, Truth & the Compulsion to Share • Matter & Objectivity • Formulating Hypotheses — Groping for Reality • Insight & Vision — Views of the Real World

CHAPTER TEN 131

    Materiality — Fine & Coarse Subjective & Objective • Meaning • Truth as Touchstone — Becoming Free of Matter-Induced Pathology • The Pitfalls & Perils of Commitment • Mind Processes & the Energy of Anticipation

CHAPTER ELEVEN 141

    Dynamics of Thought, Feeling and Action • Inner Integration — Assimilating Reality • Social Opposition & the Budding Deviant • Commitment, Integration & Transformation • Fusion, Will & Objectivity • Extrapolation & Objective Consciousness • Idea Universes, Meaning & Connectedness • Mind-Bodies & Immortality

CHAPTER TWELVE 161

    Questions and Answers

APPENDIX 197

GLOSSARY 259

REFERENCES 267

INDEX 271

QUOTATION INDEX 279

ACKNOWLEDGEMENTS

Due to circumstances beyond my control, I am master of my
fate and captain of my soul. (Ashleigh Brilliant)

This book is written in the name of man's[*] love of life and, more specifically, the guardian spirit of that love which lies dormant, undefined and undeveloped throughout much of mankind. It is dedicated to all uncompromising seekers of Truth. It constitutes a call and challenge to those souls who consciously nurture a conviction that all constraints weighing upon the human spirit can and must be eliminated. By using the highest forms of intelligence, courage and skill man can begin the sacred task of dissolving that which separates him from the fulfillment of his most cherished desires, including the desire for eternal life.

We witness man's love of life in his desire to discover all that existence can offer. We see it in his hope, his anticipation, his striving, his exhilaration and in all his adventures whether intellectual, emotional or physical. We see it in focused appreciation, during moments of quiet contemplation and in partaking of all life's pleasures.

In his love of the moment he doesn't consider his own transience as the most salient of all realities. Like the fabled grasshopper, he dances in the warmth of summer, ignoring the ant's warning of winter's approach.

A fully felt love of life implies the determination to preserve that life with every means one can muster. This does not preclude celebration, even in the face of death. Nevertheless, the principal preoccupation of someone condemned to death — as we all are — should be to work conscientiously to overcome it. Anything less implies that we have lost contact with life and with our love of it. In truth, are not all our triumphs in life, in the secret of our hearts, little triumphs over death?

Note: For ease of exposition, the pronoun "he" as well as "man," "mankind" and "humanity" will be used in the generic sense throughout this book.

This book is for those whose attachment to life remains sufficiently strong that they want to understand the reasons for their existential predicament. Herein is offered a view toward practical, concerted action for that predicament's resolution.

Sentimentality aside, in addition to friends who have offered practical and moral support I must thank my father (may his soul rest in peace), mother, wife, brother, sister, and lifetime fan, Lois. Also, there is Moe who pushed me into writing. I express special gratitude to all the philosophers and geniuses who have inspired, influenced or supported my thinking, many of whom are quoted in this work.

Worthy of special mention is Barbara McClintock, Nobel Prize-winning biologist. In her biography, *A Feeling for the Organism* by Evelyn Fox Keller, she exemplifies the creative hero in her solo attempts at what I call "Accelerated Thought." I know of no other work that describes such attempts as well, and she is quoted extensively. I owe a similar debt of gratitude to Ayn Rand, whose vivid, artistic, uncompromising portrayal of true life principles has made her a faithful ally in my struggles against the spirit of death. Her words, quoted in this book, are wielded in the name of that struggle. I feel a similar debt to Viktor Frankl, who does his best to remind us all that man is essentially a creature of meaning, and to Arthur Koestler, who sparked my thinking on creativity. Likewise I am indebted to Erich Fromm, who helped me reflect upon the act of giving.

Since the world in which we live is still largely one of restriction and obscurity, I wish particularly to thank all those who along the way had the power and opportunity to obstruct my progress but who refrained, in whatever measure and for whatever reason, from doing so. For it is probably upon them, as much as anything else, that my success in the venture that is the subject of this book depends.

Lastly, I wish to thank my teachers of Truth. They know who they are. This book is my first concrete offering justifying their efforts.

•   •   •

INTRODUCTION

The best of being a writer is the opportunity given to show man his true worth, to lift up his own idea of himself, to persuade him that trivial aims are not enough. (Paul Brunton)

Project Mind is about possibilities — real, human possibilities. It addresses the ultimate in man and his hidden capacities. Through an intelligence which for the moment lies dormant, mankind is destined to acquire a degree of mastery over the matter of this world that even science fiction has not had the temerity to portray. This yet-to-be-revealed intelligence is in fact unlimited. Potentially, man has infinite capacities. Fantastic as it may seem, if man survives he is destined for what would have to be called omniscience, omnipotence and, most important, immortality.

Most people are hard-core believers in "death and taxes" and the idea that everything that is fun must necessarily be "illegal, immoral or fattening." Not everybody has unlimited faith in mankind's potential. If they did, a book like this would not be necessary. My purpose is not to gush on about man's potential, but to illustrate the why and how of the realization of that potential and to help bring it to fruition.

More specifically, this book is about a project more critical and sophisticated than the Manhattan Project, and yet more humane than the Bauhaus or even Mother Theresa. Its object is to release the full force of intelligence imprisoned within the human form. Anyone who has had even a furtive glimpse into his own inner process of creativity has been amazed by the power lying quiescent inside. The lasting impression of such a glimpse can provide the impetus for many an adventure into art, science, mysticism, and religion.

Creative energy is elusive. As a rule, despite initial ardor one soon becomes deterred in one's efforts and diverted into conventional low-energy channels. It is not easy to split the atom, let alone set off a chain reaction. Yet analogically this is what must be done if the mind-power bottled within the human essence is to be released. Those who wish to marvel at man's untapped psychic resources often suggest that man has access to about one-tenth of his mental capacity. Occasionally, under pretense of insight into human nature, one may claim that man uses only one percent. This book will clearly show that man does not use even one-ten-thousandth of his mind and why. It also will show the process whereby man's mind can be freed from the constant taxation of distraction and thus become energized to a completely new level of emotional and mental consciousness.

One calls isolated incidents of short bursts of creative energy "Eureka" experiences, and their aesthetic equivalents "peak experiences." I call a chain reaction of Eureka experiences "Accelerated Thought," and my project to generate Accelerated Thought "Project Mind."

Eureka experiences are not that uncommon. They arise in situations where one makes concerted efforts to solve seemingly intractable problems. The more difficult the problem and the greater the effort, the more energy is released. The roles of ambition and motivation are crucial. In the rare cases, where one directs one's effort at a problem of extreme personal significance, the energy level at the moment of illumination spills over, throwing light upon other, seemingly unrelated questions. This kind of chain reaction is likely to catch a person off guard and destabilize him psychologically, precipitating a "spiritual emergency." Spiritual emergencies, like Eureka experiences, are not all that uncommon. They can cause one to reorient one's life and dedicate it to a higher purpose.

While man's hidden possibilities are important, the main thrust of Project Mind is action-oriented and aims at transforming physical matter, usually considered the domain of the "hard" sciences - physics in particular. After all, what would be the sense of enormously enhancing the power of thought if not to vastly improve and even completely alter the conditions in which man finds himself? Hasn't the bottom line of intelligence always been its application in the physical world? Physical facts and conditions are the common denominator to which all of mankind is subject — the influence before which all are obliged to submit sooner or later.

Among the restrictions weighing upon my spirit that led me to the plan outlined in this book were the multifarious human manifestations of pettiness, narrow-mindedness, shallowness and short-sightedness both in others and myself. I will show that regardless of what social or psychological forms they assume, these stem entirely from material limitations. The form of limitation most commonly encountered is the lack of "cold cash." Yet, there is another that affects us all, knowingly or unknowingly, even long before we are fully introduced to the world of money, property and greed. This is the final and most terrifying of limitations — death.

Notwithstanding reports of those who "pass over" peacefully and willingly after having lived a "full life," real encounters with death can leave indifferent only those whose constitutions have substantially lost their capacity for producing life energy, or who for other reasons are already spiritually dead. Whatever life awaits us on "the other side" cannot abrogate our responsibility or attachment to this one. Reconciliation with death is possible and even desirable, but only when the force of life in us has largely declined and no further options remain.

Before this happens, the creative life-intelligence lent us from on high offers us a chance to solve the cosmic riddle of obscurity and death. Death is not inevitable. We need a critical mass — a handful of competent researcher-visionaries — to release us from the prison of cosmic restriction and convention. Only then will the mass of men recognize that the cosmos is 99.99% spirit, the matter component constituting the mere shell of reality. Only then will the spiritual attainment dreamt of through the ages come within reach.

> *I suspect that we are not the light of consciousness in a dead universe, but the local darkness in a universe of life. (Thaddeus Golas)*

• • •

NOTE to the READER

Project Mind provides a theoretical, philosophical, psychological and metaphysical basis for Project Mind. The conceptual underpinning of this book is elucidated through a hypothetical "subject" who exemplifies a candidate for "Accelerated Thought." The final chapter consists of questions and answers to help the reader review important aspects of what is proposed and to clarify both subtle and possibly controversial points.

Since Project Mind proposes a new "essence" theory of reality, the glossary at the end provides definitions of commonly-used terms offering a new degree of precision based on the theory. Referring to them occasionally will help refresh the reader's memory of their technical meanings as assigned herein.

The appendix provides a running commentary on the main text, facilitating comprehension and providing additional depth and insight. It is strongly recommended that it be read in conjunction with the text. Most comments on spirituality have been confined to the appendix so as not to interrupt the logical development of the main theme.

Although the psychological process is described quite thoroughly, the physical plant, precise techniques and special arrangements of Project Mind are touched upon but lightly. There are many reasons for this. Some of these reasons include the wish not to overstimulate the imagination of potential candidates, the wish to avoid the oversimplification and stereotyping that can come from providing points of reference that are overly concrete, and the wish to discourage premature and hapless experimentation. To the reader who recognizes the cogency of the project, these details can for the moment be foregone; to one who does not, they would add very little.

Accelerated Thought will be shown to be the epitome of human creativity. Most descriptions attempting to explain the psychological intricacies of the creative process point to the importance of intuition and the subconscious. But many of the phenomena commonly associated with creativity do not, strictly speaking, pertain to the process of creative thought proper. These will be shown to be merely telltale symptoms of the mind trying to break out of a confused, tangled maze of conventional, distracted consciousness.

While Project Mind is about transformation, it is not restricted to "spiritual" or "inner" work. Such work has as its explicit object self-knowledge and consciousness. The kind of effort proposed in this book is patently outwardly directed, promoting change in the material world. While self-knowledge and consciousness accrue at least to some degree to the author of any kind of effort that makes him confront life, the purpose of efforts promoting "Accelerated Thought" are not specifically directed to the accumulation of inner substance or virtue. Viktor E. Frankl, Ph.D., the originator of logotherapy, has this to say:

> Self-actualization is not man's ultimate destination. It is not even his primary intention. Self-actualization if made an end in itself, contradicts the self-transcendent quality of human existence. Like happiness, self-actualization is an effect, the effect of meaning fulfillment. Only to the extent to which man fulfills a meaning out there in the world, does he fulfill himself. If he sets out to actualize himself rather than fulfill a meaning, self-actualization immediately loses its justification.
>
> In my view, excessive concern with self-actualization may be traced to a frustration of the will to meaning. As the boomerang comes back to the hunter who has thrown it only if it has missed its target, man, too, returns to himself and is intent upon self-actualization only if he has missed his mission.[*]

Even the controversial and irreverent Rushdie contends that:

> A Man who sets out to make himself up is taking on the Creator's role, according to one way of seeing things; he's unnatural, a blasphemer, an abomination of abominations.[**]

Nor is Accelerated Thought the object of the effort. It is only a process, the means to an end — that of transforming the world. The individual achieves his aim through the path he finds most meaningful, through channels that give him the most satisfaction — even if such satisfaction is seen by those more "spiritual" as being strictly egoistic.

In fact, the full force of the "self" must be harnessed through the process of Accelerated Thought in pursuit of a particular aim. Such a

---

* Viktor E. Frankl, *The Will to Meaning* (N.Y.: NAL Penguin, 1988), 38.
** Salman Rushdie, *The Satanic Verses* (U.K.: Viking Penguin, 1988), 49.

pursuit gives real meaning to the concept of "mission" or "vocation." This alone should suffice to remove Accelerated Thought from the category of spiritual work as it is normally understood (although any outward-oriented mission or endeavor, if taken seriously, should have spectacular implications for the inner life of the adventurer).

Finally, I want to dispel any notions about my own spiritual pretensions, especially concerning my convictions regarding man's potentials and the measures necessary for their realization. These convictions have come, for the most part, from brief moments of vision provoked by life predicaments. While these moments constituting the basis of my speculations have found confirmatory echoes in my spiritual practice (such as it is), intellectual speculation of whatever origins is never a substitute for spiritual work. Inner work, properly done, is purely experiential and the results never fail to surpass our imagining. While the requirements of life in no way obviate direct contact with the substance of life (contact which spiritual discipline can provide), neither does spirituality alleviate responsibility for acting in the face of the material challenges that life puts in one's path. I have met many people whose inner work surpasses mine in very great measure, and a few whose spiritual attainment to the degree that I have been able to discern its workings leaves me completely in awe. Yet even the most accomplished in this regard often differ substantially from one another when it comes to questions of ideology and practical action.

There is no accounting for individual differences. Quite apart from the different influences that "accidentally" come into our respective lives, we all have talents, tendencies, desires and temperaments that make us unique. To the extent that we are not completely brainwashed by what others think, these give us our particular way of relating to the world. The real differences that make up our potential as individuals are said to be rooted in our essence — a kind of seed — that awaits its true expression through spiritualized fertilization. This fertilization or realization comes about through direct contact with reality, something largely denied us by the artificial, agitating, distracting nature of our corrupted conditions of existence. So we sometimes resort to methods akin to meditation which provide countervailing conditions of immobility and silence in which we seek to reestablish contact with that reality and the eternal life from which it springs.

One of the main hypotheses underlying this book is that the deepest and most individuating aspects of essence are inaccessible by traditional techniques. According to one's degree of spiritual accomplishment, such techniques tend to penetrate only our superficial layers. This dilemma, I maintain, calls for artfulness, cunning, intuition, sincerity and determination on the part of every individual truly concerned with the pursuit of his destiny and true calling. Once it is found, this calling will involve him in a struggle with the substance of reality more intensely than could anything else. It is presumed that this struggle will bring into play transformational forces more powerful than those generated by other methods. General methods are better suited to preparatory inner work — keeping in mind that preparation is never finished and that the virtuoso never ceases to practice.

On the other hand, the novice pursuing any discipline, even if heavily immersed in exercises, must not be discouraged from improvising in the pursuit of his personal note. Striking results can sometimes flow from improvisation.

Caution: Please be advised that this book does not contain prescriptions for meditation, creative thinking or for mind experiments of any kind. Neither the author nor the publisher can be held responsible for psychological pathology in readers. All experimentation described in this book refers to efforts under controlled conditions, connected with and reserved for realization within Project Mind once it is established.

References to drug use and drug users are included only for illustrative purposes and are not meant to imply approval of recreational or hallucinatory drugs; nor is their use within Project Mind contemplated.

•   •   •

OVERVIEW

The Lord God is subtle, but malicious He is not. (Albert Einstein)

Considering the myriad books vying for your attention, I apologize for appearing to add to the general confusion with this one. I take refuge in claiming that this is not really a book at all, but a prospectus for the project called "Project Mind." Unlike most "books," this one is not meant to inform, educate, improve, amuse, please, satisfy or convert the reader, but rather to recruit the help of those who wish, with their whole selves, to radically transform for the best what we presently call "reality."

— T. Kun

Project Mind — the "book" — elucidates the why and how of Accelerated Thought and the role of Project Mind — the project. Project Mind is to be the pilot project and model for a new vision-driven, breakthrough-oriented science. Accelerated Thought will be the chief method of this benign new science. The aim of both this text and the project is to find candidates for participation having the will and courage to transform the world physically and spiritually through Accelerated Thought, and to help them accomplish this aim.

Just as the Eureka experience provides brief moments of brilliant insight — the divine sparks of genius and inspiration that have fueled the sudden advances in scientific progress until now — Accelerated Thought will provide sustained creative vision. This will establish an ongoing link with higher consciousness, producing a powerful cosmic current channeled through human essence (man's fundamental form and substance) from a higher dimension to fuel the transformatory breakthrough science of the future and render it holistic and comprehensive.

The accelerated creation of scientific breakthroughs engendered by Accelerated Thought will, within a few years, produce such material abundance that the pursuit of material wealth will lose all meaning. Not only will material lack, deprivation and suffering disappear from the human landscape, but greed, envy, pettiness, sloth, vice and depravity, induced in us by overindulgence and by the kind of competition that tends to turn us all into adversaries, will become irrelevant and vanish.

As the conditions of our existence become transformed and our corruption is dissolved at its root, we will be confronted with the fact that existence is 99.99% spiritual and only 0.01% physical and that we are all brothers in that spirit. Our fraternity, we will find, is based not only on equality and the shared commonalities of our Being as is normally believed, but, more cogently, on the interdependence of our unique and varied individualities. These individualities persist in finding expression mostly through such neurotic ego-phenomena as false personality, authoritarianism, careerism, racism, and fetishes and fanaticisms of all varieties. With our common consciousness released from almost universal resignation to the inevitability of "death and taxes," we will reveal through direct experience that not just the brain but our whole body is Mind.

Project Mind will prove the "essence" theory of intelligence. Accelerated Thought will be shown to be the manifestation of inborn genius sequestered within the essence-desire of every human being. Project Mind will help its participants unearth the irresistible power of essential desire — the motor of Accelerated Thought — to be found at the core of all mankind. True individuals — those of extraordinary courage and integrity who show a proclivity towards intensely independent, original thought, despite the crushing pressure of convention and conformity — will be the first to make use of the uniquely supportive environment that Project Mind will offer.

Project Mind will encourage the full, creative expression of individuality through the cultivation of Accelerated Thought. Although it will use special psychological techniques, environmental aids and sophisticated computerization, the key of Project Mind is its understanding of the fundamental nature and importance of essential individuality. To generate the ultimate expression of individuality is to release the incredible potential hidden at the deepest levels within essence and reveal the relationship of essence to consciousness, reality and truth. Accelerated

Thought as a function of objective consciousness will penetrate the deepest secrets of material reality and lead to world elimination of lack, restriction, ignorance, vice and suffering.

In some respects, Project Mind can be likened to a mineral refining process. Most important is recognizing the potential of the resource in question. The unique resource recognized by Project Mind is the essential desire of individuality. Then comes the problem of locating rich and accessible deposits, followed by the delicate techniques of extraction and refining.

The pioneers of Accelerated Thought will be those whose adult integrity and force of individuality have been built upon the act of heroic courage in childhood to say "the emperor is naked," and who sustained their belief in the utopian vision of fairy tales. They are the "accessible deposits." They must be found and recruited. The process of mining and extraction relies mainly on intuition, courage and deep-seated conviction. These empower the desire to unearth and come to terms with the essential truths underlying the question or problem each of us was born to solve. Refining corresponds to the delineation and elaboration of vision with a view to practical application. Special attention must be given to the delicate balance of heat and pressure instrumental in burning away volatile impurities of intention so as not to endanger essential substance until elemental desire begins to reveal truth and manifest as Mind.

The new science & technology will rapidly put material independence — the freedom to form and transform matter at will — into the hands of the individual. The commercial exploitation of scientific breakthroughs generated through Project Mind and its clones — replications that will inevitably spring up in science and industry — will follow its natural course. Modes of exploitation and the attitudes of those who concern themselves with commercialization will increasingly reflect a genuine concern for the welfare of others as the trend away from the covetous and cynical accumulation of wealth and power becomes established.

The utopian conditions postulated by Project Mind will not spell the culmination of humanity or signal a state of stagnation, but will be man's first real emancipation. Freed from the obscuring distraction stemming from material lack, man will discover that what he had always called "desire" and "will" was in fact impulse, inclination, appetite and craving. In feeling the first stirrings of authentic, spiritually-oriented essential desire, he will have begun his odyssey in a world of multi-layered reality, an adventure in which freedom from physical and biological restrictions will be only the first of many steps.

Reality, the newly-won friend of our essence, will be preferable to any "virtual" or simulated reality. Spiritual striving of whatever color will no longer be the uncertain, tedious, interminable, fluctuating, elitist affair it has been for millennia. Instead, it will be a universal, transparent movement in which all will share consciously — each according to his particular essence — thanks to the dissipation of the distracting and confusing influence of material lack and the pettiness it breeds in man's spirit. With unobstructed reality as our teacher, the empowered essence of each of us will unfold, revealing that its myriad facets are conditioned by unity and are in harmony with it.

•   •   •

CHAPTER ONE

Things Are Not What They Seem

There are too many distractions. You should enter a ball park as you would enter a church. (William Francis Lee III)

The notion of "distraction" is a key, lending sense to ideas and realities that would otherwise elude most readers. It is the touchstone permitting us to look at reality and at ourselves in a new way. Although psychologically and emotionally difficult to acknowledge, it offers us the possibility of a substantial opening in our capacity for understanding.

Anyone interested in verifying the implacable truth of our distracted state can do so with a few moments of sincere effort of self-observation. For instance, try to concentrate continuously upon anything at all for more than a few seconds and notice how quickly your attention waivers and random associations take you off into vaguely related thoughts and then into reverie. Ouspensky suggests this exercise:

> *Take a watch and look at the second hand, trying to be aware of yourself, and concentrating on the thought, "I am Peter Ouspensky, I am now here." Try not to think about anything else, simply follow the movements of the second hand and be aware of yourself, your name, your existence, and the place where you are. Keep all other thoughts away.*
>
> *You will if you are persistent, be able to do this for two minutes. This is the limit of your consciousness. And if you try to repeat the experiment soon after, you will find it more difficult than the first time.*
>
> *This experiment shows that a man, in his natural state, can with great effort be conscious of one subject (himself) for two minutes or less.*
>
> *The most important deduction one can make after making this experiment in the right way is that man is not conscious of himself. The illusion of his being conscious of himself is created by memory and thought processes.**

---

* P. D. Ouspensky, *The Psychology of Man's Possible Evolution* (New York: Vintage Books, 1973), 19-20.

Next, try to observe strangers in the street and make an impartial mental list of things you notice about them. Almost immediately you will begin to ruminate automatically — with or without words — on whether various people attract or repel you, or whether something about them reminds you of someone or something you like or don't like. We could go on, chewing our emotional cuds about some compliment we received, or some insult, and all this without ever really seeing the individual who triggered these self-congratulatory or self-defensive ruminations.

Few people ever actually attempt this experiment, preferring to imagine that they know very well what will happen and that they, at least to this extent, are masters of their own powers of attention. We would be genuinely horrified to see just how much of our time and energy flows into such states of reverie. Nor do we easily grasp that such inner chatter has become habitual since childhood. It is such an ingrained mechanism for justifying ourselves and condemning others, for measuring everything and anything as to whether it constitutes a force working for us or against us, that it long ago passed almost entirely out of our field of awareness. This happens in much the same way that we lose contact with all but the tiniest part of our nighttime dreams. Much like dreaming, this constant muttering has become an embedded, unconscious state underlying our overt mental activity. We recognize it only when it becomes sufficiently intrusive to attract our notice. We experience it as mood.

If our lives are reasonably balanced, in the everyday sense of the word, we don't take much notice of our moods or daydreams. Yet our general mien communicates something of our state to others. It varies with the particular axe we have to grind and with how we currently feel about things. If we make the effort to tune into the moods broadcasting from the innards of those around us, we may perceive what a given person is about: that is, the approximate contents of his inner ruminations. To understand someone's personality largely means to have insight into the coloration of his inner chatter. For despite the impression we would like to make upon others, it is the mood of this inner dialogue emanating from us that identifies us to others and gives us away to our adversaries.

At rare intervals, when conditions around us are sufficiently reassuring, we may momentarily abandon our inner reflection. For the brief moment during which we are emotionally convinced that existence is benign, we may let our inner guard down long enough to experience vibrations of peacefulness and serenity. More often, positive feedback from the environment, friendly smiles, compliments, various omens of impending good fortune, etc., are likely to amplify our inner prattling and self-congratulation to the point that it breaks through the surface as a "good mood." Regardless of how concentrated we think we are in the task at hand, it is this mood that will carry us through, for it is this substrate of self-congratulatory prattle that represents the substance of what is really going on inside us.

More often still, the environment tends to send us less encouraging messages — messages that provoke unconscious, reflective reverie of a negative and self-defensive nature. A growing overlay of anxiety can bring us to interpret even neutral signals as vaguely threatening. Thus, quite unconsciously we mistake a blank look for a critical frown, someone brushing against us as intentional aggression, or overcast weather as personal affront. Whatever imbues our inner dialogue with pessimistic or injurious content may eventually agitate our unconscious enough to break through the clouds of our minds, first as mild irritation, and later as a bad or ugly mood.

Occasionally we catch ourselves muttering inwardly about the awful state of things. We are more likely to take the contents of such a chance observation for an isolated snit rather than the symptom of an ongoing state of emotionally charged, inner dialogue. So, erroneously, we take the observed symptoms for the result rather than the cause of our mood. More often, we consider moods as conditions that mysteriously come and go like the weather. While we vaguely recognize that circumstances cause moods, we often have trouble identifying the exact reason for a mood at any given moment. Moods are occasionally interrupted by sudden noises and other shocks that jolt and awaken us momentarily from our state of reverie. Whatever it is that brings us back to the present either goes away by itself or quickly loses its startling effect. We then fall back on our confirmed psychological crutch of incessant inner talk.

We resemble, more than we care to admit, those vagrants and derelicts — the demented and the distraught — who walk the streets and halls of institutions speaking to themselves out loud. They suspect no more than we that they are in dialogue with themselves and that they, like us, talk themselves into their moods based on chance encounters and mental associations that trigger emotionally-laden trains of thought and reasoning. Completely absorbed, they no longer have any source of free attention with which to observe themselves and gain insight into their condition. Without self-observation to force an opening in this wall of talk, they remain closed and fixed. Reactions are almost always disproportionately greater than the puny stimuli which pretend to be their cause. It is likewise for the "normal" person, unless through astute introspection he can somehow become aware of his predicament.

Whether our moods are good, bad or indifferent, a durable fabric of reverie is woven by the commentary of our incessant inner chatter. The relentlessness of this inner chatter produces an almost impenetrable barrier, forming something not unlike a crust or shell that day by day grows thicker around our faculties for perceiving reality. This phenomenon is so pronounced that we become like a certain fruit that is mostly rind — for the "outer" develops at the expense of the "inner." The elements that make up this pseudo-conscious surface or veil that separates us from direct contact with life consists of little more than wishes and fears — minor fantasies that render the hard implacable world of physical reality sufferable to our weakened psyches.

Another important aspect of distraction is the psychological trait of suggestibility. The extreme reactivity of distraction — our inability to stay open and in a state of question and wonder — causes us to stick obstinately to opinions with which we strongly identify. Since our psychology cannot deal with every contingency, we tend to fall prey to doubt whenever some unforeseen situation catches us without a ready-made solution. We are fair game to anyone studied in the art of human manipulation and practiced in the technique of evoking uncertainty and doubt. We are addicted to closure and thus suggestible to any formula that answers our uncertainty without too greatly offending our already unstable ideological structure.

Our psychological husk of reflection needs penetrating so that we can be pried loose from our screen of dreams and fixed positions. We need to gain some contact with reality, at least long enough to take stock of ourselves and devise a strategy to escape the depleting effects of distraction. This is the shared objective of many, if not most, spiritual systems which use a whole panoply of methods to "still the mind." Peeling away layers of bark to gradually expose our inner cores to light is a slow, arduous process, sometimes said to take "many lifetimes." Also, esoteric, occult, mystical and other spiritual systems offer no guarantees.

The likelihood of any given individual arriving at a healthy mistrust of his habitual state of awareness or his ability to formulate meaningful goals or pursue them with any degree of constancy is very small indeed. There must be some less introspective, less obscure, less esoteric and less elitist road out of the morass of contradiction and confusion that characterizes a life bounded by the hopelessness and futility of death. Such a life reduces us all in one way or another to the pursuit of short-term, evanescent, vain and petty satisfactions — material and spiritual.

Most important, too many spiritual systems tend to condemn desire — even those emanating from our core or "essence" — as seats of corruption. Or they discount desire as a factor for inner development. Nevertheless, a truly powerful desire emanating deep from the heart of us can become the seed of an activity, vocation or project engaging one so totally as to require one to overcome his own distraction and break loose of the tissue of lies separating him from outer reality and his inner self. Through passionate struggle and friction with reality, man's multitude of fractionated desires can be welded into one indomitable will. In the process of realizing his outer goal he can almost inadvertently realize his own inner self.

Spiritual systems cannot be faulted for underscoring the dangers facing those who embark on the pursuit of truth. Sincerity in knowing what one wants, and why, has a great deal to do with what one is likely to find along the path of adventure. Purity of motive will to a great extent determine what we succeed in revealing through our powers of creativity as we dare to participate consciously in the unique, creative current of existence to which we belong. The pursuit of and occasional direct contact with our personal truth (i.e., essence-desire) will serve as a better motivator and give a better reason to strive for purity than will the pursuit of an occasional (existential) contact with some collective and largely abstract ideal expressed as a fine vibrational inner state.

This places us squarely before the question: How in practice are we to access the vast archive of aeons of recorded experience within us and benefit from what we most essentially are? What is to stop us from succumbing to the illusion that everyday intelligence (characterized in this book as "reflective" and "distracted" thought) is the "evolutionary" result and quintessence of what we, as human beings, were meant to be?

We must consider that, because of certain requirements of nature which as yet largely defy our understanding, our species has been constrained to live very superficially. As such, we are deprived of the bliss and harmony which, according to myth, is our rightful legacy. We might take stock of the inferences with which we saddle our "knowledge" and reconsider the very aims, goals and purposes we have espoused for ourselves individually and as a species. Can we admit that we have adopted these meanings without the benefit of even a fraction of the cosmic experience that under better circumstances might have accrued to us as our natural evolutionary birthright?

I have outlined some of the psychological aspects of distraction. Further on, I will touch upon the social aspects and the underlying cause of both (i.e., the restrictive influence of physical reality). My main purpose is not to catalog the phenomena of what could be termed "the pathology of conventional consciousness," nor to record the phenomenology of awakening to states of higher consciousness which constitute the natural psychic terrain for creativity. Rather, I will try to cut through the polemics and speculation, however useful or interesting these might seem, and get to what is needed. We need experimental conditions for the promotion of the spectacularly accelerated achievement of scientific and technical breakthroughs leading to universal prosperity and well-being so that the abnormal conditions of our existence which keep us prisoners in distraction may be transformed and our real needs — spiritual ones — revealed.

I maintain that our well-being will be reached only in the process of attaining to an objective consciousness. A universally credible and objective basis of hope for a better existence than is now thought possible must be established, lest we pay the final price for the distraction in which we are immersed. Accordingly, this book will stay close to the essentials of how Accelerated Thought is to be generated, especially as concerns consciousness and its transformation.

Before passing final judgment on the proposed project or on where if anywhere he might fit in, it is recommended that the reader allow time to digest this material. One is not often afforded new opportunities for self-realization. The question and answer section at the end of the book may be helpful in pinpointing problem areas.

Above all, always bear in mind the question: "After all is said and done, what does life mean to me; what is its real value?"

•   •   •

CHAPTER TWO

Lessons in Life

— Part 1 —

At four years old I was full of vitality, had no notion of wealth or poverty and had insufficient experience with deprivation to take the possibility of any form of real lack very seriously. I was the first born, warmly loved by my parents and totally convinced of their all-knowingness. If there was a question my mother couldn't answer, I would simply await my father's return from work. Life was full of joy and wonder. I looked forward eagerly to the beginning of every day; each new dawn brought new marvels and fresh possibilities in its wake. Nothing was more exciting than the prospect of getting older and gaining fuller access to life's unending mysteries.

Already, however, there was a blemish, a dark spot, on my world. The miracle and joy that was my existence had to be extinguished each night at bedtime by the dissolution of my consciousness. With vivid clarity I recall lying in bed, firmly resolved to resist sleep. Then, I suppose, came a moment of inattention or reverie and then the familiar but terrifying approach of sleep's grip gradually overcoming me. First came the paralysis of my limbs and then, when I tried to call out for help, I was unable to activate my vocal cords. Slumber deprived me of that special competence, that certain quality of intention, that connects one with his functions. Impotently and in silence, I screamed again and again. Like a man falling from a ledge and grasping at thin air for the lost purchase that could have saved him, I watched in abject horror as my inward eye, observing all this, began to succumb to the darkness. In numbness I felt the extinction of my inner light.

What a joy to awaken with the morning sunlight streaming into my room with the adventure of the day before me, and the fears of the previous night exorcised as if they had never been. I especially looked forward to going for a walk with my dearly beloved, tall, distinguished grandfather with the kind, dark, piercing eyes. We shared a bedroom. Then one day he was no longer there. "He has gone to the hospital with an illness," I was told. When I asked when he would return I was given vague assurances that he'd soon be back.

Although I was only four, I remember that particular morning. I had been sitting in our small sunlit living room, building toy log cabins with my red-brown wooden play logs that I can almost smell, even now. My mother was close by, perhaps sewing, perhaps reading, but I felt a tenseness in the house. I asked again about my grandfather. My mother appeared uneasy, then announced that he died. This meant little to me; I had never before considered death. So I asked her what it meant "to die." It was then that I received the shock of my life. My mother calmly explained, as if the matter was almost trivial, that dying was like falling asleep, only forever.

I was distressed and confused. Not only would I never again see my beloved grandfather, but if one had given me the task of inventing a fate so horrible that I wouldn't have wished it on my worst enemy, eternal sleep would have to be it. I was deeply anxious and wanted to know why such a dreadful circumstance should have overcome my dearest and closest friend.

Imagine my shock when my mother, in her wish to allay my panic, precipitously explained that death eventually comes to everyone. Suddenly my world was in ruins, its endless possibilities revealed to be a delusion. My bubble had broken and in my heart I was beaten bloody. I was on the verge of hysteria. Then, as if it were the thing I would most want to hear after receiving the terrifying, bewildering and disconsolate news of my mortality, my mother, to console me in my anguish, blurted out, "Me, too!"

In the face of this crisis I gathered all my wits and, with merciless clarity, saw that my mother was not at all what I had believed. I perceived directly, with an innocence and candor possible only to those who are free of artifice and hypocrisy, that the experience I was going through, the disillusionment and the pain, was all foreign to my mother. The bland sympathy she offered was totally incommensurate with the immensity of my distress. She was oblivious to the depth of my terror.

I know now that what I grasped in a flash was a degree of my mother's state of unconsciousness and her seeming indifference to the wondrous phenomenon that for me was life. I went stone cold inside. Somehow I knew instantly and with absolute certainty that if I failed to take immediate measures I risked losing forever the paradise that was now rapidly receding from me. I somehow understood that I could easily and irretrievably fall into that abyss of what to me had plainly become the chief feature of my mother's existence — unconsciousness — and as I came to feel much later was that of humanity as a whole. (For me, only the launching of Project Mind will signal our redemption from this state.)

I have no recollection of how I got through the rest of that day. Common sense suggests I must have had my first bout with despair, to the extent that this is possible in a normally happy four-year-old. I had lost confidence in my mother; this itself represented a trauma of no small proportion. Also, without knowing it, I was immeasurably strengthened in my individuality. In an effort of exceptional maturity I had opened my eyes, marshalled my courage and taken a stand. I had independently rejected my mother's version of the truth. In silence I resolved to find a way out of this intolerable bind, and secretly dedicated my life to that end.

My father, in true form, assured me that death is not inevitable and explained that there was a time when heavier-than-air flight was considered impossible. Ever since, the feeling that "anything is possible" has resonated strongly in me as a factor of hope. It was my father's regular insistence that absolutely anything can be accomplished if one truly sets one's mind to it. He often addressed this declaration to me, but as a child I did not have nearly enough personal confidence to credit myself with such possibilities. Having lost confidence in the protective powers of motherhood, it was only as a general principle that I could accept as real the possibility of a world without death and suffering — a world without limits. I clung to this faith with all the childish means at my disposal.

I found school terribly confining, but found solace in the love I had for a little girl in nursery school and another in kindergarten. This got me through each day. It wasn't that the other boys didn't feel similar attractions, it was simply that girls were never out of my mind; I meditated on them. While some psychologists might say I was seeking compensation for the disappointment with my mother, it was clear to me even then that I needed an ally to help me confront all forms of limitation and restriction that for me had become archenemies — the emissaries of death in daily life.

I also sought male comrades as allies, but soon discovered that through their blind submission to limits and to adult authority they had already allied themselves with all I abhorred. Losing interest in my comrades soon marked me as a loner and, already by the first grade, an outsider. Girls were different. My attraction to their beauty and the tacit understanding, current at that time, that females existed to complement, comfort and assist males, made them a natural target for my interest.

Through grade school, pain and loneliness accompanied this, my premature "adolescence." Reverie was the only relief from the constraints of school regimen and the tedium of a curriculum that didn't address itself to the existential questions that burdened me. I dreamt of love that would serve as a buffer from the stifling demands of authority, of someone with whom I could say "no" to every undue imposition or restriction, someone with whom I could unreservedly say "yes" to life. This is the state in which I spent most of the time during my school years — years that in every way represented the restriction, limitation and death from which I yearned to escape.

Happily there was the freedom of summer with all its moods. Wild thunderstorms and still, black, star-studded nights wove their web of fascination for me. Sometimes I went exploring or worked mischief with my summer comrades — the joys of vacation having granted me temporary respite from my isolation and inner attitude of revolt. Here I could enjoy the preciously genuine, naive and uncalculating kind of friendship possible to young children. Often I went out alone communing with nature, gathering a sense of boundlessness that nourished my spirit and fortified me for the months and years of loneliness and oppression ahead.

During my high school years, along with select companions who shared aspects of my search and struggle, I weathered the storm of adolescence — but not without ample gestures of nonconformity and defiance. It was a time for self-definition and confrontation with teachers who had preferred students with modest images of themselves. I always felt modesty was an over-touted virtue. I was overreaching and presumptuous with my elders: in short, a conceited smart aleck.

This awkward bearing of mine seldom perturbed my father, unless it happened to embarrass him directly. Now and again, with refreshing insight, he would put things in perspective by reminding me that, "A person has a right to be conceited, but only until he is successful." He confided to me that he himself was once considered "too big for his breeches" before his detractors were silenced by his accomplishments.

The discovery of sex opened for me a new channel of research into the eternal and mysterious unknown. I was determined that this evanescent ecstasy, so symbolic of my quest for freedom, not end up serving a debilitating, conventional marriage. As a teenager, reasonably camouflaged in the scramble for dates, I desperately sought union with someone who like me was secretly at war with limitation, death and anything that tends to compromise our sense of well-being or self-preservation. There were a few immature liaisons, yet some offered moments so perfect and so healing that I might not have survived without them.

Two incidents during high school marked me deeply and kept my life on course. One concerned a Saturday night lecture at a local university. An endocrinologist had crushed and homogenized millions upon millions of a Latin American beetle, extracted a minuscule quantity of pure growth hormone from that disgusting soup, and with it was able to generate young flesh on the back of an aging beetle of the same species. The audience was awed by the implications. In my heart was lit a new point of hope. I have kept an eye on this field ever since.

Another incident occurred one spring evening when I was 17. I was sitting quietly at my desk studying for 12th grade exams and bathed in a sense of well-being. A sudden insight of unquestionable certainty told me that there was no upper limit whatsoever to the joy and happiness that a human being can experience. This certainty has been with me ever since.

Once at university, far from home, with a sparse curriculum, liberty to skip classes, and freedom from family pressures and obligations, I was given for the first time the opportunity to think seriously about who I was and what I wanted from life. The air was full of ideas. In the cafeteria one could always find others with whom to discuss just about anything. But there was an urgency about me and an ardor that put people off. Sooner or later they grasped that I wanted more than just intellectual stimulation and casual exchange. I was after Truth.

When discussion heated into argument, I felt the cogency of what I had to say. The fire of my passion made me feel all the more intensely the urgency of the truth I was seeking, hidden within what I was trying to convey. I became increasingly identified with my position and absorbed in the subject of my quest. Occasionally, the force of my conviction kindled an insight in someone else. This inflamed my urge to influence others and encouraged me to further deepen and expand my thinking.

One quiet evening I realized I had developed strong positions on many subjects, but that these were far from integrated in my thinking and general presence. I could not always rely on the energy of passion to make my connections for me, and I began to feel incomplete and lacking in coherence. This coincided with my growing desire to formulate a comprehensive ideology that would account for what I in particular, and human beings in general, really wanted. I wished to understand how society could be organized to satisfy human needs and drives without all the deprivation, discontent, strife and suffering that everyone seemed to accept as a natural and inevitable state.

So I started for the first time to write out my thoughts and to search for points of correspondence that would unite these thoughts into a more comprehensive perspective. There was much to account for in the convictions I had accumulated over my almost 21 years. I experienced a rush of gratification each time a piece of the puzzle fit into place. Little by little I could see more clearly who I was and what I stood for. Day after day of intense reflection brought me closer to discovering what was to become the central tenet and foundation of my new understanding.

This concentrated quest for an answer to the enigmas of life dating from childhood built up a head of steam that brought about a qualitative change in my thought process. A kind of silence settled on me as the ideas and feelings circulating in my psyche harmonized within to deepen my thought and clarify my vision. I soon saw that traits such as limitation and pettiness were not inherent in human nature. The abundant energy emanating from my new state of being proved that there lies sequestered within us, just below the surface, sufficient energy and joy to overcome any adversity and satisfy any need. Witnessing this stunning truth made me want immediately to impart this good news to others.

It was only then, seeing this impulse to share arise within me, that I suddenly understood what had escaped me during my analysis of the human condition. What I discovered to my delight and astonishment was that man's almost totally obfuscated yet most characterizing drive — his most distinguishing feature — is not selfishness as is generally believed, but altruism — the desire to give to others. I suddenly realized that, deep down, all man truly wanted was to love his neighbor!

All that brought me to this realization filled me with elation and sent me on a rampage of proselytizing. I monopolized large blocks of class time arguing with my professors that the hidden and unwarranted premise behind all those psychological and social studies was man's selfishness. I insisted that such a false premise invalidated the conclusions of these studies. It was not man but a caricature of man that we were studying, and the distorted, if empirical, results were leading us away from truth instead of towards it. The fountainhead of energy and good will flowing through my body provided me with confirmation, fueling my assertions.

Some professors were more indulging of my disruptive zeal than others, and each had his or her own system to deal with me and defend established beliefs. Not one suggested that I design an experiment based on my own premise to test its validity. Little did I realize that in a world populated almost entirely by people who are caricatures of themselves, such experiments would have been impracticable. Little did I know that the need for such experiments would lead me to Project Mind.

My "cafeteria" activities flourished. Instead of attending classes, I waited in ambush to buttonhole my fellow students and expose them to my doctrine of love. My high energy drew people to me and my enthusiasm was contagious. Whenever I succeeded in imparting insight, my elation mounted. When I failed to pierce another's armor of cynicism, I keenly felt my limitations and the restriction that impeded my thought and powers of persuasion.

On my own, I could find no way to resolve the paradox of my situation. I had neither the experience nor the maturity to go it alone. I still lacked a fully elaborated, consciously assimilated ideology to handle every and any onslaught with self- possessed equanimity. I lacked a trusted companion and ally who could provide me with the grounding and shelter to calmly complete the ideological foundation that would allow me to stand on my own two feet.

Only years later did I realize how much my predicament lay within myself in a contradiction that is at the heart of the human condition, a conflict analogous to the apparent conflict between spirit and matter. I was unable to see that while I wished to share with others, I also expected reward and recognition. This impasse, this impossible contradiction between my attitude and my ideals, my ego and my essence, this premature experiment with higher forces in an unprepared psyche, called for drastic action.

Yet I did have a mentor: the only person I had ever fully admired and in whom I had implicit trust — my father. His integrity was like a shield to me. While the parents of my friends foisted their will upon their offspring, sometimes in the most summary and arbitrary fashion, my father appealed to reason, calling both himself and me to account for our actions. I was sure he would understand my pressing need and be proud of the independent and idealistic course I was forging for myself and, by implication, for others.

I was wrong. Instead, I found his courage compromised both by his fears for me and by conventional notions. Applying the full weight of the tremendous influence he had over me, he begged me to defer my search to an unspecified time in the future. There are no words to express my feeling of betrayal. Here, at the age of 21, 17 years after the great disillusionment with my mother, my father finally fell from "Mount Olympus." The spark of eternity I had always seen in him was gone. All that remained was a very worried father, and a very disappointed son.

In my despair, I could see I had no choice but to put aside my ideas for the day when I'd have the strength and maturity to bear them alone. Repressing all thought concerning them, I gradually lost contact with them and their ability to awaken the life within me. With my new sense of self throttled, I no longer knew who I was. This identity crisis melted my confidence to the extent that I had become most uncharacteristically sheepish and unable to look people in the eye.

Summer vacation reunited me with my family, but I found it impossible to communicate with my father. All I could think about was his betrayal — his refusal to abide with me for a week or two, long enough to get the substance of my ideas down on paper — and my consequent loss and suffering. My rancor irritated him constantly. My mother, distressed by all the tension in the air, tried in vain to reconcile us. My father's mere presence aroused such opposition in my that in blind, futile rebellion I would stay up nights trying impotently to reawaken my former state.

I began to make many interesting psychological observations. One day I observed a friend's pet dog. I began to understand the dog and to see it clearly for the dog-machine it was, completely determined in its reactions by its dog nature and the stimuli that impinged upon it and engaged its attention. For a short time, my analytical acuity increased dramatically. Now that I had resumed attending classes I began actively taking part, displaying perspicacious insights sufficient to gain for the first time ever the approval of professors and students alike. Sadly, this special equilibrium of attention and intelligence lasted for only a few days and then disappeared.

I realized that without the necessary maturity or corresponding external means of grounding to contain the powerful energies of what was incipient Accelerated Thought, I would just find myself in trouble again. So for the moment it seemed useless to continue along my own path.

Fortunately, during that summer I met a greatly empathetic girl to whom I could tell all. She wept openly as I recounted my story and my pain. Something in my heart that had hardened, softened. She gently but firmly ushered me back into the mainstream of life until I was somewhat my old self again, but with a difference. I had tasted "rock bottom," so fear of the unknown became less important for me that it is for most. I now knew with certainty that in my unconscious there was knowledge of tremendous force awaiting a propitious moment for its reawakening. In this spirit I completed my university studies and finally returned home.

On arrival my father handed me a newspaper and suggested I find a job, a notion that until that moment with all my psychological, spiritual, romantic and other adventures, had barely crossed my mind. Within a week I had found a position that at first seemed interesting, but after a few months drove me to boredom. I could see I was in trouble again.

Now, at age 23, I approached my father for financial backing to spend time in which to figure out what I wanted to do with myself. He agreed on the proviso that I keep regular business hours in this endeavor and commit my thoughts to paper. His acquiescence surprised me and was very likely a gesture of conciliation. He really came through this time and, somewhat in the spirit of my university experience, I sat down to do some serious thinking, but with a new twist.

Now, rather than just seeking my personal truth in the form of a coherent ideology, I was bent on forging a theoretical framework to serve as a basis for action. I was seeking a life aim, a vocation that would be worthy of my full potential and that would, in the noblest form conceivable, embody that potential and the values to which I had become committed. I intended, at the tender age of 23, to chart a course that would take into account everything that could possibly matter to me up to and including my old age.

I reflected and meditated intensively for months, sharing my insights and discoveries with my father whenever and to the extent that I could. It comforted me that my thoughts pleased and sometimes delighted him. Still, I never shared my principal conclusions with him, nor with almost anyone else for many years.

This is what I concluded:

1. My supreme value, held consciously from the age of four, was life. I deemed it imperative, one way or another, to vanquish death.

2. At the rate science was going, what remained of my lifetime would not even begin to suffice to discover the secret of immortality. Yet I knew that time and matter (including space and distance) could be overcome. I had the intense experiences of my university days as proof that insightful thought can be accelerated by staggering proportions. So I envisaged a unique method and setting for scientific inquiry that would be wholly contemplative. It would largely obviate the crutch of practical laboratory experiment to which (because of the shortcomings of our foresight, or what we call "creative" thought) we must resort each time our conviction and vision fail us. A well-orchestrated, interdisciplinary team of a few hundred minds blazing with the fire that I had experienced would rapidly reduce to nothing the limitations that physical matter, including the matter of our bodies, imposes on us.

3. To establish this, I would need a plan of action (including a detailed theoretical framework explaining its feasibility), personal credibility commensurate with such a plan, very significant financing, and allies.

— Part 2 —

I began by visiting libraries and devouring books and articles on the subject of creative thought, sometimes three or four books a day. I scanned anything even remotely connected with this subject until I understood what the thinkers on this subject had missed and why. The outlines of materials necessary to accomplish my aim and the theoretical framework I was seeking also began to grow in my mind. I pursued this research in the spirit of a sacred task. I felt as though all existence, especially the authors whose writings were feeding my enthusiasm, were benefactors supporting my cause.

With my father's help I got a job in a small company working with inventors. With the continued support of my father, I agreed to work as an unpaid apprentice so I could learn the practical, mundane business of commercializing invention. Also, I had continuing contact with a rich variety of creative people to further elaborate and verify my theories. Before long, I found myself professionally involved and fully embarked on a career that has since taken me (I am now approaching the age of 50) to many countries and has enabled me to meet thousands of inventors, scientists, specialists, officials and others involved with the creation and or practical disposition of what the trade calls "intellectual property" — the legal recognition of the crystallized results of creative thought.

During this period I made another key discovery that has fortified me in my quest. I found that there was a whole body of knowledge going back to ancient times and a whole movement concerned with overcoming the limits of coarse materiality in man in the interest of elevating his spirit, often in the service of a higher principle or deity.

Usually, the members of such schools of spirituality, mysticism or esoterism, at least the better ones, aspire to immortality through the intense, precise and systematic exercise of their capacity of attention. This inner effort can ostensibly be orchestrated in apprentices only by a "master" or by someone who has acquired some proficiency in the intricacies of balancing the many different qualities of matter and energy that live and circulate within us. Out of certain fine substances believed to derive from such efforts — efforts that often have outward manifestations that appear quite banal — new bodies are thought to develop. These correspond in their materiality to the subtlety of the spiritual energies that form them. These subtle bodies are thought to have form and function analogous to those found in the physical body. Each new body, in its turn, serves as a crucible or womb for the birth of a still subtler, and thus more nearly immortal body, and so on, until reaching the tenuity, primeness and eternal indestructibility of divinity.

Such notions seemed not incompatible with my aim. What's more, notions such as "distraction" and "waking sleep" credibly explained why, throughout life, my best laid plans regularly went astray, and why it was so difficult for me to maintain contact with what I considered my own ideas. Furthermore, I was able to meet and gain instruction from people whose level of understanding put matters in perspective for me and helped me avoid many pitfalls and blind alleys. Most important, I learned to respect my limitations of the moment and invoke the highest form of assistance possible.

At the same time something seemed glaringly wrong to me. I could see that the impediment of physical matter with its myriad impositions upon all aspects of our existence weighs too heavily on our spirits for us to fly very high for very long. It made sense to me that if we as a species and as individuals are to realize our full potential, we must tap a source of motivation and a wellspring of energy commensurate with the forces that disperse, deflect and dilute us in our purpose, separate us from our real vital interests and, in short, keep us down. I had in mind the same debilitating forces that made my mother oblivious to the incontrovertible, totally obvious truth that stared me in the face as a four-year-old, and the same disabling powers that sapped my father's courage and vision when, as a young adult, I needed him most. These are the very same dissipating influences that convince us of the eternal inevitability of death and make it difficult for me to remember my aim and strive consistently towards it, even as I struggle to write these lines.

The solution to this predicament, I believe, lies in the reconciliation and integration of science and religion (in the spiritual sense of seeking unity in man). Only in meeting the challenge that physical matter poses to our spirit will we generate the forces equal to the struggle of liberating the full potential of that spirit. To wake up to our predicament is one thing; to find ourselves transformed is another.

In marked contrast to the growth of our technical capacities, the quality of mankind's general acuity, presence of mind, moral and psychological vigor and general level of understanding gradually decline over the centuries. This happens according to little-known laws of spiritual entropy, as the superficiality and mechanicality of a more and more materialistic and automated world takes us in its grip. We become encrusted with indifference, and increasingly resigned to the inevitability of limitation and human suffering.

The tools and machines we invent for liberating ourselves from tedious and repetitious work manage to turn against us, limiting our freedom and engendering weakness and vice. Spiritually, we become their servants. By involving us more and more with external matters at the expense of introspection and self-awareness, they gently lead us further and further away from any possible understanding of our hidden inner resources. Despite physical comforts and conveniences (and, in view of our corruption, because of them), our inner life becomes ever more vacuous.

This evil cannot be fought on its own ground and terms. The very lassitude and passivity it breeds in us only strengthens its stranglehold on our minds. The very conditions of our existence must be changed. Imagine entering a chloroform-filled room, populated with unconscious people. Would you try to awaken the sleepers one by one at the risk of going under yourself, or would you seek a way to open a vent or window? Individual and organized efforts to shake people out of their torpor are doomed to failure. For each person you awaken two fall back asleep, as the experience of awakening becomes cunningly integrated into dreams of awakening. The anesthetizing influence of matter in all its forms is just too strong.

Only our highest faculty, Accelerated Thought, has the potency to pierce the veil of distraction blinding us to reality. As this book will show, the faculty of Accelerated Thought is capable of frontally assaulting the riddle of matter (including the matter of our bodies) at its root to nullify matter's restrictive influence upon our spirits. The forms of restriction that matter imposes upon humanity fall generally under the headings of distraction, dissipation (entropy) and illusion. The result? Dulled awareness, alienation, anomie, corruption, confusion, depletion and death.

Project Mind is about this fight, the necessity for it and its ramifications as far as I have been able to envisage them. I have written it because I am willing to take action and am increasingly feeling the urgency to find allies in this cause. To succeed will require the devoted support and participation of many persons. Until recently, my wife of 20 years has been my sole confidant in this undertaking. She has patiently provided the love and conditions that have allowed me to come this far. It is time for others to join in with whatever resources they can offer.

Of the many contacts over the years including family, friends and even mentors, none to my knowledge have even begun to suspect that a burning obsession dominates my life, let alone what it concerns. It is thus possible that, like "ships passing in the night," I have unknowingly crossed the paths of others having similar concerns — others who, like myself, feel reticent about openly discussing something so viscerally significant yet apparently very far removed from the hearts and minds of humanity. In writing this book I have no clear idea what kind of echo I can expect to find in my fellow man, or if anyone in unconscious distress will even recognize that Project Mind represents a real chance to escape from the limitation we accept as the "human condition."

As an individualist, I have always shunned convention and collectivities, yet I am painfully aware of the fundamental interdependence of all mankind. It is an inescapable fact which global ecological conditions are now forcing upon our attention in a most menacing way. Until now, the only massive mobilization of human resources, energies and intentions has been in the process of war where some part of humanity sought to impose its truth upon others, and where those others fought to maintain their own way of life. Only now, with the fragility of the planet's ecosystem staring us in the face, are we becoming aware of just how mutually dependent we are.

We have yet to grasp that the main lesson to be learned from our new vulnerability has less to do with the sharing of human destiny (for which we certainly must become responsible), and more with the most salient aspect of this destiny — our shared condition of mortality. We must realize that the tyrant making fools of us all from time immemorial is the mortality-bestowing matter of our bodies. Restriction and limitation are the essence of matter and the root of death. Man, through his latent intelligence, was meant to evolve into an immortal species.

The institutionally sanctioned denial of this most basic reality — our individual and collective inability to acknowledge the preeminence of the truly horrifying enigma of death — compromises our very psyche in the process of devaluing the virtue and importance we attribute to life itself. This keeps a balanced relationship with others, with the matter out of which we and our world is made, and with higher realities, quite out of reach.

I don't expect my viewpoint to be readily accepted. Yet I do believe that everyone eventually will come to recognize that, individually and collectively, our most fundamental interest lies in eradicating the tyranny of matter, restriction, limitation and death, and in freeing man's spirit to pursue the higher and nobler destiny that tragically eludes our species.

To initiate a project like this, beginning on even the smallest of scales, is a massive undertaking. The extent of the effort that will be required reminds me of one last piece of wisdom that my father, seeing my hesitation in the face of a dilemma, offered me not long before he died. He said:

Never be deterred in the goals you seek by the extent of the means that are required, regardless of how great. If you are true to your aim, the necessary means will appear at the appropriate moment.

•   •   •

CHAPTER THREE

A World in Danger —
Matter, Greed & Separation

Not only is this world not the real world, it is not even its shadow, but only the shadow of its shadow. (Paul Brunton)
The world is now too dangerous for anything less than Utopia. (Buckminster Fuller)

One would have to be either singularly poorly informed or remarkably insensitive to be unaware of the increasing level of tension and anxiety that has been invading the planet. Although strife and suffering have never been strangers to this world, until recently trouble's reach always seemed to have its limits. The individual could hope somewhere to find shelter and prospects for a brighter future, and he could at least take comfort in the firmness of the earth under his feet.

Now, along with the present growth trend of the earth's population and man's technical capacities, the scope of the mischief he was once capable of has also increased. It is now possible electronically to monitor the events of almost any spot on earth from any other, and to unleash forces of localized or even global destruction at the mere push of a button.

Greed for material advancement and effortless existence is promoted by our luxury-oriented culture and is spread far and wide by the media. Like a raging epidemic, it has managed to infect every nook and cranny of the planet with the rapacious afflictions that accompany envy and avidity. Seeing the degrading effect of greed on his countrymen, Thoreau wrote:

> *Of what significance the philosophy or poetry or religion of a world that will rush to the lottery of California gold-digging on the receipt of the first news, to live by luck, to get the means of commanding the labor of others less lucky: i.e., of slaveholding, without contributing any value to society? And that is*

called enterprise, and the devil is only a little more enterprising! The philosophy and poetry and religion of such a mankind are not worth the dust of a puffball. The hog that roots his own living, and so makes manure, would be ashamed of such company. If I could command the wealth of all the worlds by lifting my finger, I would not pay such a price for it. It makes God to be a moneyed gentleman who scatters a handful of pennies in order to see mankind scramble for them.[1]

Such frenzied grasping has always tended to promote conflict, injustice, anomie and alienation. Greed also has uniquely modern consequences. Heedless squandering and pollution of our natural resources is proceeding on a scale that permits refuge to only a shrinking minority of privileged individuals.

The term for what such conditions of existence generate in us is "alienation".[2] Alienation has many definitions and is understood differently by different psychological schools and political ideologies. It basically means estrangement — estrangement from ourselves, our families, our peers, our work, society, our belongings and all those things we consider extensions of ourselves.

In the daily scramble to find work, maintain one's life-style and get ahead in this world of material cause and effect[3], more and more people succumb to the ills of psychological pressure. Some of us just break; others live in perpetual misery or escape into physical or mental disease; still others seek release in drugs and crime.

The rest of us do our best to ignore the subtle and sometimes not so subtle feeling that everything is closing in. All the same, the message is clear: our days, too, are numbered. Intermittent lulls may allow us to retreat into the fantasy that the trend may at last be changing for the better, but eventually we reluctantly find ourselves face to face with the waking nightmare of a world going from crisis to larger crisis.

Economic, environmental and military catastrophes of global proportions do not arise overnight. They have their roots in history and in the human condition. Modern technology (which boils down to how to make or do something) has telescoped human failings into the dilemmas of humanity as a whole. In order to deal with these problems on whatever scale, we must recognize that something very fundamental has escaped our notice.

---

[1] Henry David Thoreau, *The Journal*, in *Walden and Other Writings By Henry David Thoreau*, Joseph W. Krutch, ed. (New York: Bantam Books, 1982), 431.

[2] See appendix.

[3] See appendix.

Matter — Perdition or Paradise?

We get confidently enmeshed in the glue-like processes of matter, and then wonder why it seems so hard to get out. (Thaddeus Golas)

What is the matter? "Matter" is the matter. Matter — the substrate of our daily existence — is the object of our needs and cravings, hopes and dreams. Matter[4] sustains us, it is true, but it also divides[5] and separates us from ourselves and others. It forces us to compete and ultimately to conflict with one another. All the rest is commentary.

What would happen in a world where matter and its attendant manifestations of greed, envy, passion, vice and injustice became irrelevant — actually neutralized by unlimited material abundance, security, universal health, longevity and well-being? Is it possible for the negative influence of matter to be neutralized? Should we even try to achieve this?

I am convinced that our attachment to matter can and must be eliminated as the principal cause of pathological division and conflict. Furthermore, the seemingly incredible aim of suspending our obsession with matter along with its consequences must be accomplished within the next two or three decades if we are to succeed in fulfilling our human destiny. The alternative is the catastrophe of default. Yet we don't need a new social or political system, nor a spiritual discipline nor a religious dogma of inspiration or renunciation.[6]

Paradoxically, what we need is an empirical method to accelerate dramatically our already growing mastery of matter. This implies a transformation of science, scientific method and, consequently, what we call industry. This transformation is predicted by Nobel prize laureate Dr. Barbara McClintock and is, to some degree, prefigured in her own style of research:

> *In her view, conventional science fails to illuminate not only "how" you know, but also, and equally, "what" you know. McClintock sees additional confirmation of the need to expand our conception of science in her own — and now others' — discoveries.*
> *As she sees it, we are in the midst of a major revolution that "will organize the way we look at things, the way we do research." She adds,*

---

[4] See appendix.

[5] See appendix.

[6] See appendix.

"And I can't wait. Because I think its going to be marvelous. We're going to have a completely new realization of the relationship of things to each other.

"What we label scientific knowledge is lots of fun. You get lots of correlations, but you don't get the truth. . . Things are much more marvelous than the scientific method allows us to conceive."[7]

McClintock's faith in the future is to her credit. But how are we to pass from "correlations" to "truth?" Science at its best (which it rarely is) is the wholehearted pursuit of truth. Bohm expresses it thus:

Behind the intellectual drive of the great creators in science, a deeper force seems at work. I believe that at some intuitive level of his awareness, the scientist senses that nature is simple, subtle, interconnected and one. Without this idea or something like it, it is difficult to account for the way scientific genius operates. Why should one equation expressing nature's workings be truer and better than four, three, or two? The drive to unveil this inner structure and to express it in the beautiful and elegant language of mathematics seems similar to the mystic's insistence that behind the multiplicity of appearances there lies the unity of reality.[8]

Truth & Freedom

These are the men who have renounced matter, the men who believe that the values of their spirit cannot be brought into material reality. (Ayn Rand — Atlas Shrugged)

If the truth ever does "set us free," it will be from restriction — spiritual and physical. Breton and Largent concur:

In the end, scarcity doesn't describe reality but our perception of reality. If we accept closed-system premises, we regard scarcity as an iron law. But the so-called law describes us, not what's out there. We create scarcity from the limits of our knowledge and the narrow uses of our creativity. No matter how much scarcity makes us feel trapped in limits, the walls binding us are our own.[9]

Throughout this work, reference will be made to the changes to be expected in a world set free from the restrictions and conflicts matter has

---

[7] Evelyn Fox Keller, *A Feeling for the Organism: The Life and Work of Barbara McClintock.* (W. H. Freeman and Company, 1983), 203-7, reprinted by permission.

[8] David Bohm, "The implicate order and the super-implicate order" in *Dialogues With Scientists and Sages: The Search for Unity.* Renée Weber. (London & New York: Routledge & Kegan Paul, 1986), 23-51.

[9] Denise Breton and Christopher Largent, *The Soul of Economies* (Wilmington: Idea House, 1991).

imposed upon humanity from the beginning of time. This is not to imply that an unlimited abundance of what we call wealth and power is the whole answer to man's happiness and salvation, nor that satisfying greed or pandering to vice will extinguish human failings. Rather, a growing consensus and consciousness concerning the vanity of materialism will result. While we have all paid lip-service to this ideal, the very real perspective of matter not mattering will give teeth to this sentiment.

Violence, passion and craving are gross distortions of our natural needs, stemming from psychological and systemic imbalances induced in us by societies preoccupied with material considerations. By physically eliminating the foundation of these evils — the addictive power of material possessions — the young will be freed to develop without vice and depravity and the old will be relieved of many of the already accumulated stresses and pathologies of envy and competition. Technically backward nations, rich and poor, will be relieved of the corrosive humiliation of craving the advanced products they took no part in creating, while social and political adjustments will allow the revelation and expression of their own inner, creative capacities. In a world that awakens our appetite for reality, vice and escapism lose all meaning. They become obsolete. Thus the abundance envisaged by Project Mind must not only answer our real, immediate physical needs, but also must be so encompassing as to alleviate the irrational basis for our impulse to own things.

The need for ownership can represent various levels of attachment to the matter of this world. And while this need can account for legitimate needs and real vulnerabilities that pertain to the physical nature of our body, the extent to which we exaggerate these needs suggests how little we acknowledge the non-physical side of our nature. That some people can, paradoxically, seem completely satisfied by materiality, can be attributed to the anesthetizing effect that abundance can have on our personality. We constantly seek to tranquilize our anxieties by trying to compare favorably with others through the instrumentalities of wealth, power and status — all materially determined and determining.

Nor does illusion of security mitigate the intransigent reality of our vulnerabilty.[10] The threat of global holocaust and the anxiety it induces in us is merely repressed, and the profusion of palliatives that society offers

---

[10] See appendix.

in compensation threatens to drag our consciousness downward towards unrelieved distraction.

Ironically, while all the time blinded to the truth of our deteriorating situation, we persist in the belief that we are making progress. Progress for contemporary man, "New Age" literature reminds us, consists of a consciousness-eroding trend towards more and more leisure filled with increasingly mindless indulgences. We take pride in our technological culture while all the time becoming technologically and culturally less and less literate. We glory at the technological conveniences at our disposal while, through the abuse of these amenities, we allow our spirit to slip imperceptibly into oblivion. Thoreau says:

> *Most of the luxuries, and many of the so called comforts of life, are not only not indispensable, but positive hindrances to the elevation of mankind. With respect to luxuries and comforts, the wisest have ever lived a more simple and meagre life than the poor. The ancient philosophers, Chinese, Hindoo, Persian, and Greek, were a class than which none has been poorer in outward riches, none so rich in inward.*
> *Our inventions are wont to be pretty toys, which distract our attention from serious things. They are but improved means to an unimproved end.* [11]

With science advancing at an unprecedented (some would say excessive) rate, one might reasonably expect widespread bewilderment — "future shock"[12] — and major, disruptive civil dislocation. To the contrary, we find society adjusting rather nicely. Those isolated incidents in which the unions offer short-lived, pitifully inept, token resistance to the introduction of this or that new technology merely underscore our sophistication and eagerness to adapt one way or another to any promising new modality of comfort and escapism. For as long as technology serves to pollute us physically, culturally and spiritually, it will perpetuate and deepen our distraction.

Science is working overtime in the service of mass addiction to provide us with state-of-the-art techniques for the sweet sleep of self-indulgence and self-tranquilization. Thus we become ever more entangled in a web of illusion of our own making. In our perverted and unnatural pursuit of the unreal, our natural capacity for adaptation — nature's key to survival — has been turned against us and now threatens to spell our perdition. Bronowski hammers this point home:

---

[11] Thoreau, "Walden," *Walden and Other Writings*, 115-44.
[12] See appendix.

The history of other animal species shows that the most successful in the struggle for survival have been those which were most adaptable to changes in their world. We have made ourselves by means of our tools beyond all measure more adaptable than any other species, living or extinct; and we continue to do so with gathering speed. Yet today we are afraid of our own shadow in the nine o'clock news; and we wonder whether we shall survive so over-specialized a creature as the Pekinese.[13]

We soon acquiesce to conditions of existence that not so long before would have appeared outrageous to us. The norms of only 20 years ago now seem quaintly naive to us, almost a lost paradise, and give rise to whole industries dedicated to nostalgia. We have become so buffered from shock, so desensitized to reality, that even as we teeter on the brink of global disaster we carry on with business as usual. What then could serve to shake us out of this suicidal complacency and alert us to the individual and collective danger of our condition?

As long as true breakthroughs remain few and far between, and science continues to advance at a conventionally regulated rhythm (however rapid), the shocks and dislocations of innovation will be minimal. This allows the individual and society to adjust to an increasingly pathological situation at a more or less convenient and comfortable rate. Blasé towards the miracle of creativity, and having brought innovation down to our level by crassly exploiting it for trivial or destructive ends, we have checkmated ourselves into a no-win situation which leaves us grasping at imaginary straws. We grasp at such straws in an unconscious bid to keep intact the psychological cocoon protecting us from even a glimmer of painful awareness of our real situation. The main feature of that situation is our mortality.[14]

Once matter is sufficiently devalued, ownership becomes irrelevant. Unreal matter-related desires need no longer be satisfied since, with their bases of deprivation and invidious comparison removed, they evaporate. The potential effect of general abundance is illustrated by More:

The ambassadors stayed there one or two days and observed that so much gold was thought so little of, and saw that it was despised there as much as it was honored in their own country. When they also learned that the chains and fetters of a single runaway slave took more gold and silver than all the trappings of the three of them, their feathers drooped and in shame they laid aside all that finery of which they had been so arrogantly proud. This came

---

[13] J. Bronowski, *The Common Sense of Science* (Harvard University Press, 1953).
[14] See appendix.

about especially after they had spoken more freely with the Utopians and learned their ways and opinions. For they are amazed that any man can be pleased with the feeble glow of a little gem or stone, when he can gaze at a star and the very sun itself; or that anyone is so crazy as to think himself more distinguished because of a thread of finer wool; for however fine a thread it may be, a sheep once wore it, and all the time it was nothing more than a sheep.[15]

We know from everyday experience that all appetites vanish once they are satisfied and don't return until the feeling of lack returns. Complex lacks and appetites, especially when they include artificial and acquired aspects, are more difficult to satisfy. The appetite for ownership has five main drives: comfort, power, jealousy, prestige and security. They can be further defined as follows:

1. Comfort — behind the obvious fact that a certain degree of abundance can free us of real deprivation (e.g., starvation, exposure, disease, etc.) and its associated anxieties, the use of material means to cultivate and satisfy acquired needs, artificial needs and vice-related needs engenders the illusions upon which the quest for comfort power, prestige and security are based. Once the means exist to satisfy all physical needs, real and imagined, the foundation for generating illusions concerning the general importance of such satisfactions will be undermined.

2. Power — Material advantage bestows power over others, either directly (through the real and addictive needs of others — "wage slaves") or indirectly (through politics). With universal abundance no one will need to depend upon the material wealth of others.

3. Envy — There is always someone who has more of what is generally considered worth having. To be the focus of others' admiring attention enhances one's sense of existence. Even he who has most will want to increase his lead and prestige. When material advantage disappears, envy will gravitate to objects of finer materiality such as aesthetics, knowledge and wisdom, and will empower them.

4. Prestige — the adulation of the envied affluent who serve as models for those less "fortunate" — creates fashion that pro-

---

[15] Sir Thomas More, *Utopia*, trans. by Peter K. Marshall (New York: Washington Square Press, 1966), 69-70.

vides status symbols (props) which support emulation and amplify envy. When the objects of people's interest change, those who embody higher values will become prestigious. The higher the values, the finer their objects and the more difficult to counterfeit and use as props for emulation.

5.   Security — Material advantage is often better equipped to defend itself against deprivation, aggression and disease. This encourages the unconscious illusion of immortality concerning those who appear to be privileged in all things. Once the means become available for objectively increasing health and security for all (without distinction), and the prospect of physical immortality becomes real, anything other than reverence for life and the values that enhance life will be inconceivable.

Once new conditions of existence ushered in by Project Mind deliver us from these aspects of lack and deprivation, we will soon become aware of other, more essential, more spiritual, insufficiencies. We will at last realize what Socrates meant when he said that those who pursue wealth and honor are distracted from the pursuit of truth, wisdom and virtue. Once we have nothing to gain from our neighbor's deprivation and everything to gain from his well-being (virtue, unlike material benefits, cannot be appropriated), loving our neighbor will be our only remaining option. We will discover that each individual's uniqueness complements our own and can help us reveal aspects of higher reality to which, by his very uniqueness, our neighbor is closer. Then, acting in concert, we will be able to work through a new science of biology toward eliminating the root of all shameful attachments (the only remaining objective basis of our vulnerability — mortality) by assailing our primordial Achilles' heel: the materiality of our body.

Released from the psychological and cultural prison of distraction that matter has imposed, a new breed of man will emerge from the present miasma of vanity and confusion. This new man will be much freer and more capable of realizing his hidden potential — a potential hinted at in myth. Ouspensky quotes Gurdjieff as saying:

> *"Man's possibilities are very great. You cannot conceive even a shadow of what man is capable of attaining. But nothing can be attained in sleep. In the consciousness of a sleeping man his illusions, his 'dreams' are mixed with reality. He lives in a subjective world and he can never escape from it. And this is the reason why he can never make use of all the powers he possesses*

and why he always lives in only a small part of himself.[16]

The prospect of waking up to reality and taking full possession of their faculties has always interested certain men. They deeply intuit that no virtual or simulated reality nor other fantasy, however vivid, can compare to the natural, holistic reality that awaits us.

• • •

---

[16] P. D. Ouspensky, *In Search of the Miraculous* (New York: Harcourt, Brace & World, 1949), 145.

CHAPTER FOUR

False Bases of Hope

Yet when I surveyed all that my hands had done and what I had toiled to achieve, everything was meaningless, a chasing after the wind; nothing was gained under the sun. (Eccl. 2:11)

Throughout the ages, various spiritual, psychological and even political systems have invited us to rise above the restrictions imposed by the physical nature of the mundane world. Whatever successes these systems may claim, the present lamentably unhealthy state of humanity suggests that they and mankind must largely have failed in this transcendent undertaking. Berg underlines this failure for us:

> *While it is true that science, the arts, religion and philosophy, capitalism, socialism, communism, ethical humanism, and host of other isms, each in their own way may have contributed to the awareness of certain individuals and perhaps may have even improved the living conditions of segments of the general population, humanity as a whole seems no closer today, and in some respects farther than ever before, from achieving what is, or should be, its true objectives of harmony, freedom from want and hunger, and world peace.*
>
> *Human history stands as an indelible reminder of the failure of sometimes good ideas to penetrate the human heart. The precepts of major religions, for example, have been articles of faith for centuries, yet the benefits of religion pale in the shadow of the horrors of wars fought in their names.*
>
> *That such difficulties persist establishes an overwhelming indictment against all of our cherished beliefs and institutions. New creeds and doctrines seek to account for this, but no sooner are they expressed than humanity again makes manifest some new outrage and we watch in horror as the whole philosophical, political, or religious edifice tumbles like a house of cards.[1]*

---

[1] Philip S. Berg, *Power of Aleph Beth* (Jerusalem - New York: Research Centre of Kabbalah Press, 1988), 2:108-9.

While political and economic systems recognize that the material question is fundamental, they embody vision that falls short of recognizing that material needs, real or imagined, are only an expression (if a coarse and distorted one) of needs of a finer, more essential nature. It is this failure of vision that has put us in our present predicament. The final consequence and proof of our failure would come with the total destruction of our species. But why wait passively for events to overtake us? Albert Einstein says:

> *The atomic bomb has changed everything except our way of thinking. And so we drift helplessly toward unparalleled disaster.*

There remain a few who still believe in "Ban the Bomb" type activism, and that the survival instinct of the masses will somehow counteract the folly and corruption that matter induces in us. However, this view presumes that conscience in the average man is still significantly operative. Others claim that mind-bending discoveries of the "new physics" and the growth of spiritually oriented groups in the West[2] will in time (through paradigm shift) transform the social landscape. This trend, including "New Age" fads, is rife with delusions and is still too young to be certified positive or even benign, but it could open minds to the need for Project Mind.

Peter Russell[3] argues tantalizingly how trends in technology are influencing human perceptions and life-styles in the direction of Marshall McLuhan's "global village." He offers analogies from nature suggesting that the forces now at work must almost inevitably bring about the hoped-for transformation of mankind.

One germane factor that he and others in his camp seem to miss is that the social trends giving rise to this optimism are seldom due to enlightenment from within, but rather from the measure of hope that certain technologies (notably transportation, communications and computerization) have generated by eliminating some of the restrictions to our freedom as individuals.

Problematic as it is from other standpoints, technology has raised standards of living and relieved us of some of the drudgery of laborious, repetitive work. Russell also overlooks that, while ancient forms of inner, spiritual work indicate a desirable direction, they do not offer a challenge to which most modern men can relate. It is hard to imagine the masses

---

[2] See appendix.
[3] See Peter Russell, *The Global Brain* (Los Angeles: Tarcher, 1983).

sacrificing illusions and physical comforts for the uncertain and pro-tracted pursuit of spirituality, or even joining the bandwagon of environ-mentalism. Some trust that (short-sighted) "technological assessment" will find a way to curb technology's worst excesses. Some vainly hope that the horror of our situation alone may provoke a lifesaving, worldwide "consciousness" revolution.

There exists a growing sense that as a species we have lost control. Only some kind of miracle or some very fundamental breakthrough radically changing the quality of our daily lives could produce a general awareness sufficiently benevolent to counteract the forces of destruction already afoot. Harman and Rheingold emphasize this need:

> It is a peculiar fact of life for those of us alive today, of all the generations since our ancestors descended from the trees and began to shape rocks and tools, that without a near-future breakthrough into a true realization of our familyhood, there will be no future generations. Let us envision utopia, and thus bring it into existence. There is no reasonable alternative.[4]

But today's visionaries and prophets of transformation are still far too vague. While they consider as possible and even necessary a world that is alive and conscious (without limits or boundaries), they fail to be explicit about how even the best intentions can change deeply ingrained, centuries-old beliefs concerning the limitations that govern our lives.

New Possibilities for a New Age

Let no one deceive you. Your capacities, aspirations and conceptions prove that you are not formed for time, but for eternity. (Max Theon)

Notwithstanding the current widespread disappointment with science and technology, some people are beginning to recognize that the break-through we need will be revealed through the faculty of creativity. Rogers suggests:

> In a time when knowledge, constructive and destructive, is advancing by the most incredible leaps and bounds into a fantastic atomic age, genuinely creative adaptation seems to represent the only possibility that man can keep abreast of the kaleidoscopic change in his world. With scientific discovery and invention proceeding, we are told, at a geometric rate of progression, a generally passive and culture-bound people cannot cope with the multiply-

---

[4] Willis Harman and Howard Rheingold, *Higher Creativity* (Los Angeles: Tarcher 1984), 219.

ing issues and problems. Unless individuals, groups and nations can imagine, construct and creatively devise new ways of relating to these complex changes, the lights will go out. Unless man can make new and original adaptations to his environment as rapidly as his science can change the environment, our culture will perish. Not only individual maladjustment and group tensions but international annihi-lation will be the price we pay for a lack of creativity.[5]

Such urgings are fine, but how are we to proceed? A new theory of creativity and an explicit path to world transformation through Accelerated Thought is exposed in this book. Initially, only men of exceptional courage and spirit, in the framework of Project Mind, will be able to break through the barrier of distraction and transform our physical conditions of existence and, with them, the paradigms that hold us in a prison with invisible walls.

Only by neutralizing the causes of the matter-related obsessions that estrange us from our humanity and inner potential will challenges of a completely new order be revealed to the rest of us. We will lack the means or even the desire to banalize the shocking yet encouraging revelation that mankind will have enlarged its very capacity for understanding and that this major step in human evolution — in consciousness — was a result not of machine-assisted thought, but of thought liberated from distraction. But until these changes begin, we will remain largely blind to anything beyond common consensus.

Mind Over Matter — Misconceptions & Possibilities

Ask of me, and I will make the nations your inheritance, the ends of the earth your possessions. (Psalms 2:8)

The conquest of matter must begin with an act of mind. "Mind over matter" is more than just a phrase. It implies that matter, by the very nature of things, must submit to the intelligence of a mind capable of manipulating, forming, transforming, transcending and eventually understanding it. Ultimately, through "mind" we shall be able to merge[6] with matter in all its phases.

---

[5] C. R. Rogers, "Toward a theory of creativity," *ETC: A Review of General Semantics,* 11 (1954):250

[6] See appendix.

According to David Peat, "mind and matter are not distinct substances but two sides of one reality."[7] Orders emerging from this common spectrum contain more subtle orders that are important not only on the subquantum level, but also in the evolution of life and the operation of society.

That matter by its very existence weighs upon man's spirit may not be immediately evident to everyone. That the matter around us including that of our bodies is only an accessory aspect to reality, like a husk or shell, is probably even less obvious. Yet even a superficial understanding of this most fundamental issue could help us reorient our lives to more fulfilling purposes than we have now.

Matter is like a small ripple on this tremendous ocean of energy. (David Bohm)

Like a gargantuan blowfish, matter overwhelms us with a spectacular cosmic display of mass and expanse. It fills our senses and intoxicates us with the illusion of its primacy and ascendancy. We look at the stars and our minds are boggled. We come away with the impression that they, not we, are meant to dominate reality.

Yet according to many religious cosmologies[8] (and physics is ever gravitating towards the Big Bang theory), all the matter in the universe once fit neatly into a space so small that it could be called dimensionless — infinitely smaller than our own bodies. Perhaps we take the world of physical matter too seriously. After all, according to physics matter itself is almost all empty space anyway. It is the rapid movement of atomic particles that gives the impression of solidity, just as the spokes in a rapidly rotating wheel can produce the illusion of a solid surface. Remember that man, not matter, has the spiritual prerogative of free will. The matter of the universe is at our disposition; we need only learn its secrets.

The question of "matter versus spirit" is one that has ever dominated theology, philosophy, spirituality and, more recently, physics. These two fundamental aspects of reality and the challenge of the existential riddle they represent emerge naturally as mankind finds itself imperiled by converging threats to world peace, world ecology, world economics and world health. Not only is it becoming clearer that our future well-being

---

[7] F. David Peat, *Synchronicity: The Bridge Between Matter and Mind* (New York: Bantam New Age Books, 1988), 214.

[8] See appendix.

will depend on our grasp of this enigma, but a very likely instrument of our destruction — thermonuclear war — is our most tangible manifestation (outside the phenomenon of life itself) of an interface between a lower and a higher dimension. Atomic energy provides external, consensual proof that matter has expressions belonging to realms beyond our world. These expressions include the sun and stars which, together with "empty" space, comprise almost everything we know beyond our planetary existence.

If the threat of nuclear holocaust doesn't weigh you down, perhaps it is taxes, or the month's bills or mortgage payment, or the children's education, or the need of a car — or a job. For the rich, the material question also takes on many forms, not the least of which are personal security, the risk of accident and the ever-present threat of illness. That through our bodies we have a physical dimension makes us subject to all the vagaries and happenstance to which coarse matter is subject. So after a brief lifetime of more or less suffering we are, because of our material component, condemned to die.

Now we find ourselves on the threshold of the era of its transformation — an era ushered in with a horrifyingly convincing demonstration of Einstein's classic formula, $E=MC^2$, for the conversion of matter into energy. More important than the actual means for transforming matter into energy was Einstein's introduction of the very notion of transformation into our general understanding — an understanding restricted until recently to only a tiny minority of thinkers — primarily spiritual thinkers.

It could be argued that conventional chemistry also transforms matter from one form to another and that even simple combustion, practiced in the form of the cooking fire by our Stone Age ancestors, qualified as a modest version of transformation. Nevertheless, even the most modern and complex chemical reactions do not evoke the sense of awe produced by phenomena of a truly cosmic order. It is the scale of the results we see in nuclear and fusion reactions that tells us we are dealing with a process bridging dimensions — a process that truly merits the term "transformation."

One could always speculate that, given enough time, resources[9] and energy (perhaps from solar energy, fusion or even "zero point" energy) to pursue our present course, we might eventually have found how to transform anything into anything. In principle, there is no technical

---

[9] See appendix.

problem regarding matter that can't be solved in the normal[10] progression of science and technology — given enough time.

But the time for conventional solutions is running out. We now find ourselves choking on the polluting influences of a corrupt and corrupting science and faced with the growing specter of apocalyptic catastrophe. Political leaders and statesmen are showing us the way with about as much initiative, vision and leadership as the average pet dog that runs on ahead as if to guide, yet repeatedly (and anxiously) looks back to see if his master is still there, "following."

The hope and promise[11] of universal prosperity and well-being originally held out by modern science and technology is materializing too slowly and with too many hitches and complications. The credibility of that promise is stretched thinner with each passing day as more problems than solutions are created. Technical progress — our growing mastery of matter — is happening in a very lopsided manner, more often than not benefiting some sectors of humanity at the expense of others. Prosperity in one part of the world unwittingly tends to cause hardship elsewhere.

Certain types of technical problems are selected to receive attention and funding for reasons some consider worse than arbitrary. Defense projects, for example, and those with military implications of any kind continue to receive priority in almost all societies. Such priorities spread their pervasive influence to all levels, either directly to those who compete for public resources, or indirectly to the rest of us. This happens through economics and culture — agencies shaped by the very disposition of such resources. Just as most people demonstrate belief in the primacy of matter in their relentless pursuit of ownership, entire nations are consumed with their obsession with territory and national security.

Technological progress is like an axe in the hands of a pathological criminal.
(Albert Einstein)

As a consequence, growth patterns of scientific knowledge become so impossibly skewed that culture, and in particular the artifacts of our material culture (produced by what was aptly dubbed "the military-industrial complex"), end up compounding and feeding back to us the means for further cultivating our already advanced state of matter-induced intoxication. If the bulk of the means at humanity's disposal had from the beginning (thanks to some miracle or quirk of fate) been allowed

---

[10] See appendix.
[11] See appendix.

to flow into research determined by less wasteful criteria, the prosperity and general well-being to which we all aspire might by now have been within sight. At least the lives of hundreds of millions of this planet's inhabitants (those in the "third world" in particular) would be less desperate, and global conditions less critical on all counts.

Breakthroughs will increasingly localize and individualize control over the means of production and bring about the true democratization of physical materiality. For example, Drexler, in his *Engines of Creation,*[12] describes how universal abundance could come about. He convincingly speaks of nanotechnology, nanocomputers, molecular engineering, nanomachinery, gene synthesis machines, cell synthesis machines, cell repair machines, assemblers, replicators, etc. He lovingly calls these "engines of abundance" and deeply regrets their delay. He easily envisages molecular-sized nanomachinery supported by nanocomputers manufacturing or "growing" for you, before your eyes, a home or car or steak dinner, using almost anything including sewage and garbage as raw materials. Furthermore, bread, fruit, meat and vegetables made in this way will be indistinguishable from the real things, except that they will contain all the organic nutrients they should while sparing animal and vegetable life we now destroy so mechanically.

Regardless of what technical means become available, we must realize that it is the limits of our vision — consciousness — that determine the risks of abuse and pollution. Technological assessment can barely see over the next hill and is less than a band-aid to the gaping, polluting wound produced by distraction-inspired technology, owing to its non-holistic, non- comprehensive nature. Without the benefit of Accelerated Thought, technology will continue accelerating our rush to oblivion.

Fortunately, last-ditch solutions sometimes do work. But before outlining how we are to be spared the worst influences of our relationship with matter, there is at least one other manifestation of "mind over matter" to be noted. The case in point concerns mind actually replacing matter, as illustrated by progress in electronics and by computerization.

It is common knowledge that the transistor, printed circuitry, integrated circuitry (i.e., microchips) and, most recently, superconductivity, have made possible the miniaturization and subminiaturization of a multitude of clever gadgets that continue to shrink in size even as this is

---

[12] See K. Eric Drexler, *Engines of Creation* (New York: Anchor Books, 1990).

written. These display an ever-growing range of novel functions applicable to many fields of endeavor and enquiry.[13]

When one thinks about it, miniaturization — the art of getting equal or better performance from a smaller package — involves replacing matter with intelligence or "mind" in the sense that a 1950s room full of tons of electronic tubes, heavy equipment and miles of wiring (representing much matter indeed) is today reduced to a chip that will sit comfortably on the tip of your little finger. That "silicon" chip, seen exclusively from the perspective of matter, is basically a pinch of common sand. The rest is intelligence — mind. Just as the restriction of mind by matter occludes mind, the restriction of matter by mind reveals mind.

The intelligence of the chip consists of very special dispositions of matter, including highly specific material compositions, circuitry and other complex, functional patterning, all of which could be included under the term "form." It is this form embedded in the "silicon" of the chip that constitutes the essence of its intelligence. While the composite substance of that chip is the best material that could be found for the job until now, it is inevitable that newer and more "intelligent" materials will soon replace them (e.g., gallium-arsenide, etc.). With technical progress, the marriage between form and substance grows more and more intimate, and the resulting "matter" expresses more intelligence and becomes more lifelike.

In terms of the constraints matter imposes upon us, inventions use this same principle of economy. They simplify and facilitate existing tasks and make it possible to address new ones. Technology simplifies life (at least the physical side of life) by transferring the burden of existential constraint to the tools with which we contend with matter.

"Functional complexity" is form imbedded in matter. We see that as matter becomes more intelligent, the form that it embodies becomes more intricately structured. As matter and the form contained within it become ever more compatible and more perfectly mated, they eventually become indistinguishable from one another until we can no longer discern where one ends and where the other begins. As intelligence becomes manifest, the aspect of matter seems to recede into the background. The perfect union between matter and form is to be found in the phenomenon of life, and more particularly, human life.

---

[13] These include artificial intelligence, neural networks and simulated virtual reality (cyberspace).

Undoubtedly we will some day learn to measure and quantify intelligence. I believe this will then make possible the elucidation of a formula as elegant as Einstein's $E=MC^2$ to show the spectacular inverse relationship between matter and mind. Observe the diversity, flexibility, richness and subtlety of function in the human being — a miraculously compact package of capacities. Yet in material terms we are over 90% water, and the rest merely biological precursors to an urn full of dust and ashes. The essence of this "package" is the intelligence innate to our humanness — truly a triumph of mind over matter.

•   •   •

CHAPTER FIVE

Creativity & Breakthrough — Conventionality & Distraction

Since the time between now and Armageddon is so short, we ought to hold nothing back but give people the chance to obtain full Truth. (Paul Brunton)

Only with the neutralization of matter's restraining influence upon the expression of our mind's potential will we be able to assimilate presently unthinkable, indigestible realities. These realities will be rendered palatable to the rest of us by the pioneers of Accelerated Thought. Through the fruits of their exceptional courage, insight and initiative they will eliminate the root causes of the existential fears and anxieties, passions and vices that play such an important role in restricting the exercise of "mind."

Perhaps from the beginning, this privileged, pioneering role and responsibility, along with the extraordinary energy level that goes with it, was reserved in the cosmic plan for those who will forge the way. The rest of us will be granted a somewhat lesser ecstasy. In the words of Puccini:

> *The great secret of all creative geniuses is that they possess the power to appropriate the beauty, the wealth, the grandeur, and the sublimity within their own souls, which are a part of Omnipotence, and to communicate those riches to others.*[1]

One way or another we are destined to pass from the inner slavery and stagnation inherent in our overbearing preoccupation with what we have — whether that "having" relates directly to matter itself or to human attributes that we covet as we covet matter — to the inner freedom and development intrinsic to the exploration and discovery of what essentially, as human beings, we are. We have yet to learn to relate to ourselves and to others not as objects, but rather as process — that miraculous, dynamic, developmental and intelligent process we so glibly call "life."

---

[1] Arthur Abell, *Talks with the Great Composers* (Garmisch-Partenkirchen, Germany: G.E. Schroeder-Verlag, 1964).

To make up for lost time and usher in a new age of universal prosperity and well-being, at least some human beings will have to leap ahead in developing mental capacities capable of producing scientific and technical breakthroughs at a rate and with a regularity unheard of until now. While he extols breakthroughs, Koestler bemoans the pedestrian pace that otherwise prevails:

> The collective advances of science as a whole, and each of its specialized branches, show the same alternation between relatively brief eruptions which lead to the conquest of new frontiers, and long periods of consolidation. In the case of the individual, this protracted chore has its natural limits at three score years and ten, or thereabouts; but on the historical stage, the assimilation, consolidation, interpretation and elaboration of a once revolutionary discovery may go on for generations, and even centuries. The new territory opened up by the impetuous advance of a few geniuses, acting as a spearhead, is subsequently occupied by the solid phalanxes of mediocrity; and soon the revolution turns into a new orthodoxy, with its unavoidable symptoms of one-sidedness, over- specialization, loss of contact with other provinces of knowledge, and ultimately, estrangement from reality.[2]

In the future, breakthroughs will have to be frequent, significant, striking and inspiring. Only this will take the edge off the desperation and suffering that plagues a substantial portion of humanity. Only this will rekindle the hope of mankind.

The process of Accelerated Thought that these pioneers will embody is somewhat akin to the "Eureka" or "peak" experience — the climax to what we commonly call "creative thought" or simply "creativity." Candidates for Accelerated Thought will be creatively inclined and, if not leaders in their technical specialties, at least highly conversant in some discipline or field of enquiry.

They may be considered creative geniuses. At times we find such individuals tend to display character traits of audacity, impudence, nonconformity, rebelliousness, unconventionality, obsessiveness, intolerance, impatience, arrogance, unsociability, eccentricity, etc. This is why the genius is usually excluded from establishment situations, and especially from the higher echelons where conformity and political finesse are vital to professional survival. One dictionary definition of genius describes it thus:

> Genius. Exceptionally high mental superiority demonstrated by creative achievement, usually in a specialized field of activity. Nonscientific litera-

---

[2] Arthur Koestler, The Act of Creation (London: Pan Books, 1966), 226.

ture has often hinted that genius is akin to psychosis, and while this thesis is without convincing support, neither has it been wholly disproved. The genius indeed presents an "abnormal" pattern of personality. He is, as a rule, withdrawn, egocentric, and either indifferent to, or impatient with, affairs beyond the perimeter of his special interests. His self imposed "exile" from the contemporary social stream creates the impression that he is socially maladjusted.[3]

Following is a sample of what Koestler has to say about genius and the status quo:

One of the conspicuous handicaps is the conservatism of the scientific mind in its corporate aspect. The collective matrix of a science at a given time is determined by a kind of establishment, which includes universities, learned societies, and, more recently, the editorial offices of technical journals. Like other establishments, they are consciously or unconsciously bent on preserving the status quo — partly because unorthodox innovations are a threat to their authority, but also because of the deeper fear that their laboriously erected intellectual edifice might collapse under the impact. Corporate orthodoxy has been the curse of genius from Aristarchus to Galileo, to Harvey, Darwin, and Freud; throughout the centuries its phalanxes have sturdily defended habit against originality.[4]

The real talents of those who float to the top lean more often than not towards public relations and diplomacy, although in their technical fields these people also must command a reasonably high degree of expertise and perhaps have moments of inspired ingenuity. For purposes of conventional science this competence accounts to a large extent for the good work that is done. The manifestation of real genius, however (the kind equal to the task of producing conceptual breakthroughs), is tragically rare in organized science. As a rule, it tends to gain recognition only in those unusual cases where, thanks to freak circumstances (and in spite of society), genius somehow manages against all odds to find some concrete, physical embodiment.

Leonard provides an exception that proves the rule. In his work *The Transformation* he points out that without undeniably compelling proof, new revolutionary views of reality can occasionally gain ground through some surprise verification. His case in point is the anomaly in Mercury's apparent orbit which confirmed Einstein's theory of general relativity.[5]

---

[3] James A. Brussel and George La Fond Cantzlaar, *The Layman's Dictionary of Psychiatry* (New York: Barnes and Noble, 1968), 98.

[4] Koestler, *Act of Creation*, 240.

[5] George B. Leonard, *The Transformation* (Los Angeles: Tarcher, 1981), 123.

Unfortunately, far-reaching new insights and theories, unlike discoveries that are ripe to be made, have very few points of correspondence with existing, empirical knowledge. This does not mean that, apart from these freak breakthroughs, astonishing discoveries aren't made from time to time within established science. Yet "establishment breakthroughs" arrive as a matter of course, more naturally than one would think, along the front of expanding knowledge. Koestler agrees:

> One should not underestimate ripeness as a factor facilitating discoveries which, as the saying goes, are "in the air" — meaning, that the various components which will go into the new synthesis are all lying around and only waiting for the trigger-action of chance, or the catalyzing action of an exceptional brain, to be assembled and welded together. If one opportunity is missed, another will occur.[6]

And Briggs confirms:

> Simultaneous discoveries in science seem to indicate that the fires of the individual vision are considerably less important to the discovery process than the fires of the zeitgeist. In this view, says University of California psychologist Dean Keith Simonton, "Individual creators must be little more than interchangeable agents."[7]

David Bohm would attribute this to what he calls "implicate order"[8] — that all there is to know is already embedded in a higher reality which sooner or later becomes revealed. But opportunities take time to occur.

What is it that constrains genius and the discovery of breakthroughs? There is no formal policy or elitist conspiracy to hold back progress. Quite to the contrary, there is plenty of rivalry, competition and incentive to egg scientists on. Yet no artificial constraints need to be imposed upon thought when that thought is already fettered by conventional, distracted consciousness. Society siphons off our energy and conditions us to a low grade, "reflective" form of thought that we mistake for real, conscious thought. This is the key to understanding why things rarely go exactly the way we want them to and how we are so easily deflected from our purpose no matter how resolved we believe ourselves to be.

When we reflect — like the moon which is passively illuminated by the sun — we do not generate energy. We simply allow the energy of attention already present in us — lent to us from on high — to focus on

---

[6] Koestler, *Act of Creation*, 110.

[7] John Briggs, *Fire in the Crucible* (Los Angeles: Tarcher, 1990), 229.

[8] See David Bohm, *Wholeness and the Implicate Order* (London: Routledge & Kegan Paul, 1980).

whatever holds our interest. Subjectively, we may very well experience the effort of focusing as an active gesture. But as a rule, the object of our interest, whether it be a sensory impression or an idea, adds little if anything to the force of our attention. Yet it would if it were actively assimilated into the light of our awareness. Associative reflection absorbs most of what little attention we do have, limiting us basically to observing or thinking about one thing at a time.

We can, of course, create compound concepts and enlarge our ideas. Through them, we can enlarge our conceptual perspective just as we develop skills and routines that increase the scope of our mental and physical manipulative capacities. But we achieve these things only by repetitiously and painstakingly programming them into our nervous circuits of brain and body. Their presence does not increase our awareness any more than programs render computers conscious. Rather, they enhance our capacity for reacting automatically to complex situations with the modicum of attention at our disposal. As new habits and skills become ingrained in us, our attention is again freed to repeat the process and complete yet another layer of programming in mechanistic mimicry of awareness.

Mechanical, reflective thought is easily mistaken for true thought. Reflective thought, like driving a car, is basically a mechanical act, although it can be performed with more or less attention and on many levels of proficiency. While such mechanical thinking can bring many material benefits, it cannot raise consciousness. Hofstadter observes:

> A formal system is said to be capable of reflection if it can reason about itself. Gödel was the first person to discuss such things in detail. Nowadays reflective systems are the bread and butter of many a logician. However, computer modeling of logic is just now reaching the point where reflection is being seriously explored.
>
> The idea is very enticing, but I think it has less to do with genuine progress in AI than it does with progress in elegant formal systems. It all has to do with one's ultimate view of what thought is. If you believe that thought is intimately tied up with some strict notion of truth and reasoning, and that exquisitely honed deductive capacities are the Centerpiece of mentality, then you will naturally be drawn toward reflective reasoning systems. If, on the other hand, you believe, as I do, that reasoning is a far, far cry from the core of thought, then you will not be too inclined to jump toward such systems. [9]

---

[9] Douglas R. Hofstadter, *Metamagical Themas: Questing for the Essence of Mind and Pattern* (United Kingdom: Penguin, 1985), 544.

It is not uncommon for thinkers to explain man's limitations in the sphere of consciousness in terms of being stuck in the prevailing social paradigm. It is often implied, if not said straight out, that if one could break out of this culturally defined straitjacket to thought there would be no further obstacles to clear, unbiased, unrestricted consciousness. There is a grain of truth in this. The reach of paradigms can go considerably beyond the scope of what we know as ideation when they relate to a much larger, undefined reality. This "larger" reality cannot be grasped by the head-brain alone but requires what is known in modern "new age" lore as the "body-mind." In this usage, paradigms correspond to levels of awakening and of existence. But the paradigms we are likely to encounter are the concept-bound paradigms of reflective thought.[10]

Another serious limitation of reflection is that in absorbing the bulk of our attention, the object of our interest largely deprives us of the energy to guide our thoughts and follow them in a straight line. We become easily distracted by thoughts and events that catch our attention. Our thoughts turn round in circles more than we care to admit. Without realizing it, if we don't happen to be in grooves of a well-ingrained routine to keep us on course, we are constantly returning to the point where we got lost in reverie. This helps explain why there is so little original thought. Reflective thought is the basic mechanism of our state of distracted awareness. The conditions of existence around us are designed to absorb our energies and keep us on this level, not unlike the way governments "mop up excess liquidity" to keep their economies from "overheating." Leonard shows insight into this process:

> In normal circumstances, the culture rather effectively controls what particular fraction of existence each individual is able to bring to awareness. The rest is relegated to dreams, symbols, or rare genius. This control of awareness serves as perhaps the major stabilizing force in any society. The tightness of the control and the narrowness of individual awareness present few problems in a stable, slow-changing society beset by no significant challenges.[11]

Although no particular "villain" can be singled out, and there is no intention here to anthropomorphize society, it would still seem as though there existed deeply embedded in society's *modus operandi* a strategy of "divide and rule" served by the forces of distraction. This "strategy" effectively prevents society's various constituent elements (individuals,

---

[10] See appendix.
[11] Leonard, *Transformation*, 110.

groups, institutions, associations, etc.) from conferring, coordinating and eventually rebelling in the name of their own paradigm. Such vision might just contain the seeds for overthrowing the governing authority and its ideology. This cosmic "strategy" evokes the legend of the multiplication of "languages" in the Tower of Babel in which, because no one was able to understand the exact meaning of his neighbor, the construction of the tower, aimed to reach heaven, was thwarted.

The dispersion and dissipation of our conscious energies by the structure and dynamics of our cultural life undermine the optimum functioning of all but those heroically determined and sometimes obsessed minds we habitually stigmatize with the label "inventor" or "eccentric genius." Accordingly, established scientists hypnotically bound by the status quo rarely find the energy to rise above accepted theory and paradigms of thought long enough to seriously consider revolutionary new perspectives occasionally proposed by their less conventional colleagues. Such colleagues are soon branded as eccentric or worse if they persist in trying to wake fellow scientists out of their cultural trance. The complexity of language and the distracted and distracting psychological matrix from which language springs nicely masks real meanings and issues which, like rays of sunlight through dense cloud cover, break through only with the utmost difficulty.

The inability to communicate new meaning to others, especially to those in our own field, discourages us and saps our energy. Thus the forces of distraction inherent in matter-dominated society prevent all but the rarest of inspirations from becoming breakthroughs and from disrupting the mind-debilitating, ego-soothing reality-consensus that shields society from the change that novelty always imposes.

Insights are rarely gained by mere associative ruminating in the process of forming new and valuable combinations. In addition to saturating ourselves with the elements of a problem, a special quality of alertness and attentive watchfulness is necessary in order to recognize a promising combination, even in those oft-cited instances where chance plays a disproportionately important role. The more energy we have available for this kind of intensely profound, ongoing vigilance, the less chance needs to play its role in the creative process. The more we are able to "see," the less we are in need of happy circumstances to shock us into these isolated instances of seeing. Incisive seeing is what McClintock strives for:

*What is it in an individual scientist's relation to nature that facilitates the
kind of seeing that eventually leads to productive discourse? What enabled
McClintock to see further and deeper into the mysteries of genetics than her
colleagues?*

*For her, the smallest details provided the keys to the larger whole. It was her
conviction that the closer her focus, the greater her attention to individual
detail, to the unique characteristics of a single plant, of a single kernel, of a
single chromosome, the more she could learn about the general principles
by which the maize plant as a whole was organized, the better her "feeling
for the organism."* [12]

The more deeply the intensely focused mind probes the data that the
cosmos presents, the more we understand the overall cosmic pattern and
the less we will be distracted — our energy depleted by the dissonance of
this or that out-of-place feature. Keller, speaking for McClintock, confirms:

*When scientists set out to understand a new principle of order, one of the first
things they do is look for events that disturb that order. Almost invariably it
is in the exception that they discover the rule.* [13]

The better the quality of attention, the more economical we are with
our energy and the better the quality of our thought, in a rising spiral of
efficiency. Refinement and accumulation of attention offer us a modality
of experience which, unlike anything else we know in life, is self-
generating and potentially limitless.

Creativity is inherent in the cosmos as it is in mankind. So evidence
of the proposition that some people are vastly more creative than others,
like the phenomenon of greed, is only an artifact of the distraction induced
in us by matter. It effectively masks the creative intelligence lying at the
heart of each of us. Peat puts it this way:

The source of all reality is an unconditioned creativity. [14]

Autism is a rather spectacular, if sad, illustration of this principle.
Certain autistic individuals display uncanny talents for music, art, figur-
ing out problems, and so on. For example, a teenager unable to do simple
addition names, within seconds, the days that given dates fall upon and
vice versa, or says which dates and days coincide in which years. He does
this without method or intellectual effort as we know it. Or a girl of five,
after listening to a symphony, can sing individually and faultlessly, from

---

[12] Keller, *A Feeling for the Organism*, 101-199.

[13] Ibid., 123.

[14] Peat, *Synchronicity*, 217.

beginning to end, the score for each and every instrument in the orchestra. Or a school-aged youngster without artistic training draws accurate portraits of buildings viewed from his school bus window — renderings that would easily pass as professional work.

These "idiots savant" represent a certain class of individual who, in childhood, make a fateful kind of choice. They "choose" to maintain contact with something inner at the expense of outward integration. They preserve certain primordial channels to higher intelligence at the expense of the skills upon which social development depends. These channels, as in the preceding examples, are "visible" to the outside observer to the extent that they produce results recognizable as "useful." And while they remain highly restricted in the scope of their mundane application, the natural virtuosity of such skills is undoubtedly a clear indication that these channels run very deep. Limited and restricted as they may be, in the narrow domains of the performance they govern, these channels represent a capacity for concentrated attention beyond anything we normally experience or imagine.

How can we even begin to guess at the quality of inner life these apparent "subnormals" (including those who don't display capabilities we recognize as having merit by our common standards) have preserved for themselves? Are we so sure the delights of "normalcy" and the intelligence of conventionality, as exemplified in our own lives, would measure up if objective comparisons were possible? Of course, significant comparisons are not possible. Even the pathetic, maladapted and limited exercise of Accelerated Thought evinced in examples such as those just cited is totally incommensurate with ordinary intelligence. As such, it defies methodical analysis and leaves us stymied. It matters little whether the medical condition of autistic individuals is defined as "psychological," "neurological" or some combination thereof. Whatever the cause, such capacities confront us with living manifestations of man's hidden possibilities.

The retreat into the distraction-reduced environment of the isolation tank, pioneered by Dr. John C. Lilly,[15] seems to produce a limited simulation of autism. Lilly reports that the tank, through sensory deprivation, provided him with distraction-free shelter from the physical and psychological pressures of the world and enabled him to think and solve problems with unusual rapidity. With the experience amplified by the

---

[15] See Jeffrey and Lilly, *John Lilly so far . . .* (Los Angeles: Tarcher, 1990), 85-137.

hallucinogen LSD, he claims that this environment gave an unheard-of efficiency to the functioning of his brain.

Many thinkers still cling to the simplistic formula that the intelligence manifested through creativity is a function of "divergent" or "lateral" thinking — what we more commonly call "open-mindedness." Hudson recognizes this error:

> Much writing on creativity rests on the assumptions that creative people are open, flexible and unconventional, and that the uncreative are inflexible and authoritarian. On this argument, it is the divergers (and perhaps all-rounders) who break new ground, while the convergers plod along cautiously in the rear. My own evidence suggests that this assumption is mistaken.[16]

Haddon and Lytton expand on this point:

> Despite the attention which "Creativity" has received as a fashionable topic for research there is, as yet, as Vernon (1964) and Hudson (1966) point out, no clear evidence for the assumption that high scorers on tests of 'divergent thinking' in Guilford's terminology, will be particularly fertile in creative original production in their own life situation. Nor is there evidence for the converse, that high scorers on tests of 'convergent thinking' alone, will lack such creativity. The best way of looking at this question probably is to regard high scores on divergent thinking as an indication of lack of anxiety about nonconformist responses, a necessary, but not a sufficient condition for creative work.[17]

That some people are more open than others to higher dimensions within themselves and have moments of conscious insight is more a question of circumstance than of inherent potential. Owing to conditions of life on our planet, the development of creative vision is universally stifled and some of us are simply slightly less inhibited than others. Peat seems to recognize this:

> Clearly creativity pervades every element of nature. But if this is indeed the case, then why is creativity not more evident in our own lives? For unlimited creativity is generally taken to be a special gift, something that is unique and associated with those occasional geniuses who emerge in the arts and sciences. Most people, by contrast, feel that their capacity for creativity is seriously limited, for they are caught up in the day-to-day activities of work, relationships, and family that allow them little energy or latitude for change.

---

[16] L. Hudson, "The question of creativity," *Contrary Imaginations* (Methuen, 1966; Penguin books edn., 1967), 11.

[17] F. A. Haddon and H. Lytton, "Teaching approach and the development of divergent thinking abilities in primary schools," *British Journal of Educational Psychology*, 38 (1968):171.

So whatever creativity does take place in a person's life is generally channeled into rather narrow limits that are established by circumstances and the various customs, beliefs, and restrictions of society.

Many people, when they attempt to overview their lives, sense that they are trapped by time and history. Thus they feel the victim of childhood traumas, the failures of the school system, their parents' economic and social standing, bad judgments made at work, and trapped in the neighborhood or city and the country they happen to live in. Even society, and the nation itself, appears to be a victim of its past mistakes, which make present conflicts inevitable, so that truly creative solutions seem out of the question.[18]

Like gravity, distraction and its consequences are everywhere. Whatever sparks of intelligence we do manifest are simply the residue of our capacity for vision — a higher form of intelligence that distraction has eclipsed.

We're all Infant Prodigies . . . (Thomas Mann)

Human intelligence, fundamentally, is one. That there seem to be distinct as well as higher and lower forms, including automatic skills of mind and body appearing to be autonomous and unrelated to creative vision, is distraction's way (through the agency of reflective thought) of throwing sand in our eyes. Sterile, uninspired, mechanical mentation, feeling and movement appear, for all the world, to be independent faculties quite free and unrelated to intuition, insight and vision. They are in fact all that is left of true thought after the creative core and soul of thought — consciousness — has been compromised. Alienated from our intelligence, we are alienated from ourselves. Laing puts it this way:

I am not merely spinning senseless paradoxes when I say that we, the sane ones are out of our minds. The mind is what the ego is unconscious of. We are unconscious of our minds. Our minds are not unconscious. Our minds are conscious of us. Ask yourself who and what it is that dreams our dreams. Our unconscious minds? The Dreamer who dreams knows far more of us than we know of it. It is only from a remarkable position of alienation that the source of life, the Fountain of Life, is experienced as It. The mind of which we are unaware is aware of us. It is we who are out of our minds. We need not be unaware of the inner world.[19]

Conditions of existence around us provide little opportunity for the unbridled development of creative consciousness with which we are all born. Culture soon infects us with the virulent infirmity of distraction

[18] Peat, *Synchronicity*, 215-16.
[19.] R. D. Laing, "Transcendental Experience in Relation to Religion and Psychosis," *Spiritual Emergency*, Stanislav Grof and Christina Grof, eds. (Los Angeles: Tarcher, 1990), 56-7.

through the good services of our distraction-afflicted families and the servile and sclerotic complicity of the educational system. Only the victims of autism and of some forms of insanity are, in a sense, immune. It is the mission of Project Mind to extend immunity to others in whom the spark of life has, through obsessive loyalty and unrelenting suffering, somehow survived the ordeal of solitude and oppression reserved for those who dare defy common standards of inner Being.

For the rest of us, this spark — this residue of consciousness — except for rare moments of peak experience and creative inspiration, languishes in our unconscious. Yet even this undeveloped, saving remnant can be burned out of us if the distraction of our conditions becomes too harsh. We have all met burned-out salesmen, housewives, managers, executives, laborers, students and teachers suffering from this particularly devastating form of depletion. From burnout, so symptomatic of our times, nervous breakdown is not very far. Cattell and Butcher offer us an interesting perspective on how we become depleted:

> There is a relevant, detailed discussion by Broadbent (1958) of the application of information theory to brain action, in which one of his main propositions is that as long as you use a lot of the channels for input, you have too few free channels for scanning. That could explain a good deal here. The typical extrovert conceivably has too many channels taking in information — or at least, alert to the external trivia of everyday life — and not enough for scanning accepted material. Or, to quote Wordsworth instead of information theory: "The world is too much with us." And if we paraphrase his next line: "Talking and visiting, we lay waste our powers." [20]

Given this context, it should not be difficult to see how breakthroughs in established science, when they do occur, are almost always hit-and-miss affairs. Given the over-accumulation of data around the focal point at which breakthroughs are made, they could almost be said to be inevitable occurrences rather than acts of penetrating vision as we would wish to believe.[21]

Thus it turns out, quite ironically, that the prodigious significance of isolated instances of genius — truly nonconformist vision — tends to be masked by the spectacular nature of these considerably more common, serendipitous, almost inevitable "establishment" discoveries. The sense of forward movement this conventional brand of breakthrough provides

---

[20] R. B. Cattell and H. J. Butcher, *The Prediction of Achievement and Creativity* (Bobbs-Merrill, 1968), 290.

[21] See appendix.

has the effect of reconfirming our confidence in our institutions and reinforcing our pride and sense of cultural affiliation. We are gratified and reassured by what we take to be sensational testimony to the efficacy of science, and we are led to assume that, as a species at least, we are living up to our potential.

Creativity, Eureka & Accelerated Thought

With You is the fountain of life; in your light we see light. (Psalms 36:9)

Accelerated Thought implies a far more rapid rate of progress — one freed from the constraints of social and professional norms, traditions and habits. Even more important, Accelerated Thought is free of the depleting effects of distraction. It implies a psychological state seldom encountered in daily life — one that embraces an intensity of experience almost totally foreign to mankind in its present state.

Literature on creativity is replete with reports of mental activity somewhat reminiscent of Accelerated Thought. This phenomenon is sometimes called the "Eureka" experience in honor of Archimedes' revelation of how to determine the volume of an irregularly shaped object through liquid displacement. Having left the problem aside to take a bath, Archimedes was ripe to recognize that the rising level of his bath water was the measure of his own body's volume. According to this well-known legend, the shock of this realization and the emotional energy it released propelled him out of his bath to run naked through the streets of ancient Athens shouting, "Eureka."

When a discovery comes to us in this way, we are intuitively certain of its correctness. Our resulting level of exhilaration depends on our stake in the projected outcome. McClintock bears witness:

> *"When you suddenly see the problem, something happens that you have the answer — before you are able to put it into words. It is all done subconsciously. This has happened too many times to me, and I know when to take it seriously. I'm so absolutely sure. I don't talk about it, I don't have to tell anybody about it, I'm just sure this is it.*
> *"What is ecstasy? I don't understand ecstasy, but I enjoy it. When I have it. Rare ecstasy."* [22]

This elation derives either from our sense of release[23] from a restrictive circumstance or problem that held us prisoner or, by corollary,

---

[22] Keller, *A Feeling For The Organism*, 103-204.
[23] See appendix.

from the anticipation of rewards to flow from newly revealed possibilities.

Although the Eureka experience is not exactly Accelerated Thought, it is very closely related and its habitual exercise is the trademark of creative genius. Just as a salutary shock at the right moment to a prepared mind can produce a Eureka experience, a series of Eureka experiences under favorable conditions in a properly prepared psyche can induce a chain reaction which can develop into Accelerated Thought. Accelerated Thought is a high-energy mental process whereby realizations (consisting of problems and solutions) arrive second by second in rapid-fire sequence rather than once a week, once a year or once in a lifetime as is typical with Eureka experiences under a regime of reflective[24] thought.

The intensity of this experience, described later in detail, is accompanied by a spectacular increase in vitality and a feeling of elation. There is an accumulation of awareness for real possibilities that lifts the mind and the individual as a whole (for in these moments he *is* mind) to a more integrated and conscious level of functioning than before. Increased integration and increased energy are but two sides of one coin — the coin of consciousness.

Creative Individuals as Subjects for Accelerated Thought

Never doubt that a small group of thoughtful, committed citizens can change the world; indeed, it's the only thing that ever has. (Margaret Mead)

Project Mind is based on the premise that it is possible to arrange conditions favoring the occurrence of Eureka experiences as precursors of Accelerated Thought. I will show that this induction process and Accelerated Thought itself can be induced, maintained, contained, modulated and ultimately harnessed to the benefit of mankind, and particularly to those who undergo the process. This has long been the fondest dream of professionals in the creativity field,[25] a dream that has been stymied and forestalled by impaired vision and the chronic inability to reconcile spirit and matter.

Much empirical testing and experimentation will be necessary to fine-tune environmental conditions and optimize their management to

---

[24] See appendix.
[25] See appendix.

help ensure that the process of Accelerated Thought ultimately may be successfully fostered in a wide[26] range of human types and personalities.

To begin with, it will be necessary to work with subjects already substantially predisposed towards Accelerated Thought — those who during their lifetimes have had fairly frequent Eureka experiences and, in some rare cases, perhaps even short, self-induced bouts of Accelerated Thought. These are people one would have to consider truly creatively inclined (in terms of this project).

Creative individuals, in fighting to preserve their independence of spirit, inevitably must sacrifice at least some of the comforts of conformity for an existence of relative social isolation. Such sacrifice affords them a corresponding measure of inner freedom. Very early in life, we are forced to compromise ourselves and our sense of what is right to conform to the dictates of those who wield authority. When we are very small, almost everyone is bigger and stronger than we are. Yet we all have had our moments of rebellion and personal heroism when we clung to some truth we cherished — some vision we valued — rather than sell out to the comfort of a warm, hypocritical, soul-sacrificing bath of communal acceptance.

There are those who, for one reason or another, fight harder than the rest to preserve their sense of unique identity and independent spirit. The price they pay in social dissonance and maladjustment (and sometimes in psychological imbalance) is often very high. This undoubtedly accounts to a considerable extent for the anti-social traits popularly associated with highly creative individuals. This attitude of determination and rebellion is well expressed by Weil:

> I do not want to be adopted into a circle, to live among people who say "we" and to be part of an "us," to find I am "at home" in any human milieu whatever it may be . . . I feel that it is not permissible to me. I feel that it is necessary and ordained that I should be alone, a stranger and an exile in relation to every human circle without exception.[27]

Having accustomed themselves to foregoing a certain degree of approbation as the price for preserving and cultivating a corresponding measure of freedom of thought, these people, somewhat more than others, become adept at breaking out of conventional frameworks of thought and seeing from fresh new angles. This facility could be of priceless benefit

---

[26] See appendix.
[27] Simone Weil, *Waiting for God*, trans. by Emma Craufurd (New York: G.P. Putnam Sons, 1959), 54.

to science and industry in formulating novel hypotheses, in radical extrapolating and in proposing revolutionary new technological capabilities. In reality it tends to become either diverted from, or suffocated within, the highly structured environment of formal organizations. Despite the opportunities and enticements business seems to offer, the truly creative individual is plainly going to be discouraged by the bureaucratic group-think of industrial and commercial environments with their mundane and narrowly defined mission-oriented mandates and conformist hierarchies. Leary had rules for pursuing unconventional ends — in his case, psychedelic drug studies — in institutional settings:

> *Rule number one: work with influential officials on the fringes of the system. Rule number two: use the prestige of the institution while remaining as far as possible from its center. Rule number three: find closet individualists within the system to protect you.*[28]

Leary's strategy paid off for a time, but he soon had to move out of the mainstream of society in search of conditions in which he could pursue his truth, in (relative) safety.

Existing Conditions Discourage Creativity

Test me, O Lord, and try me, examine my heart and my mind. (Psalms 26:2)

The creatively inclined existential loner tends to be relegated to roles at society's periphery where more tolerance exists towards individualism and independent thought. But even at the fringes such an individual rarely finds a framework to support the full and free expression of his particular creative bent. Even the most liberal and innovative businesses and institutions tend to be encumbered by the constricting requirements of conventional society with which they must interact in order to survive. Thus with most avenues of expression and development blocked, there is a tendency for creative people to remain indistinguishable from their pedestrian neighbors aside from their telltale proclivity towards antisocial expression. Ghiselin comments:

> *One might suppose it easy to detect creative talent and to recognize creative impulse and creative work. But the difficulties are considerable. Because every creative act overpasses the established order in some way and in some degree, it is likely at first to appear eccentric to most men. An inventor ordinarily must begin in isolation and draw the group to himself only as it*

---

[28] Timothy Leary, *Flashbacks*, (Los Angeles: Tarcher, 1990), 153.

is discovered, sometimes very slowly, that he has invented some part of what they are in need of. At the beginning of his struggle for realization his originality may achieve no more striking manifestation than an extreme dissatisfaction with established order.[29]

Normally, it is only in light of proven achievements that creative genius is finally recognized. Hard facts impose themselves upon us whether we like them or not. Our patience is sorely tried by pretentious claims to vision. Without concrete proof, a new theory even when accompanied by elaborate explication requires of us bystanders either corresponding powers of vision or at least considerable effort for the theory's assimilation — effort few are willing to make. McClintock learned this the hard way:

It is commonplace about scientific discourse that the more a claim is at odds with accepted beliefs, the more resistance it encounters. (It is also the case that any divergent claim is by its nature hard to understand, even for those who listen with good will.) And the results that McClintock reported in 1951 were totally at variance with the view of genetics that predominated.

Would she be able to communicate her "understanding" to others? She was sufficiently aware of the disparity already present between her own thinking and that of her colleagues to know that many of them would have difficulty seeing the implication of her new findings.

McClintock was right to be apprehensive. Her talk at the Cold Spring Harbor Symposium that summer was met with stony silence. With one or two exceptions, no one understood. Afterward, there was mumbling—even some snickering — and outright complaints. It was impossible to understand. What was this woman up to?

She had unveiled her creation, a beautiful explanatory model with full supporting evidence, the object of six years of loving attention and grueling hard work, and her colleagues had turned their backs.[30]

We do not so readily accept such pretensions in others until we are confronted with irrefutable proof or are otherwise coerced by circumstances (e.g., social consensus or physical force) to make this effort of comprehension and ego adaptation. In his youth, Einstein himself was considered a dullard and had to struggle to get by professionally, at least at the early stages of his career, until his work was eventually confirmed.

In the mid-1800s, Hungarian physician Ignaz Philipp Semmelweis discovered that bacteria was the cause of infectious disease. Despite a spectacular drop in mortality in the wards under his control, he was

---

[29] *The Creative Process*, Brewster Ghiselin, ed. (New York: Mentor Books, 1964).
[30] Keller, *A Feeling For The Organism*, 138-145.

ridiculed, ostracized and forced out of his post at Vienna General Hospital. Nothing he did succeeded in overcoming barriers of envy, suspicion and ignorance. Almost predictably, he lost his mind and committed suicide. Harman and **Rheingold** sum it up this way:

> *The course of history has been profoundly affected by precisely those experiences that most people find hardest to believe. In science and the arts, we have seen how those who were derided by their contemporaries as crackpots or lunatics were often hailed by later generations as geniuses or visionaries. The same seems to be true in the realm of spiritual experience, at least in certain notable instances.*[31]

Manifestly brilliant young people judged by their peers "most likely to succeed," more often than not become rather pedestrian scientists, educators and the like, if not outright failures. So how are we to judge? Hudson has this to say about intelligence:

> *That the conventional intelligence test has failed to predict who will do outstanding work in science (or any other field) there is little question. MacKinnon's work is the most telling in this respect. He finds little or no connection between adult I.Q. and adult achievement above a minimum level, which lies somewhere in the region of I.Q. 120. That is to say, nearly all of his eminent men and women produced scores above this level; but amongst them, the relation between I.Q. and originality was virtually nil. A mature scientist with an adult I.Q. of 130 is as likely to win a Nobel Prize as is one whose I.Q. is 180.*[32]

That we tend to recognize creative genius only in retrospect is not just because we are petty and deny credit to those who threaten to reveal our mediocrity. We have genuine difficulty in distinguishing truly original thought from mere pretentious nonconformity and other forms of gratuitously defiant deviance.

This difficulty arises directly from our own pedestrian level of thought and awareness which deprives us of the energy necessary to break out, even momentarily, from our lethargic routine. Thoreau conveys this idea forcefully:

> *To him whose elastic and vigorous thought keeps pace with the sun, the day is a perpetual morning. It matters not what the clocks say or the attitudes or labors of men. Morning is when I am awake and there is a dawn in me. Moral reform is the effort to throw off sleep. Why is it that men give so poor an account of their day if they have not been slumbering? They are not such poor calculators. If they had not been overcome with drowsiness they would have*

---

[31] Harman and Rheingold, *Higher Creativity*, 122.
[32] Hudson, "The question of creativity," 104.

performed something. The millions are awake enough for physical labor; but only one in a million is awake enough for intellectual exertion, only one in a hundred millions to a poetic or divine life. To be awake is to be alive. I have never yet met a man who was quite awake. How could I have looked him in the face?

We must learn to reawaken and keep ourselves awake, not by mechanical aids, but by an infinite expectation of the dawn, which does not forsake us in our soundest sleep.[33]

Thus true creativity is the immediate, ongoing, waking vision of a unified intelligence. Yet traditionally, creativity is seen to be comprised of discrete stages including self-application, incubation, Eureka, elaboration, etc. — depending on the point of view. This insistence upon separate phases rests on the virtually universal misconception that the ignition phase forms an integral and inseparable part of the creative process, and thus must be repeated anew for each creative thought or act. But the ignition of a process or engine is, or at least should be, nothing more than incidental to its running. In these terms, the process of creativity as popularly perceived is likened to an automobile that stalls every few inches and never actually gets going. "Elaboration" similarly presumes that the process is soon over and that the details are worked out as a denouement in a prosaic frame of mind. Creativity is almost universally considered to be an inherently brief condition and not the continuing state of Being that, potentially, it is.

For much the same reasons thinkers often fail to distinguish between unconscious processes (including skills and habits of thought, perception, feeling and action that we have programmed into ourselves, not to omit the neurotic and psychotic ones) and the subconscious. Hypnosis gives some credence to the popular belief that the unconscious includes a record of everything we have experienced since birth and perhaps earlier The unconscious and its programmed routines, like instinct, can normally be trusted to operate reliably below the level of awareness. The subconscious is our inborn, hard-wired, coded knowledge of the world that forms an integral part of us. It contains all that is knowable to man and is the functional complexity of our "soul" impressed by nature onto the material of our essence. It can be awakened to any significant degree only through intense, direct contact with reality and, to some extent, through the exercise of intuition that aims at the heart of essence. Instinct provides the only common ground shared by the unconscious and subconscious.

---

[33] Thoreau, *Walden*, J. W. Krutch, ed., 172.

Instinct is recorded in essence and rendered manifest through automatic, unconscious action. One could say that the unconscious contains "forgotten" experience while the subconscious contains innate knowledge not yet experienced.

In the distraction of daily life the only contact we normally have with our subconscious is the occasional insight during particularly intense moments when the inevitable struggle with life arouses the cosmic truth imprinted on essence (the "root" or "seed" of our unique individuality). Even then, only the outer layers of essence are usually concerned. While the constant stream of impressions we receive from daily life may impinge on essence, they are largely deflected.

> One's own self is well hidden from one's own self. Of all mines of treasure, one's own is the last to be dug up. (Friedrich Nietzsche)

A great deal also has been written about dreaming and dream-like states where the inhibitive effects of our habits of thought break down and allow the "bizarre" within us to surface. As a rule, these analyses beg the question of what in us has both the capacity and the inclination to break out of the straightjacket convention imposes. What slips by unnoticed is that the core function of creativity is vision. Keller says of McClintock:

> Arguments in cytogenetics employ an interplay of qualitative and quantitative reasoning in which the quantitative analysis rests on a host of prior judgments that remain necessarily qualitative. In particular, before the effects of specific genetic crosses can be counted, distinct phenotypic and cytological traits need to be identified. Both of these processes of identification require kinds of experience not easily communicated to those who have not participated in the actual observations. They require an extensive training of the eye. And McClintock's eye was surpassingly well trained. "Seeing," in fact, was at the center of her scientific experience.[34]

Seeing becomes vision when what is seen is a discovery — a newly perceived reality. Preliminaries are thus necessary for priming Accelerated Thought, but they also could be said to be a necessary "evil," required by the listlessness of our reflective thought and distracted state. In principle, the need for "priming" declines as channels to the subconscious are established and vision grows.

---

[34] Keller, *A Feeling For The Organism*, 147-8.

The Need for Self-Knowledge

A man who strays from the path of understanding comes to rest in the company of the dead. (Proverbs 21:16)

That our state of distracted awareness almost completely inhibits the possibility of vision escapes the understanding of those who study creativity. It escapes simply because they consider themselves already conscious and largely free of the restriction of spirit imposed by matter although they are as much subject to it as anyone else.

Creativity researchers quite rightly attribute the rarely observed psychological phenomena associated with creativity to the subconscious, but they do so for the wrong reasons. The subconscious is the repository of cosmic truth emanating from essence. This is our potential for contacting reality, not some magic problem-solving mechanism serving our indolent existence.

The subconscious remains submerged because the truth it guards is totally incompatible with our illusions. Once our relationship with the material world begins to reflect cosmic reality (and this is the objective of all the great philosophies, ways and religions), the truth buried in this subconscious need no longer fear the light of day. It can meet and merge with the existential reality to which it corresponds through the agency of a unified consciousness which is our greatest potential — our birthright. Janov expresses something similar in a therapeutic context:

> *Some of us prefer the neurotic never-never land where nothing can be absolutely true because it can lead us away from other personal truths that hurt so much. The neurotic has a personal stake in the denial of truth, and it is this we must face when stating that a truth has been found. To find truth is to find freedom. It means to eliminate neurotic choice which is no more than rationalized anarchy. The neurotic who wants to be free to see all sides often cannot believe that he may proceed directly to what is true — not my truth but his. He has only to journey inside himself, which is a lot closer than India.*
>
> *Science is the search for truth, which does not preclude finding it.* [35]

We will begin to recognize true innovators and reduce the superfluous pain and trouble we wreak upon them only when we gain a clearer notion of our own inner makeup. We must discover how, through creativity, information can be integrated within consciousness to become

---

[35] Arthur Janov, *The Primal Scream* (New York: Dell, 1975), 422-3.

real knowledge, and how our minds can integrate with matter in a new, rectified way.

The field of art seems to be free of many constraints that inhibit creativity. The raw materials are relatively inexpensive (when compared, for example, with the tools of science) and creativity is widely acknowledged to be inseparable from the very nature of art. Nor, provided he has independent means, does the artist need the active sanction, cooperation or approval of others, at least at the creative stage of the work. He brings down flashes of vision, giving them form, however vague, to serve as signposts to those who will attempt to travel farther along these same roads.

Everywhere I go, I find a poet has been there before me. (Sigmund Freud)

The main problem facing the artist concerns the abuse of this very freedom. In the functional world of science and technology, "the proof is in the pudding." A theory or an invention, whether expressed as a product or a process, either works or it doesn't, is useful or it isn't. Very little subjectivity[36] enters into it. Criteria of validity and value are less clear-cut in matters of aesthetics,[37] and largely leave the rigors of sincerity in the hands of the artist himself. It is difficult to be stringently impartial with oneself and with one's work.

The inventor is kept honest by the heartless, unyielding laws of physics. But without hard and fast criteria for art,[38] and original art in particular, what is to keep the creative artist's work tied to any reality?

Thus conditions for the successful expression of creative genius include not only the freedom to exercise one's hard-won flair for original thought, but also the requirements of inner consistency, fortitude and discipline necessary to overcome difficulties, doubts and uncertainties.

All my life I have struggled to make one authentic gesture. (Isadora Duncan)

This degree of integrity is hard to find even in men of the cloth, let alone in poets, artists and others pretending to creativity. These, like most people who pursue creativity (being generally predisposed to dissension, rebellion and non-conformity), tend to gravitate toward the fringes of society where both deviation and laxness are tolerated. There, for lack of communal support, most artists tend to languish impotently with little else for comfort than the cloying taste of prideful revolt and their fantasies of what they might have become in a better world.

[36] See appendix.
[37] See appendix.
[38] See appendix.

On the other hand, those creatively inclined people who find accommodation by compromising somewhat within mainstream society usually do so at the expense of having to live what remains of their nonconformist impulses, thoughts and aspirations largely in the solitude of their own hearts. To further relieve the dissonance and discomfort of this existentially lonely "corner" of their psyche, they may make one concession too many. Forsaking their secret defiance towards conformist banality amounts to surrender (self-betrayal), breaking their already tenuous contact with that mysterious, unborn reality. In this way, most connections with inner truth die stillborn, and with them the creative fertilizing germ for ushering truth into this world.

In summary, one could say that the process of creativity and, ultimately, Accelerated Thought, is purchased at the price of having to contend with and prevail against the limitations matter imposes upon our spirit both directly, through our sensory apparatus, and indirectly, through the influence of material-obsessed society. Inversely, abdicating the struggle in favor of the relative comfort and peace of conventionality cuts us off from the energy and exhilaration of discovery and possibilities for inner growth.

Abstraction & the Illusion of Freedom

Set me free from my prison, that I may praise your name. (Psalms 142:7)
Yet, there is still another class of individual who, like the artist, appears to be free of many social and material restraints and could be thought of as an exception to this rule. Take the case of today's computer "whiz-kid." This free-wheeling program writer has a very high degree of freedom in developing, testing and applying any program he devises. With his personal computer substituting for laboratory, workshop and scientific personnel, it would seem that the world is his oyster.

Like mathematics, computer science concerns itself primarily with relationship, referents for which are presumed to be found in the real world. Thus most programming and most uses of mathematics concern themselves with the ever-increasing efficaciousness of handling data from such other disciplines as physics, chemistry, engineering, economics, accounting, etc. Besides being the handmaiden of science, industry and commerce, computer science is a science in its own right. Although, strictly speaking, a program is nothing more than a set of instructions to manipulate data, matter, other programs or even itself, the consequences of such manipulation are not always foreseen and can be far-ranging indeed, as the work done so far in artificial intelligence, virtual reality and neural networking shows. But computer science is just in its infancy and is still undergoing rapid mutation.

The hypotheses of sciences concerned with relation and abstract form use constructs that describe, map, model and understand the unknown. While all science is concerned with relation and the exploration of reality, computer science and mathematics, taken exclusively as independent tools of discovery, concern themselves principally with concepts of relation. Unlike physics and chemistry, these are only indirectly concerned with matter as such. Poincaré observes:

> *The genesis of mathematical creation is a problem which should intensely interest the psychologist. It is the activity in which the human mind seems to take least from the outside world, in which it acts or seems to act only of itself and on itself, so that in studying the procedure of geometric thought we may hope to reach what is most essential in man's mind.*[39]

It might seem that computer scientists and mathematicians, unencumbered by many constraints that normally impede creative thought, would be revealing the unknown more rapidly than anyone else. The increasingly unlimited manipulations of computer text and graphics lend credence to this expectation. Shouldn't scientists in these "matter-free" disciplines[40] be piercing cosmic mysteries at a far faster rate than their matter-bound counterparts?

To derive meaning from thought, man's mind needs to work with forms that refer more or less directly to his world — his realm of reality. Theorizing in mathematics and computer science can soon reach a point where conceptual forms and patterns become so rarefied, so abstract, so far removed from experience as to become completely enigmatic. The progression of such constructs proceeds blindly according to the rules of some proposition, principle or thought game. Similarly, the ability to control forms on a computer screen is worlds away from the control of matter. Form is infinitely more pliant than matter.[41]

In other words abstract concepts, to the extent that they become bereft of significant referents to the known world, tend to lose meaning

---

[39] H. Poincaré, *The Foundations of Science* (Science Press, 1924), 383.
[40] See appendix.
[41] See appendix.

and usefulness until an internally consistent abstract theory is found to correspond to some real phenomenon or, at very least, to fit into some existing theory. This is especially true of mathematics:

> The mathematical facts worthy of being studied are those which, by their analogy with other facts, are capable of leading us to the knowledge of a mathematical law just as experimental facts lead us to the knowledge of a physical law. They are those which reveal to us unsuspected kinship between other facts, long known, but wrongly believed to be strangers to one another.[42]

Kinship or relationship reveals meaning. But the battle for meaning starts from and ends in the known — in forms and functions which relate in some way to life experience or to knowledge derived from such experience. Between these two anchorage points such a campaign can roam far afield into the "netherworlds" of conjecture.[43]

Unfortunately for the mathematical genius and his computer-bound cousin, the rather abstract relational aspect of their medium and the material with which they work greatly inhibit them from developing the depth of commitment necessary for fueling the process of Accelerated Thought. Abstractions lacking firm referents have a way of slipping through the fingers of the mind. Mental constructs derived more or less directly from the material world are so much more accessible, more concrete, more "real" and more readily retained by our reason, such as it is.

The image of creative genius so often projected by professionals in these and many other fields derives mainly from the gift of associational facility — the ability to easily grasp, retain and manipulate ideas and bits of information. It is at a premium in professions dominated by the subtleties of abstraction. Associational facility, often confused with intelligence itself, has the effect of amplifying our reflective capacities and underscores the little-known fact that reflection is a corruption of abstract thought. However, gifts can also be impediments:

> It would be a fundamental error to believe that a man's vocation coincides with his most indisputable gifts . . . sometimes it runs contrary to them. There are causes — such as Goethe's — in which the multiplicity of gifts troubles and disorients the vocation, or at least the man which is its axis.[44]

---

[42] Ibid., 386.

[43] See appendix.

[44] Jose Ortega y Gasset, *In Search of Goethe from Within*, trans. by Willard Trask, in William Phillips and Philip Rahv, eds., The New Partisan Reader, 1945-1953 (New York: Andre Deutsch, 1953).

Even a small dose of creative courage can go a long way in the world of conventional achievement when amplified with such a gift. Yet the moment courage lacks, the individual, confronted with a problem that requires much more than the merely manipulative faculty of ideational fluency, is stymied like everyone else. To understand an idea, one first has to envision it, then take hold of it and finally become one with it. New ideas (including old ideas which are new to the one exposed to them) display a certain pristine resistance to suitors of insufficient virtue.

All this does not preclude discovery or even Eureka experiences in computer science or mathematics. It does mean that the unusual freedom of exploration afforded by concepts only tenuously connected to the world of what we call "matter" is purchased at the expense of the added difficulty of engaging and coming to practical terms with such concepts. And it is precisely the practical implications of any discovery (or in the wider sense their significance, importance or meaning) that have the capacity to excite the researcher and ultimately galvanize him to the energy level at which Accelerated Thought operates. The illusion of freedom from conventional matter-imposed inhibitions grows in direct proportion to the detachment of concepts from significant referents in the real world.

Form as Intermediary Between Mind & Matter

He knows how we are formed, he remembers that we are dust. I was woven together in the depths of the earth. (Psalms 103:14, 139:15)

This alerts us to the ubiquitous presence of forms, both in the matter of the world and in the representational functions of the mind. Concepts, feelings, sensations and perceptions are the mind-forms with which we maintain and create representations of outer reality. Just as certain dispositions of matter lead to the release of given forms of energy, so special, meaningful configurations of the forms of thought, feeling and sensation can release corresponding energies and awarenesses.

All matter is created out of some imperceptible substratum . . . nothingness, unimaginable and undetectable. But it is a particular form of nothingness out of which all matter is created. (Paul Dirac)

It is important to understand the terms "matter," "form," and "energy" — actually three aspects of one thing. When we talk about levels of materiality, we mean coarser and finer forms of matter: for instance, solid, liquid gas and plasma. Or, to take a more concrete example: ice, water, steam and super-heated steam.

These different forms of matter imply different energy levels. Anyone who has been burned by steam knows that it packs much more force than boiling water at the same temperature. The energy difference pertains to the difference of form assumed by the water when it becomes steam. The different life forms — mineral,[45] vegetable, animal and human — also display progressively finer levels of materiality, not only in their physical appearance and complexity of organization, but also in that elusive quality we call "life-energy," "consciousness" or "intelligence." Lacking the notion of levels of materiality and levels of consciousness restricts us to a flat- earth view of reality. Like a rat's maze, it subjects us to the oppression of limitation, obstruction and difficulty wherever we turn.

One interesting criterion that can help us differentiate levels as they apply to life forms is noting the principal foods these life forms require. Animals can manage on coarser food than can humans (raw meat, rough vegetation, decaying matter, etc.), while plants get by on still coarser fare (inorganic matter). Now, thanks to Einstein, it is becoming common knowledge that matter is itself a form of energy. This idea is quite different from the conventional notion of combustion, which is simply a chemical reaction whereby oxygen combines with "fuel" substances to produce heat, water and oxidized by- products. The difference according to Einstein's formula $E=MC^2$ (energy = the mass of matter multiplied by the speed of light squared) is that matter disappears completely and energy appears in its place. This is a truly cosmic transformation or change of form, although by no means the final one. This is because energy is also matter, albeit of a much finer consistency. It will eventually be shown to be transformable again and again into still finer forms of matter and energy appertaining to the higher cosmic dimensions to which these finer forms belong.

Living creatures participate in similar processes. The cells of our body, including brain cells, burn food for energy in complex oxidation-like processes. Our minds, however (and by "mind" I refer here to the capacity of consciousness that derives from our ability to sense, feel and think), have spectacular transformational possibilities on a cosmic scale strangely evocative of Einstein's famous formula. Virtually all the great

---

[45] See appendix.

traditions, in one way or another, tell us we have the incredible ability to embrace virtually all cosmic levels of energy and matter, including those yet undreamed-of by science. Science still has a long way to go before it comes to terms with such phenomena as thought, feeling, attention, consciousness and life as forms of energy and matter.

Just as there are intermediate, mundane levels of material transformation (the instance of oxidation was just given) whereby relatively modest amounts of energy are released through the interaction of rather large amounts of matter, our brain — the generator of mind — in its commonly known manifestations also has a correspondingly moderate, low-grade efficiency range of functioning. This range includes mind processes with which we are most habitually concerned — mind processes which embrace almost all our social interaction.

Besides occasional Eureka experiences and despite the constraints of distraction, communal life permits at least vestiges of higher level, quasi-cosmic type transformational mind-processes. These usually come in the form of "peak experiences" — short bursts of heightened awareness and feeling — in the spheres of identity formation, rites of passage, romantic love, parenthood, religious revelation, sports (participative and spectator), ceremonies (communal, religious and others) and death. The radiance of certain lovers, brides, new and expectant parents, born-again Christians, Jews, etc., is a telltale sign that their awareness has changed from that of those around them. Persons undergoing this temporary transformation know instinctively that they are participating in a larger, extraordinary reality granting them a finer sense of existence than the everyday one charged with energy and wonder.[46]

The most common and elemental peak experience is the sexual orgasm. This brief taste of paradise, of eternity, provides for many the only respite from banality — the only transcendence — ever experienced. Orgasm[47] bears a hint, not always heeded, that somewhere there are higher, more divine sources of gratification than those to which nature normally grants access. It mimics the perpetual ecstasy of potentially permanent states of consciousness yet unattained. Happily, many of us are blessed with varied, if transitory, tastes of higher reality. But the one thing all "peak experiences" have in common is the exhilarating release from the restriction that our distracted state normally imposes upon feeling.

[46] See appendix.
[47] See appendix.

Feeling also can be released by external means by vividly evoking that which evinces hope. By exalting our values through his vision and talent, the artist sustains our mood and morale. The sports fan, thrilled by a brilliant play or the achievement of a new record, witnesses excellence which to him represents the extension of the limits of what was heretofore possible. People in love are convinced of their future happiness and for a time feel certain they have left the constraints of loneliness and despondency behind; each finds in his partner the promise of a continuing high-energy experience of self.

Unfortunately, for most of us these breakthroughs are mostly passive, lived as replays evoked from artistic representation. We depend on others to create the inspiration upon which our elevated state depends. The wave of feeling we ride is based on invocations of hope vibrating on the wavelength of shared values. In our chronic state of spiritual deprivation we sometimes crave moments of transcendence. If we weren't granted occasional release through these furtive peeks into eternity — these reminders of the possibility of higher level functioning and awareness within ourselves — what sources of inspiration or depth of meaning would be left to us altogether?

There are also moments during which, spontaneously, we suddenly wake up to the feeling that life is passing us by — that we have forgotten to live it and to explore its possibilities. The most notable of these "moments" is depression, and especially the depression known as "mid-life crisis." On the surface we can appear to be mourning for our lost youth. We are actually suffering from the anxious realization that we may have missed the boat, and from disorientation concerning what boat exactly we have missed. We find ourselves at a loss as to where to turn in a world largely indifferent to this kind of realization. Society usually finds a way to tranquilize our disquiet. But in ignoring this mid-life alarm — this S.O.S. flare sent out from essence — and in consenting to rejoin communal anesthesia at this critical juncture, we are cut off, perhaps irrevocably, from life's most substantial transformational possibilities. Only a person who is pursuing his true vocation, or some line connected to that vocation, will be spared the worst of the pain inherent in this "valley of the shadow of death." The more his transformational prospects are rooted in the matter of this world, the more he will benefit from the reminder it represents.

Just as matter can be shaped and formed or even completely transformed into energy, concepts and images (which are the representations by which matter is retained by thought) can be molded through imagination and transformed[48] into awareness. This can happen if these forms join in special energy-releasing combinations corresponding to still finer forms of materiality in the process of throwing light on some new, yet-unrevealed reality.

A new idea or form is revealed as a reality simultaneously with its meaning. And meaning, in the end, boils down to usefulness, even if that use is temporarily restricted to merely aesthetic or intellectual realms. Its place is defined by its known function. When some form acquires a new function, it takes on new meaning. The psychic energy generated through acts of creativity, and more specifically through Accelerated Thought, derives from the discovery of forms bestowing new meanings to life. In other words, they grant us new possibilities, new (external) functions, and concomitant new perspectives and understandings. This act of discovery is an unveiling of light hitherto obscured by old and coarse forms.

The discovery of each new possibility suggests to man, at least unconsciously, the prospect of removing all that limits him and bars his way to paradise. "Paradise" is our poetic euphemism for unlimited joy, omnipotence, omniscience and, above all, immortality. At the slightest hint of these prospects, man's spirit soars as a great energy of hope and anticipation begins to circulate in him. This is the energy of Accelerated Thought.

The key to the treasure is the treasure itself. (John Barth)

• • •

---

[48] See appendix.

CHAPTER SIX

Thought Transformation —
the Search for Meaning & Purpose

A man's work is nothing more than this slow trek to rediscover, through the detours of art, those two or three great and simple images in whose presence his heart first opened. (Albert Camus)

Early candidates for Project Mind will, of necessity, have gained considerable mastery over their chosen field of endeavor or at least in areas pertinent to those of nature's secrets they wish to penetrate with Accelerated Thought. Ghiselin recognizes the importance of competence:

> *Even the most energetic and original mind, in order to reorganize or extend human insight in any valuable way, must have attained more than ordinary mastery of the field in which it is to act, a strong sense of what needs to be done and skill in the appropriate means of expression. It seems certain that no significant expansion of insight can be produced otherwise, whether the activity is thought of as work or not. Often an untutored beauty appears in the drawings of children, and we rightly prize the best of them because they have wholeness of motive, but they have scarcely the power to open the future for us. For that, the artist must labor to the limit of human development and then take a step beyond. The same is true for every sort of creative worker.[1]*

More important still, these candidates will be predisposed towards creative thought although most, through caution and common sense, will have avoided venturing solo very far into Accelerated Thought. The prime reason for this avoidance has its roots in the very valid fear, conscious or unconscious, of the psychologically harmful consequences of pushing themselves unprotected beyond certain limits of concentration. Passing from any given mode of functioning to any other means altering one's inner state of dynamic equilibrium, implying an intermediate state of imbalance — a delicate, even precarious indeterminate point between the old and the new.

---

[1] Ghiselin, ed., *The Creative Process*, 29.

Energy trapped in a restricted loop must be freed and fed into larger, less constrained circuits. The shorter circuit contains less resistance, does less useful work and thus is inherently more stable for any given energy level. This is analogous to the higher stability of the more fundamental elements whose electrons maintain few and tight orbits around their nuclei. To sacrifice this stability in the interest of higher, more complex functioning permitting more points of contact with larger realities involves considerable effort. Such attempts initially trigger subjective reactions including fear and revulsion.

Any new state of equilibrium is just that — new — and requires time to accumulate the increased energy necessary for its own stability. This delicate and perilous passage can place the individual at considerable risk, especially in environments intolerant to unconventional psychological manifestations. On the other hand, there are always those rare individuals who, despite this fear, feel somehow compelled to summon their courage and try to realize what they intuitively feel to be the potential of their creative faculty.

Some tend to be attracted by the adventure offered by experimentation itself, especially the excitement and elation that unfailingly accompany creative thought. Others are motivated by the rewarding results anticipated from such an adventure, among which can be counted the power that tends to accrue to those who possess unique knowledge. For most, the prospect of contributing substantially to and becoming appreciated by one's fellow man represents an important source of motivation. But all such instances have in common a burning passion for life and a healthy impulse towards action. Kierkegaard recognizes the importance of passion, courage and action:

> Thus our own age is essentially one of understanding, and on the average, perhaps, more knowledgeable than any former generation, but it is without passion. Every one knows a great deal, we all know which way we ought to go and all the different ways we can go, but nobody is willing to move. If at last some one were to overcome the reflection within him and happened to act, then immediately thousands of reflections would form an outward obstacle. Only a proposal to reconsider a plan is greeted with enthusiasm; action is met by indolence.[2]

He sees that distraction — what he calls a "reflective condition" — saps courage and passion and undermines action:

---

[2] Sören Kierkegaard, *The Present Age*, trans. Alexander Dru (N.Y.: Harper Torchbooks, 1962), 77-8.

Reflection is not the evil; but a reflective condition and the deadlock which it involves, by transforming the capacity for action into a means of escape from action, is both corrupt and dangerous, and leads in the end to a retrograde movement. The present age is essentially one of understanding lacking in passion.[3]

The courage and passion animating candidates for Accelerated Thought represent that premium of vitality that has survived distraction. There are many impulses that can animate an individual's inclination towards this kind of mind-adventure, but they could all be summarized under the general heading of "the search for meaning." This book is all about meaning: how it is sought, established and transformed, but most important, how meaning forms the basis of life itself.

There are those among us who, from time to time, awaken to a feeling from deep within carrying at least the whisper of a conviction that we are destined for something greater than the ordinary. That feeling or intuition[4] expresses an ambition far beyond the idea of success or even exceptional achievement within existing frameworks. The very difficulty in speaking of these feelings and aspirations derives from the fact that they issue from that little-known domain in ourselves — essence.

Life is a maze in which we take the wrong turn before we have learned to walk. (Cyril Connolly)

A genuine search for meaning implies a striving for some kind of redefinition of things and, ultimately, for self and world transformation. It is an inner impulse to break out of the constraining obscurity of accepted, habitual modes of reflective thought, feeling and action dictated by social frameworks governed by distraction — frameworks which must cultivate conformity if they are to survive. Kierkegaard again:

If, for a moment, it should seem as though an individual were about to succeed in throwing off the yoke of reflection, he is at once pulled up by the opposition of the reflection which surrounds him. The envy which springs from reflection imprisons man's will and his strength. First of all the individual has to break loose from the bonds of his own reflection, but even then he is not free. Instead he finds himself in the vast prison formed by the reflection of those around him. He can only escape from this second imprisonment through the inwardness of religion, no matter how clearly he may perceive the falseness of his situation. With every means in its power reflection prevents people from realizing that both the individual and the age

---

[3] Ibid, 68.
[4] See appendix.

are thus imprisoned, not imprisoned by tyrants and priests or nobles or the secret police, but by reflection itself. . .[5]

For Kierkegaard, the search for meaning implied religion. Others favor different approaches. Some of us explore through sounds, some through words, some through abstractions, some through images, others through feeling and still others kinetically. Then there are the various combinations of these. Exactly how we select our chief modalities of reality processing is hard to say. Yet it would be safe to speculate that competitive pressures in our formative years force us to lean on those functions that serve us most readily. This, in time, tends to orient us towards professional vocations requiring these specific forms of cognitive facility. Thus, faculties that might have become functional channels for the expression of creative impulses usually end up serving the narrow, egoistic interests of the individual and of the society that maintains itself through the encouragement of such reductive modalities of Being.

It is true that some societies seem more progressive than others concerning the latitudes of thought and expression they permit. But given the scale of the problem, such distinctions are trivial. This freedom, for most of us, constitutes nothing more than an illusion. It is an insidious trap preventing us from seeing the reality of our condition which, like sleep, is a sort of prison with invisible walls. Whatever meaning can be found within the framework of any common society, regardless of how liberal, does not begin to answer to the definition of "meaning" as something that connects us with eternity.[6]

Vision of Truth & Utopia, Fundamental to Our Humanity

Truth is completely spontaneous. Lies have to be taught. (Buckminster Fuller)
Candidates for the intense creative effort needed to initiate Accelerated Thought carry within them a profound, usually inarticulate faith that things are not at all as they seem, and that bright, clear vision could free us from the aimless and confining routine that life in society usually offers. For psychologically obvious reasons they dare not admit, often even to themselves, that they aspire to a fairy-tale world where existence

---

[5] Kierkegaard, *Present Age*, 48.
[6] See appendix.

glows with bright, almost psychedelic luminosity and color, where virtue and evil are extant for all to see and where virtue must always prevail.

It is not to deceive or to poison their minds that the young are fed children's stories and fairy tales. On the contrary, these tales and the atmosphere they breed evoke curiosity, wonder and vitality in children who very naturally believe not only that the world is benign and that good prevails over evil, but that life is a wonderful adventure leading them to untold treasure and happiness. Small children find it easy to believe that all that limits, separates and leads to hurt (or worse) can be vanquished. As naive as it may seem, we might do well to ask ourselves if this is not the reality for which we were truly destined. Berg conveys this sentiment eloquently:

> Into this mysterious universe we are born, with no apparent set of instructions, no maps or equations, no signs or guideposts, nothing but our equally unfathomable instincts, intuitions and reasoning abilities to tell us where we came from, why we are here and what we are supposed to do. What we do possess — perhaps it the key to our survival as a species — is an almost unquenchable need to know. A human being comes into this world with a passionate sense of wonder and inquisitiveness and an equally powerful need for self expression. Yet, somehow these seemingly indelible primal imperatives become eroded, as a rule, after only a few years exposure to modern "reality" and contemporary educational methods.[7]

It seems that the human need for this vision is so fundamental that even repressive, thought-censoring society cannot afford to deny us at least limited exposure to such "dissident propaganda." In fact, the establishment does not abolish fairy tales for fear of crippling our psyche and rendering us unfit for productive socialization. There exist conventional psychological explanations, almost apologies, for the need for fairy-tale material during early childhood. Yet the one thing these explanations do not recognize is that the vision this material offers the child is a possible one — one demanded by its very nature. Thoreau concurs:

> Shams and delusions are esteemed for soundest truths, while reality is fabulous. If men would steadily observe realities only, and not allow themselves to be deluded, life, to compare it with such things as we know, would be like a fairy tale and the Arabian Nights' Entertainments. If we respected only what is inevitable and has a right to be, music and poetry would resound along the streets. When we are unhurried and wise, we

---

[7] The Zohar Parshat Pinhas, Philip S. Berg, trans., comp. and ed. (Jerusalem - N.Y.: Research Center of Kabbalah Press, 1987), Vol. 1, preface xix.

perceive that only great and worthy things have any permanent and absolute existence, — that petty fears and petty pleasures are but the shadow of the reality. This is always exhilarating and sublime. By closing the eyes and slumbering, and consenting to be deceived by shows, men establish and confirm their daily life of routine and habit every where, which is still built on purely illusory foundations. Children, who play life, discern its true law and relations more clearly than men, who fail to live it worthily, but who think that they are wiser by experience, that is, by failure.[8]

We could all use the guidance of those with this kind of attitude. But as a rule, counselors and psychologists are intent on helping others adjust and conform to the norms of an already existing social "reality." Establishment professionals are rarely revolutionary in their outlook, and almost never utopian. They and the establishment they unwittingly promote glibly overlook the most profound of truisms, that "the child is father to the man" and that we make our most crucial decisions in youth, precisely when we are least competent to make such decisions (according to those who tend to deprecate intuition and extol conventional experience). In the nursery we are already expressing preferences, including values and modalities of perception, which will significantly influence our fate. Bassis recognizes this search:

The reason that the infant so eagerly seeks new experiences, experiments with himself and his environment, is continually creative and innovative and develops his human potentials is due to the "will to meaning." I challenge anyone to observe a one-year-old for a period of time and then explain his purposive behavior and joie de vivre *on the basis of need satisfaction and drive reduction without being guilty of sub-humanizing the humanness of the young.*[9]

The child becomes lost in the shuffle as those in authority impose their own synthetic version of reality upon their sacred charges. The bulk of the socialization process involves teaching children to table their immediate desires in the name of cooperation. The child quickly learns the supreme value of peer popularity and role playing. He learns that values are group defined and to aspire and judge group eyes. Personal idiosyncrasies are encouraged only when they conform well to existing frameworks. We like to think of teachers, healers and counselors as guides and mentors seeking our best interests, but Thoreau counsels us to become our own guardian and guide:

If we have thus desecrated ourselves — as who has not? — the remedy will be by wariness and devotion to reconsecrate ourselves, and make once more

---

[8] Thoreau, "Walden."

[9] Edward M. Bassis, unpublished paper.

a fane of the mind. We should treat our minds, that is, ourselves, as innocent and ingenuous children whose guardians we are, and be careful what objects and what subjects we thrust on their attention. Read not the Times. Read the Eternities. Conventionalities are at length as bad as impurities. Even the facts of science may dust the mind by their dryness, unless they are in a sense effaced each morning, or rather rendered fertile by the dew, of fresh and living truth. Knowledge does not come to us by details, but in flashes of light from heaven.[10]

There comes a fateful moment in early childhood when we come head-on with disillusionment. As soon as our reason can grasp it, something inevitably forces upon us the awareness that the world is not the benign wonderland that fairy tales advertise. Our parents are revealed to be less than gods and, worst of all, we learn that everything alive is programmed to die. Each of us responds differently to this news, but one thing is sure: no one embraces constraint with open arms, and no one gladly exchanges an open-ended paradise for the restricting limitations of hell on earth. It is very hard for us even to begin to conceive of the dimensions this trauma represents for us or to measure its repercussions throughout life. One moment everything is rolling along fine as we contemplate the satisfactions waiting at our destination. The next, our whole life has been irrevocably changed.

The young child is totally vulnerable and without guile or defense mechanisms. He experiences everything with the whole of himself and innocently takes everything at face value. The child's collision with restrictive reality arrives with crushing force. (This is the source of what Arthur Janov calls the "Primal Scream.") The result is usually a pathetic compromise ranging from autistic retreat to total surrender to fate and authority — a paralyzing accommodation that allows only a bare minimum of utopian hope to cohabit a psyche reconciled to "death and taxes." From then on, everything we think and do is conditioned by this compromise. It defines the limits of our willingness to engage reality and thus the limits of our realizable potential. This is society's most reliable, built-in protection from non-conformist and utopian impulses.

In only the rarest of cases (i.e., the future candidates for Accelerated Thought) does the small child manage to resist the steam-roller of convention and refuse to allow his spirit to be compromised by the belief in the preeminence of limitation. In clinging with his whole Being to the ideal that has represented his life for his first three to five years and all his

---

[10] Thoreau, "Life Without Principle," in: *Walden and Other Writings*, 369.

expectations for the future such a child is subjected (in the face of the undeniable forces of restriction) to the contradiction of these two realities. In resolutely refusing to allow his utopian spirit to be obliterated by the unavoidable, encroaching vision of crushing restriction, his whole essence is exposed to a momentary but immensely intense, deeply penetrating experience. If ever an irresistible force is to meet an immovable object, it is here. In this kind of traumatic, cataclysmic, but immensely worthwhile encounter lies the seed for all search for truth, individuality and struggle with the world of matter.

Later in life, thanks to certain intuitive, artistic and other subterranean channels hopefully left intact by the ravages of socialization, it is sometimes possible for those of us who have had at least a semblance of this heroic encounter to gropingly select life goals and vocations that in some way correspond to our essence — our inner nature. These channels of precocious, pre-conscious knowledge (if any survive the brainwashings and our endless concessions to convention) are all that remain of what might permit some degree of communication between our essence and what we call our "mind" or "consciousness."

Were it not for the tragic violence of conventional socialization, the external knowledge we acquire as children might integrate harmoniously with self-knowledge. These two different but fundamentally compatible elements blend naturally when we learn directly from experience. Communing with nature is one such learning modality:

All my life I have felt close to nature. Her presence was real to me long before I knew anything of the laws by which she worked - a child's pre-reflective though definite awareness of nature's being. Looking back, I realize that since my earliest childhood I have sensed "something" in nature's background and even in the foreground. The beautiful and lavish variety of her forms has been a source of real meaning in my life, and from the beginning I felt a kinship with nature's offspring - animals, plants, rocks, forests, water, earth, the sky, and even the remote stars and galaxies. No one taught me this; I simply awoke to the world with the conviction of my relatedness to these things. The feeling, common in childhood and often lost as we grow up, has remained with me.[11]

During the routine acquisition of theoretical knowledge we are compromised by being required to "swallow" as real, information that is not in some way personally verified. It is not only our personal participa-

---

[11] Renée Weber, *Dialogues with Scientists and Sages: The Search for Unity* (London & New York: Routledge & Kegan Paul, 1986), 2.

tion in this unnatural act that compromises our integrity so severely, but also the violence done to our very process of "understanding" in the broadest sense of the word—the way we process reality. The adult world, which for most children is the final ruling authority in all matters, actually prescribes this warped form of reality testing while paying little more than lip service to the importance of "hands-on" learning experience. Our basis for developing independent judgment thus sabotaged, we are set up as dupes for established authority and the view of life it wishes to offer us.[12, 13]

Speaking of his childhood, one of Janov's patients describes his handling of this existential predicament:

"I took me away from Me. I killed little Jimmy because he was rough and wild and boisterous and they wanted something tame and delicate. I had to get rid of little Jimmy in order to survive with those crazy parents of mine. I killed my best friend. It was a bad deal, but it was the only deal I could make."

Another put is this way:

"If I were smart when I was young, I would have died because I would have known that they hated me. I had to be dumb to survive. I just shut off part of my brain. I've noticed the bright, alert look in very young children, and then something happens to change them."

Janov adds:

Instead of being himself, he struggles to become another version of himself. Sooner or later the child comes to believe that this version is the real him. The "act" is no longer voluntary and conscious; it is automatic and unconscious. It is neurotic.

To understand why thirty years after being faced with a shocking realization a person is still reacting to it, we must bear in mind that the young infant is wide open. He is defenseless, and this means that he can perceive in a direct feeling way. What he may perceive in his earliest months or years may be too much to bear. So he covers. He may develop symptoms or dull his senses, yet the painful perception is still waiting to be felt. In one case a patient at the age of two and a half saw the deadness in his parent's faces. He began to perceive the utter lifelessness of the existence of those around him and of his own existence. He did not feel that feeling completely. He developed asthma.

Some of us get the idea in early life that our parents do not want us to be exuberant and really alive, soon learn to go around almost holding our breath out of fear of doing or saying the wrong thing, being too loud or boisterous, laughing too uproariously. Sooner or later this fear strangles the

[12] See appendix.
[13] See appendix.

feeling into a taut throat, a tight chest, and a clenched stomach. Because of this clamping off process, the voice tends to be higher- pitched; it is a voice not connected to the whole body.

We have underestimated how much deprivation goes on in the first months of life and how that deprivation affects us for the rest of our lives. [14]

The candidate for Accelerated Thought is thus someone in whom some of his blissful, childlike vision has survived socialization. The small child's courageous impulse to face the oppressive specter of restriction head-on and say "no" is primary. But exceptionally wise parental guidance is also necessary to prevent the child from being completely crushed by conformist forces. Later in life, the lingering memory of the possibility of a better existence will reflect some aspect of the vivid glow, maybe even a hint of the enticing scent[15] that evokes nostalgia for a lost paradise. This occasional feeling of vividness gives expression to the conviction that just behind the veil of everyday life lie real, accessible, realizable, utopian possibilities.

The reason we like precious jewels so much is they remind us of planes of consciousness we've lived on where those are the pebbles. (Aldous Huxley)

Some individuals will have lacked the self-discipline to hold on to the substance of the truth for which they fought, yet may have retained some of the feeling associated with that truth. Such persons remain emotionally convinced of the existence of truth — in itself, good. But without a matching intellectual infrastructure they tend to latch on to fanatical causes that appeal to the intellectually naive. Hoffer explains:

The fanatic is not really a stickler to principle. He embraces a cause not primarily because of its justness and holiness but because of his desperate need for something to hold on to. Often, indeed, it is his need for passionate attachment which turns every cause he embraces into a holy cause.

The fanatic cannot be weaned away from his cause by an appeal to his reason or moral sense. He fears compromise and cannot be persuaded to qualify the certitude and righteousness of his holy cause. But he finds no difficulty in swinging suddenly and wildly from one holy cause to another. He cannot be convinced but only converted. His passionate attachment is more vital than the quality of the cause to which he is attached.

What matters is not the contents of the cause but the total dedication and the communion with a congregation. He is even ready to join in a holy crusade against his former holy cause, but it must be a genuine crusade - uncompromising, intolerant, proclaiming the one and only truth. [16]

---

[14] Janov, *The Primal Scream*, 25-166.

[15] See appendix.

[16] Eric Hoffer, *The True Believer* (N.Y.: Harper & Row, 1951), 80-82.

Because of their passion for truth and the vitality that animates their fervor, it is reasonable to assume that certain individuals with a fanatical bent could be introduced to Accelerated Thought, provided they could be made to see that their hopes and frustrations stem both from the potential and the restriction that matter represents to mankind. It might be possible to convince a portion of such individuals of the virtues of intensely focused thought as an avenue to the truth, whose feeling so inspires them. It is about time the power of fanaticism was harnessed to benign and constructive ends.

In the beginning, however, Project Mind will be seeking those who have in mind some specific intellectual orientation that has explicit implications for the transformation of matter. Of these rare individuals, one could reasonably surmise that a certain proportion will be interested in benefiting from unique practical "arrangements" tailor-made to help them pursue their truth and destiny through the exercise and development of their capacity for Accelerated Thought. Carefully regulated conditions could help reduce the risk of psychological mishaps[17] and enhance chances for a successful experience.

From such expected results one anticipates not only the subjective satisfactions that derive from discovery and self-realization but, even more important, the practical, usable findings one expects to issue from the faculty of invention — findings that by their very nature impose new material conditions upon human existence. Individuals can disagree on ideology, they can sidestep meaning and they can shut their eyes to truth, but they cannot escape the influence of their environment that to an ever-increasing degree consists of technological culture. In the future, this cultural environment will be increasingly molded by the irresistible results of Accelerated Thought.

• • •

---

[17] See appendix.

CHAPTER SEVEN

Special Conditions Needed to Promote Accelerated Thought

This is the gate of the Lord through which the righteous may enter. (Psalms 118:20)

An experimental framework or pilot plant, Project Mind, will be created in order to demonstrate the viability of Accelerated Thought. Candidates will recruited and screened. Mature, psychologically and spiritually trained specialists, including those having experience with and insight into the process of creativity and its risks, will act as guides for participants.

Guides will be responsible for their comfort and ensure that all their physical and environmental needs are met. Guides will be selected who will thoroughly familiarize themselves and identify with subjects' intentions and aspirations and, when needed, provide encouragement. This has nothing to do with the mutual stimulation of group dynamics or brainstorming. To the contrary, if a subject's essence-desire is not sufficiently operational to function on its own in a protected environment, beyond the odd Eureka experience no amount of priming will help.

The main input guides will provide is a high quality of attention, empathy, comprehension and esteem to be accorded subjects. Nor will subjects be brought in contact with one another and risk cross-contaminating their psyches with the internalized distraction inherent to the subjectivity of each. State-of-the-art computerization and on-line data retrieval will furnish "objective" input needs-imaging capacity, scientific data, etc. pertinent to each subject's quest.

At times, guides will be called upon to help ground subjects by managing overexcitement. Empathy and the sharing of realizations will serve as reserve psychic capacity while the subject adjusts to the impact of new insights. In cases where excitement becomes unwieldy, the guide will function as a damper to absorb agitation (e.g. graphite damping rods or heavy water in nuclear reactors). At this point the subject needs the convincing assurance that even if his new awareness is lost in the imperative descent to a lower energy level, he will be helped to find this source of potency again after suitable preparation. Perry speaks of spiritual emergency:

> The most fragmented "thought disorder" can become quite coherent and orderly within a short time if someone is present to respond to it with compassion. Such a relationship is far better than a tranquilizer in most instances. A haven where there is attentiveness to inner experiences and where, removed from the context of daily life . . .

> This rationale of handling spiritual emergencies, no matter how disturbed the person, is that in the high-arousal state when the archetypal unconscious is energized and activated, the psyche autonomously does its own work in its own fashion. What it needs for this is not "treatment" but rather a coming into close and deep relationship with another individual who empathizes and encourages but does not interfere.[1]

Emergency, or not, we more readily accept stress management suggestions from those we are convinced understand the basis of our difficulty and the uniqueness of our situation, and are committed to our success.

Provisions will be made for the care and lodging of participants, and remuneration to help compensate for family and other responsibilities which will be neglected. Relative isolation is necessary to prevent outside influence on the subject's efforts to generate the concentration needed to spark the chain reaction of Accelerated Thought. However, the effort and the desire to press on relentlessly must, in the end, be his. Whitfield emphasizes depth and mutuality of commitment as keys to effectiveness:

> An organization has a "psychological contract" with its members as well as a legal one in terms of their commitment to its aims and the depth to which they are prepared to be involved intellectually, emotionally and morally in the enterprise. If it is asking for total commitment, it must be prepared to give genuine reward . . .[2]

Project Mind will optimize the relationship between itself and participants in providing them with conditions to do what they were born

---

[1] John Weir Perry, "Spiritual Emergency and Renewal," *Spiritual Emergency*, ed. Grof and Grof (Los Angeles: Jeremy P. Tarcher, 1990), 69-75.

[2] P. R. Whitfield, *Creativity in Industry* (United Kingdom: Penguin Books, 1975), 147-148.

to do. It will befriend their essence. A better ally than that would be hard to imagine.

Thought Compression — Focusing to Break Out of Distraction

Try? There is no try. There is only do or do not do. (Yoda)

The process of Accelerated Thought is initiated by applying unusually sustained "pressure" to conventional reflective thought. This means intensely concentrating or meditating on a problem to which we are most deeply committed to solving. This will not merely increase our awareness of the terrain we have chosen for struggle, but also will change the quality of our awareness of it. In unearthing from within ourselves a better quality of attention than we have known until now, we also begin repairing our faculty of independent vision, subverted in childhood. Branden grasps that this is where significant contact with reality begins:

> *The choice to focus one's mind is primary, just as the value sought, awareness, is a primary. It is awareness that makes any other values possible, not any other values that antecede and make awareness possible. Awareness is the starting point and precondition of goal directed (value directed) human action—not just another goal or value along the way as it were. The decision to focus one's mind (to value awareness and make it one's goal) or not to focus, is a basic choice and cannot be reduced further.*[3]

The subject must concentrate on his problem at the expense of all else, in the spirit of high adventure, in the hope of revealing relationships, aspects and meanings never before encountered. Thoreau comments on the subject of concentration:

> *The intellect is a cleaver; it discerns and rifts its way into the secret of things. I do not wish to be any more busy with my hands than is necessary. My head is hands and feet. I feel all my best faculties concentrated in it. My instinct tells me that my head is an organ for burrowing, as some creatures use their snout and forepaws, and with it I would mine and burrow my way through these hills. I think that the richest vein is somewhere hereabouts; so by divining rod and thin rising vapors I judge; and here I will begin to mine.*[4]

The motivation to pursue this kind of effort in the face of one's own distraction, and the obstacles in the world which are the crystallized

---

[3] Nathaniel Branden, *The Psychology of Self-Esteem* (New York: Bantam Books, March, 1971).

[4] Henry David Thoreau, "The Journal," p. 431.

consequences of distraction, presupposes intense desire. It requires the melding of our multitudinous, fractionated desires into one dauntless, indefatigable will, strong enough to carry our efforts to term. On the subject of desire, Strauss comments:

> *I can tell you from my own experience that an ardent desire and fixed purpose combined with intense inner resolve brings results. Determined concentrated thought is a tremendous force ... I am convinced that this is a law, and it holds good in any line of endeavor.*[5]

As his efforts advance, the subject becomes increasingly captivated by his research, and motivated in the extreme to find the "secret" that leads to a new theory, understanding or invention. We must bear in mind that the key to inducing Accelerated Thought is powerful inner motivation. Tesla, for instance, believed that his work was a matter of life and death.[6]

Total commitment is necessary if the consequences are to crack the psychological shell of convention and touch the subject's innermost Being. Buber suggests just what single-minded, self-application requires:

> *It demands of you a reaction which cannot be prepared beforehand. It demands nothing of what is past. It demands presence, responsibility; it demands you. I call a great character one who by his actions and attitudes satisfies the claim of situations out of a deep readiness to respond with his whole life, and in such a way that the sum of his actions and attitudes expresses at the same time the unity of his being in its willingness to accept responsibility.*[7]

Such an effort must gradually bring about a radical modification in the functioning of the subject's mentation, in the way he experiences himself, and in how he experiences outer reality. As he delves more and more deeply into the idea universe of his problem, our adventurer gradually loses interest in commonplace matters and in the worries and preoccupations that habitually vie for his attention. Briggs comments:

> *Psychiatrist Rollo May claims that "absorption, being caught up in, wholly involved" in a work is the hallmark of the artist.*
>
> *Some creators — perhaps many — justify the vast amounts of idle time necessary for absorption by focusing on the creating activity as an escape from what they feel are the inadequacies and pressures of their everyday life.*[8]

---

[5] Abell, Arthur. *Talks with the Great Composers*, (G.E. Schroeder-Verlag: Garmisch-Partenkirchen, Germany, 1964), p. 25.

[6] Nikola Tesla. *My Inventions* (Zagreb: Skolsa Kjiga, 1977), p. 44.

[7] Martin Buber. *Between Man and Man*, trans. Ronald Gregor Smith (New York: Macmillan Paperbacks, 1965), p. 114.

[8] John Briggs, *Fire in the Crucible* (Los Angeles, Jeremy P. Tarcher, 1990), p. 200-205.

The subject's sense of mission grows as he gives himself over to the problem at hand. His mind becomes increasingly saturated with the problem's components. Ghiselin elaborates:

This self-surrender so familiar to creative minds is nearly always hard to achieve. It calls for a purity of motive that is rarely sustained except through dedication and discipline. Subordination of everything to the whole impulse of life is easier for the innocent because they are not so fully aware of the hazards of it or are less impressed by them, and they are not so powerfully possessed by convention.[9]

The self-surrender that Ghiselin evokes (or "self-effacement," as it is sometimes called) corresponds closely to the experience of "ego annihilation" so basic to classic spiritual training. It is not unreasonable to assume that those interested in the trenchant effort that leads to Accelerated Thought tend to be self-assertive and, as such, steer clear of traditional, explicitly "self-effacing" forms of inner work.

The advantage in the ruggedly independent orientation of the self-assertive type is audacity and originality of thought. His strength lies in his ability to preserve part of his mind inviolate from the pressures of social influence. The strength of those who intentionally sacrifice their own willfulness to the purpose of finding integration in a larger reality is the stability and balance that come from "Being." While one does not necessarily preclude the other, in practice, those persons with integrative tendencies engendered through selling out to the convention from childhood have thereby undermined the processes that breed individuality. At a later stage, if they are lucky, they may get the chance within some organized framework of inner work to preserve and enhance, through Being, whatever spirit has survived the prosaic but crushing forces of distraction.

Those in whom self-assertive tendencies have developed in the service of preserving some vision of truth (in contradistinction to those who aggressively and selfishly pursue conventional goals) tend to be repelled by the common belief, in many ways fallacious, that spirituality requires self-abnegation and the "subjugation" or "death" of the ego. Those who manage to overcome obstacles sufficiently to approach a school of esoterism, often find themselves rejected by students and teachers alike whose attitudes reflect this fallacy. Having sacrificed their own true individuality in early childhood, these students and teachers end

---

[9] *The Creative Process*, Brewster Ghiselin, ed. (New York: Mentor Books, 1964), p. 24.

up feeling threatened by the unrefined, self-assertive expression of such individuality in others. Largely denied the stabilizing virtues of inner work that might enable individualists to develop a more generalized and deeply rooted presence as ballast against the heady effects of original thought, such individualists lack any framework where they can receive the enlightened support and the guidance they need and deserve.

In accelerated, or simply "creative" thought, the guide and master to whom one surrenders, is not another person or even a "higher influence," but rather one's own destiny in the form of the deepest, most intimate and powerful desire one is able to release from essence. It is with this desire that Project Mind aligns itself and upon the authenticity of which it most depends.

In pursuing his desire, the subject's ardor intensifies as new, hitherto unperceived relationships begin to emerge among certain conceptual elements of the problem upon which he has chosen to focus. Each small discovery fuels the enterprise with the promise of success. Each new light shed on the problem helps to illuminate the subject's mental field of view, providing the energy to reduce it further to the essential kernel of truth he is seeking. The subject can become absorbed in his thoughts much longer than we conventionally consider normal or proper for an act of concentration. He becomes, for a while, psychologically self-contained, delving deeply for truth. Ghiselin again:

> *The concentration of such a state may be so extreme that the worker may seem to himself or others to be in a trance or some similar hypnotic or somnambulistic state. But actually the state of the so-called trance so often mentioned as characteristic of the creative process or of stages in it differs markedly from ordinary trance or hypnosis, in its collectedness, its autonomy, its extreme watchfulness. And it never seems to be directly induced. It appears rather to be generated indirectly, to subsist as the characteristic of a consciousness partly unfocused, attention diverted from the too-assertive contours of any particular scheme and dispersed upon an object without complete schematic representation. In short, the creative discipline when successful may generate a trance-like state, but one does not throw oneself into a trance in order to create.*[10]

Ghiselin rightly emphasizes that the state into which the subject enters is the means and not the purpose. The purpose of creativity at its best is the search for truth. But this truth, when retrieved from the depth of his psyche (whether or not it represents a newly revealed truth about

---

[10] Ibid., 25.

the external world), by virtue of being the focus of all his available energy and of what means most to him will also be his own personal truth. This is the truth upon which, to a remarkable extent, he has chosen to make his stand and stake his claim. Investing his faith, energy and resources — in short sanity itself — in such a project could be said to be following his destiny, assignation or calling.

I'm doing what I can to prolong my life, hoping one day I'll learn what its for. (Ashleigh Brilliant)

Maurice Friedman offers this insight:

Each man has need of the personal confirmation that can come only when he knows his "calling" — his existence in the fullest sense of the term — as an answer to a call. No man is able simply to confirm himself. He may be able to do without the admiration of crowds, but he cannot do without the silent dialogue, often internalized within himself, through which he places his efforts within the context of a mutual contact with what is not himself. He needs to feel that his work is "true" — both as a genuine expression of the reality that he encounters in his life and as a genuine response to some situation or need that calls him.[11]

By virtue of having selected[12] this quest from all others and having made it his vocation — the purpose and center of his existence — he will have made a definitive statement about himself. Each revelation concerning this truth also will be a revelation of self-truth such that, to the extent that his commitment is genuine[13] (confirmation of which would be the appearance of high-energy inner phenomena) he will be revealed to himself by the illumination this energy provides.

The minute you begin to do what you want to do, it's really a different kind of life. (Buckminster Fuller)

Eventually, the subject narrows his vision to a nuclear complex of elements that becomes the embryonic nucleus of a new consciousness. As will be shown later, this nucleus has the strategic function of defining the role and thus the relative meaning of all the other elements or secondary associations within the subject's ideational repertoire revolving around it. As the excitement peaks, the subject, to his amazement, discovers that the pursuit of truth contains a uniquely personal key to self-understanding and inner coherence which in turn leads him to a new, rectified integration with the world at large.

---

[11] Maurice Friedman, *Problematic Rebel: An image of modern man* (New York: Random House, 1963), p. 365.

[12] See appendix.

[13] See appendix.

The process of thought-compression is not merely a conceptual process involving an economy of the forms of thought. Ideas which have a potential for evoking meaning within the given context attract and focus the energy of attention. An efficacious effort of intentionally focusing attention on problems or ideas, charges them, in turn, with the light of awareness, investing them with meaning and rendering them potent and able to attract even more energy. Thus there is little question but that intense motivation is the prime ingredient fueling the beginnings of creative thought, since only assiduous, concentrated self-application can enable us to lift ourselves out of the quagmire of distraction.

The degree of freedom from unwanted thoughts and the degree of concentration on a single thought are the measures to gauge spiritual progress. (Ramana Maharishi)

It seems that almost all psychological analyses of the creative process insist upon at least a dual aspect of effort. This includes a self-assertive component whereby the individual applies his mind to a problem, and an integrative phase whereby the subconscious — free of the waking habits of thought — is free to form novel combinations that are then allowed into awareness by a conscious mind is sufficiently prepared to recognize the relevance and value of what is served up by the subconscious. This is what happens when conventional minds dabble in creative thought and flirt with unconventional modes of energy modulation.

The commitment of such minds is equivocal and halfhearted: in short, impure. Rather than waging all-out "holy war" on the limits imposed by conventional thought, these thinkers wage limited-action forays into the zone of non-distraction. This they do less in the single-minded pursuit of truth than for the rewards of self-aggrandizement. These ambivalent creatures, content to live as neither fish nor fowl, will have only the briefest moments of accord with the truth hidden within. They condemn themselves to endlessly repeating unreliable, fluctuating contacts between their truth-laden essence and their minimally sincere waking search for the cosmic truths imprinted within that essence. This, as a rule, is the fate of those who choose to serve conventional science.

Only single-minded commitment — the constant returning to the problem — helps get the process going and, more particularly, keeps the energy needed for driving the process from dissipating into the everyday reveries and distractions of life. The interest generated by intuition — interest that forges connections between essence and the problem at hand

— helps keep the devotee on track and anchored in his inner self. McClintock provides a living example:

> But, there was always a direction in which she was headed. The more complex and confusing the data grew, the more essential it was to have a point of reference to remind her of that direction, and sufficient ballast to keep her on course. Her point of reference was provided by her inner vision and the ballast by her extraordinary confidence.
>
> "It never occurred to me that there was going to be any stumbling block. Not that I had the answer, but [I had] the joy of going at it. When you have that joy, you do the right experiments. You let the material tell you where to go, and it tells you at every step what the next has to be because you're integrating with an overall brand new pattern in mind. You're not following an old one; you are convinced of a new one. And you let everything you do focus on that. You can't help it, because it all integrates. There were no difficulties." [14]

Thanks to his new and hard-won vision and clarity of thought, each new act of self-discovery reconfirms our subject's confidence in having chosen this path, and in the power and efficacy of his own spirit for having guided him to it. His confidence moves ever closer to certainty each time some new step reveals actual possibilities for action and releases psychic energy from the anticipation of success of such action.

The concretization of vision is a powerful part of generating new vision. As he progresses, the working of the subject's mind less and less resembles the process of "reflective" thought in which concepts are only fleetingly illuminated in the light of attention. His central idea begins to glow with its own energy — the energy of meaning — and subsequently illuminates all other ideas with which it associates actively. This again concentrates, reinforces and increases the scope of his attention, gradually transforming it into a "higher," less fragmented form of awareness (primarily, at this stage, self-awareness). [15] To some extent, this awareness also includes relations the subject has with external things. These "things" are forms assimilated from the outside world, forms with which he has some natural affinity.

But before vision can become operative, we must pass through certain experiences which result from efforts to redeploy attention from the distraction of convention to the wholehearted pursuit of a personal truth. One of the meanings of the word "experience" in French, Hebrew

---

[14] Keller, *A Feeling For The Organism*, p. 125-6.
[15] See appendix.

and other tongues is "experiment." Our efforts are, in fact, experiments in living — in how to be. We experiment with the functional configurations of what we could reasonably call our "energy field," which is the experiential testing ground from which emerges our experience of ourselves — our Being. The advantage of this kind of experimentation, as opposed to external, scientific experimentation, is that the equipment at our disposal (even if we lack expertise in its use), is the most elaborate possible — the human form, the body. The observations it allows us to make as we gain in expertise are direct and immediate, forming an integral part of the effort-experiment.

Our understanding of these observations is crucial since it largely determines the mold and character of later experimentation. It is here that honesty with oneself really counts. For without the testimony of a physical artifact embodying the truth we are pursuing, we are on the "honor system" and remain the sole judges of the results of our own inner experiments. We pay for any deceit in the currency of our integrity as we strive relentlessly towards our truth. Little children, with their lack of artifice, are the purest of "scientists" as they probe and discover reality with the whole of themselves.

External, "scientific" experiments, on the other hand, although lacking in most of these advantages, do have the virtue of public reproducibility and corroboration. In this kind of struggle, however, it is our reflective thought that is exercised and not our Being. Information is accumulated, not consciousness. The only major increment of Being that can be gained through this reflective process is through the occasional boost of intuition, whereby the researcher only momentarily abandons the false security of reflection in a soul-felt effort to find his existential bearings and come up with an original hypothesis or experimental design. As a rule, these short forays into the subconscious are too brief for an experience-experiment to form, and the individual gleefully snatches his paltry booty from what he might call his "creative" prowess. He grinds his ego's axe at the expense of what might loosely be called his soul and, having sold his birthright for a Eureka-inspired "mess of pottage," rejoins the world of distraction with no regrets, all the more confirmed in his idea of what it means to "experiment."

In a moment of conscience, he may require himself to remain in the mode of intuition longer than it takes for a quick flash of insight, in which case he may eventually begin to suspect that life itself has another, "meaningful" dimension and begin to experiment more systematically with experience-experiments.

Meaning & Awareness — Knowledge & Reality

The unexamined life is not worth living. (Socrates)

It is a fundamental mistake of Man's to think that he is alive, when he has merely fallen asleep in life's waiting room. (Idries Shah)

Most people like to believe they are self-aware, "at home," present to themselves. Precious few ever realize that a repertoire of good habits and clever responses does not comprise an integral presence — or even a conscious part of ourselves. That we often automatically know what to do, and when, speaks well of our memory, philosophy and the organization and mechanical integration of our knowledge. But it creates an illusion of awareness, both for ourselves and for others. The social sciences are barely beginning to make distinctions between our functions and the awareness with which these functions may be infused.[16]

Harman and Rheingold in their *Higher Creativity*[17] trace the problem these sciences have in dealing with the subject of consciousness.

Not only do we avoid looking at the question of consciousness, but Georges Bernanos affirms that we have every reason to fear the vision of what, in default of consciousness, we have become:

Many men never give out the whole of themselves, their deepest truth. They live on the surface, and yet, so rich is the soil of humanity that even this thin outer layer is able to yield a kind of meagre harvest which gives the illusion of real living . . . How many men will never have the least idea of what is meant by supernatural heroism, without which there can be no inner life! Yet by that very same inner life shall they be judged . . . Therefore when death has bereft them of all the artificial props with which society provides such people, they will find themselves as they really are, as they were without even knowing it — horrible undeveloped monsters, the stumps of men.[18]

This underlines the fact that it is not so much a problem of seeking a scientific consensus on consciousness (once consciousness research is

---

[16] For more information see Stanford M. Lyman and Arvin B. Scott, *A Sociology of the Absurd* (New York: Meredith Corporation, 1970), p. 2-3.

[17] See appendix.

[18] Georges Bernanos, *Diary of a Country Priest*, trans. Pamela Morris (New York: The Macmillan Co., 1937), p. 108f.

seriously undertaken), although this alone would represent some progress. Rather it is one of awakening from within ourselves a conviction that a real life exists above the somnolent one we are now living.

We are reluctant to admit the horrifying fact of our conscious non-existence until we become convinced experientially of the possibility of change. Only moments of real self-awareness induced by attempts at Accelerated Thought, long spiritual practice, chance peak or Eureka experiences, sincere introspection, or even certain hallucinogenic drugs and techniques, can show up our normal state for what it is — a strategy to enable us to react mechanically to situations. And this we do, as consistently and efficiently as possible, while remaining virtually unconscious — one could almost say soulless. Thoreau bears witness to such a moment of awakening from routine oblivion:

> *Sometimes, after coming home thus late in a dark and muggy night, when my feet felt the path which my eyes could not see, dreaming and absent-minded all the way, until I was aroused by having to raise my hand to lift the latch, I have not been able to recall a single step of my walk, and I have thought that perhaps my body would find its way home if its master should forsake it, as the hand finds its way to the mouth without assistance.* [19]

We can encounter our mechanicality when trying to concentrate — on writing, for instance:

> *The problem of creative writing is essentially one of concentration, and the supposed eccentricities of poets are usually due to mechanical habits or rituals developed in order to concentrate. Concentration, of course, for the purpose of writing poetry, is different from the kind of concentration required for working out a sum. It is the focusing of the attention in a special way, so that the poet is aware of all the implications and possible developments of his idea, just as one might say that a plant was not concentrating on developing mechanically in one direction, but in many directions, towards the warmth and light with its leaves, and towards the water with its roots, all at the same time.* [20]

There is no place in us for something truly new, without first recognizing the very frightening limitations of the old. We are reluctant to let go of our vain and costly dependency on the old without the assurance of having some stake in the new. We must have some compelling reason to face the identity-annihilating chaos of transition.

---

[19] Thoreau, "Walden," p. 230-231.

[20] Stephen Spender, "The making of a poem," *The Creative Process*, ed. Brewster Ghiselin (New York: Mentor Books, 1964), p. 113.

A Clear Direction

He who has a why to live, can bear most any what. (Friedrich Nietzsche)

Some problem, some issue or idea will have to matter enough to us for this vicious cycle determining our conditions of existence to be broken. Some of us will have to care enough about some aim to wrench our attention away from convention-conditioned habits long enough for newly released energy to begin to fill our whole body-mind with an altered general awareness of the world and of ourselves. The pioneers of Accelerated Thought, by virtue of their heroic effort and its transforming effect upon matter, will lift from our minds the veil — the excessive weight of distraction — now preventing most of us from even glancing in the right direction.

When it happens, this new life-condition will relieve the inner faculties of the rest of us from the worst of matter's impairment. But freeing these faculties from distraction cannot relieve us of the task of developing them. To the contrary, in a world largely free of trouble and anxiety, where work for material gain is no longer necessary or interesting, we will be obliged by want of materialistic directions, to apply ourselves to that which remains — the neglected side of ourselves: our spiritual lack. Meanwhile, as long as distraction and the obscurity of this material world cloud our vision, it is left to the initiative of heroic pioneers to break the spell that keeps us from perceiving the higher reality that surrounds and permeates us.

He who would know the world, seek first within his being's depths; he who would truly know himself, develop interest in the world. (Rudolf Steiner)

So our subject, guided by intuition, intensely focuses the cutting edge of his attention on that aspect of reality most akin to his essence. He seeks to free himself from the weight of incomprehension in the hope of better serving the purpose of his existence. Although effort is directed at solving some problem and effecting some change in the outside world, the greater part of the change is yet inward. The individual, often without even noticing, begins to gain new insight into his own possibilities.

Archimedes, for instance, had good reason to be pleased at his discovery of how to measure the volume of an irregularly shaped object. He could perhaps look forward to being rewarded by the king, but more than this or even the feeling of having gained knowledge, his inner sense of Being and of being able was increased at having been released from one of matter's prisons. For a moment he became acutely aware in his feeling nature, if not in his mind, that within himself lay the capacity to overcome any obstacle and reach any achievement. Archimedes had a small peek at a world unencumbered by matter, and a brief taste of immortality. It was this sense of freedom, more than anything else, that propelled him out into the street exploding with elation. Interestingly, recurring accounts of those who have undergone a near-death-experience also include reports of elation at becoming free of the material plane. Tesla, describing a Eureka state, attests to just such elation:

> *I cannot begin to describe my emotions. Pygmalion seeing his statue come to life could not have been more deeply moved. A thousand secrets of nature which I might have stumbled upon accidentally I would have given for that one which I had wrested from her against all odds and at the peril of my existence . . . For a while I gave myself up entirely to the intense enjoyment of picturing machines and devising new forms. It was a mental state of happiness about as complete as I have ever known in life . . . When natural inclination develops into a passionate desire, one advances towards his goal in seven-league boots. In less than two months I evolved virtually all the types of motors and modifications of the system which are now identified with my name.* [21]

In order to join and swell this growing pool of awareness, conceptual forms must not deflect the light of attention sent their way. The beam of attention must be sufficiently powerful and coherent to illuminate a maximum of contour and detail that the form (problem or idea) under consideration presents to the individual. This form has to be compatible with the current configuration of the subject's awareness. It has to mesh neatly with his "meaning" to contribute to the lucidity of awareness — his now dynamically expanding energy-breeding conceptual framework which constitutes the beginnings of his new, personally-generated consciousness.

While he will still have the capacity to take notice and reflect, externally illuminating such forms as before, if his meaning is very restricted in its scope a great many phenomena from the observable world will be insufficiently relevant and thus insufficiently compatible in form to be absorbed into his awareness. Only objects of thought compatible with the already animated, light-infused forms comprising his present consciousness will be able to nourish the flame of expanding awareness.

---

[21] Nikola Tesla, "My Inventions."

Energy Accumulation & Illumination

This is the gate of the Lord through which the righteous may enter. (Psalms 118:20)

Fortunately, marshalling an exhausting and sustained effort of attention is necessary only during the early stages in order to prime the process. Later, when the subject discovers the essence of the idea most important to him, his understanding of the issues with which he has been grappling changes. The vision of his newly, defined truth releases him from the energy-depleting burden of doubt and uncertainty. Once the subject's objective (the object of his hopes, dreams and personal struggle) is revealed to lie in one clear direction, distracting irrelevancies are brushed aside and tremendous energy is freed for use. Hesse artistically expresses the value, force and function of discovering this principle of unity operating within ourselves:

> *From that hour Siddhartha ceased to fight against his destiny. There shone in his face the serenity of knowledge, of one who is no longer confronted with conflict of desires, who has found salvation, who is in harmony with the stream of events, with the stream of life, full of sympathy and compassion, surrendering himself to the stream, belonging to the unity of all things.*[22]

His direction and circumstances now simplified, our subject's consciousness is suddenly able to accumulate energy and evolve. Thoreau expands:

> *I learned this, at least, by my experiment; that if one advances confidently in the direction of his dreams, and endeavors to live the life which he has imagined, he will meet with a success unexpected in common hours. He will put some things behind, will pass an invisible boundary; new, universal, and more liberal laws will begin to establish themselves around and within him; or the old laws be expanded, and interpreted in his favor in a more liberal sense, and he will live with the license of a higher order of beings. In proportion as he simplifies his life, the laws of the universe will appear less complex, and solitude will not be solitude, nor poverty poverty, nor weakness weakness. If you have built castles in the air, your work need not be lost; that is where they should be. Now put the foundations under them.*[23]

Our subject's energized thought system, due to energy saved from the process of distraction and the energy-efficient mode of its functioning, now begins to acquire the possibility of becoming self-sustaining.

---

[22] Hermann Hesse, *Siddhartha*, trans. Hilda Rosner (New York: New Directions Paperback, 1951), p. 139.

[23] Thoreau, "Walden," 343.

This is somewhat analogous to the stage in the birth of a star which in the fledgling state, as a huge ball of gas, accumulates sufficient pressure and mass to produce the intense heat necessary to trigger the fusion chain-reaction that renders stars the brilliantly luminous suns that they are. In reaching this stage, a star, like our candidate for Accelerated Thought, begins in a highly diffuse state gathering substance at a very slow but gradually increasing rate. As substance and energy accumulate the star heats up, causing matter and energy to merge in the creation of incandescent plasma.[24]

It is this stellar, pre-fusion reaction state that best characterizes our subject's present condition. Although no longer as vulnerable as before to environmental distractions, our subject's consciousness is not quite ready to extend its influence outward through what in a newborn star would be the radiance of its light.

The subject still has to consolidate his new inner awareness by reprocessing, reinterpreting and reassimilating his old knowledge and feelings, bringing them into line with his new internal order. The last vestiges of his passive, reflective thought system must be reintegrated and actively absorbed into the light of his new consciousness. Whatever forms the subject's new consciousness is unable to absorb actively must be abandoned as dead capital, stored in memory, or forgotten. The subject must come to accept that certain of his old attitudes and ideas no longer fit with his new vision.

Had most of his thoughts and feelings been incompatible with his original intuition, this intuition (really an incipient awareness) would never have been able to grow into a new consciousness at all. The bulk of him would have been at odds with the intuition and stifled it. The rejection of the bulk of one's personal repertoire from one's consciousness implies a narrow consciousness of limited scope — a restricted mind. If the subject is sufficiently programmed with conventional notions and attitudes, any intuition or fleeting new vision will be starved for compatible mental associations which might otherwise serve as fertile ground or culture in which a new awareness could grow.

---

[24] A plasma is an extremely hot, incandescent, energized, gaseous state of matter, dissociated (ionized) in a balanced manner into equal quantities of positive and negative ions, and thus electrically neutral and highly conductive. After solid, liquid and gas, plasma is often called the fourth state of matter. Some thermonuclear reaction experiments are carried out within plasmas.

Thus many people turn to science fiction and other fantasy material in an often poignant bid to open the door of their psyches to new, unconventional possibilities that might arouse from within them some unique intuition of their own. Meanwhile, they live this possibility vicariously through the all too often cynically and commercially motivated intuitive ruminations of others. They grope through this literature for an atmosphere sufficiently fresh and potent to lift the dull, oppressive weight of conventional thought from their heavily socialized minds.

For most of us, given the difficulties we encounter daily, it is almost impossible to develop a strong faith in the chances of success of some idealistically motivated course of action. Nor is it easy for us to find exemplary individuals as models to inspire such faith in us. One of the highest functions of art is to supply just such models and to inspire faith in the "worthwhileness" of pursuing our ideals. When we identify with the hero of some story, we share emotionally in his success and in the vindication of his stand maintained against all odds. Ayn Rand says:

> *Amidst the incalculable number and complexity of choices that confront a man in his day-to-day existence, with the frequently bewildering torrent of events, with the alternation of successes and failures, of joys that seem too rare and suffering that lasts too long — he is always in danger of losing his perspective and the reality of his own convictions. Remember that abstractions as such do not exist: they are merely man's epistemological method of perceiving that which exists — and that which exists is concrete. To acquire the full, persuasive, irresistible power of reality, man's metaphysical abstractions have to confront him in the form of concretes (i.e., in the form of art.)*[25]

When we borrow the artist's vision of where our ideals should take us, we tacitly oblige ourselves to take steps to realize that vision. Otherwise we betray ourselves and the artist who gave of himself to help further those ideals. When we betray those ideals we sabotage our own vision and are left to drown in the anomie of meaninglessness. In the words of Camus:

> *All I wish is to regain some peace of mind in a world that has regained a meaning. What spurs me on is not ambition but fear, my very reasonable fear of that inhuman vision in which my life means no more than a speck of dust.*[26]

That this condition is the rule, rather than the exception, is expressed in this famous passage by Thoreau:

---

[25] Ayn Rand, *The Romantic Manifesto* (New York: Signet Books, 1975), p. 23.
[26] Albert Camus, *Caligula and Three Other Plays*, trans. Stuart Gilbert (New York: Vintage Books, 1958), p. 22.

The mass of men lead lives of quiet desperation. What is called resignation is confirmed desperation. From the desperate city you go into the desperate country, and have to console yourself with the bravery of minks and muskrats. A stereotyped but unconscious despair is concealed even under what are called the games and amusements of mankind.

It appears as if men had deliberately chosen the common mode of living because they preferred it to any other. Yet they honestly think there is no choice left. But alert and healthy natures remember that the sun rose clear. It is never too late to give up our prejudices. No way of thinking or doing, however ancient, can be trusted without proof. What every body echoes or in silence passes by as true to-day may turn out to be falsehood tomorrows. . .[27]

At this stage of self realization, the subject's consciousness gradually reaches a crest of inner integration displaying plasma-like qualities of homogeneity and steady incandescence. The subject now knows his own mind and also what his destiny requires of him. Since "no man is an island" (John Donne), it is now time for our subject to reorient his attention towards the outer environment — physical matter itself. This is what we normally think of as the domain of science. But now, using the force of his new consciousness which is beginning to manifest the process of Accelerated Thought, he can bring a whole new energy to bear upon the task of understanding and mastering matter. The embryo of a new, transformed science will have formed.

In summary, this second, self-sustaining, plasma-like, self-awareness stage on the way to Accelerated Thought contains within itself the illuminated idea universe which constitutes the core of interest that the world and life hold for the subject. This includes all those aspects of himself and the outside world that prove to be pertinent and thus are actively integrated within his new consciousness. Thought has become truly organic when it becomes sufficiently integrated to be experienced or "felt" as one unified whole, rather than as fragmentary associations continuously following and impinging upon one another. Feeling begins to be organic when our sense of self is no longer easily usurped by some transient interest or complaint. Everything our subject feels he is, is included within consciousness. He fully feels what he has become.

On the other hand, this consciousness is limited to self-consciousness because the contents of this awareness — alive, active and self-consistent as subjective consciousness — remain, for the moment, restricted to "personal or subjective interests and meanings." And yet,

---

[27] Thoreau, "Walden," 111.

that this glowing body of awareness has limits and cannot continue to expand unrestrained plus the fact that almost all of what constitutes reality including the physical universe is still excluded from it suggests that a new kind of effort and process will soon be required.

The third, most exciting and most treacherous leg of his journey now begins as our subject shifts his rectified attention from the subjective world of abstract and aesthetic forms and relationships towards the more concrete world of matter. He need no longer concern himself with old familiar details — aspects of the world that have since become reinterpreted and reintegrated into his glowing plasma-like awareness. In the fullest sense of the word, these are now part of him. All those aspects, relationships, forms, possibilities, and manifestations of matter that have yet to be discovered, identified and integrated into consciousness now constitute the unknown for him.

Conventionally it is the job of science to reveal the laws governing matter. It is the role of industry to invent uses for this knowledge for the benefit of mankind. As already explained, all this progresses at a fairly conventional rhythm, notwithstanding occasional leaps deriving from those rare scientific breakthroughs produced by the giants of science — those exceptionally creative individuals who seem to appear on the scene only every few generations. Their unconventional vision is often so at odds with that of their colleagues, and so far in advance of their field, that these geniuses — when finally recognized — are sometimes suspected of having brain structures very different from normal.

Researchers in a postmortem operation went as far as to seek structural abnormalities in Albert Einstein's brain. Of course they found none. His new vision of matter, his genius, was part and parcel of a new awareness, a new relationship which he himself developed towards himself, time and matter in flat disregard for and irreverent defiance of convention. He could not have attained this vision without a burning interest in his subject, sufficient self-respect to take his own intuitions seriously, and the conviction necessary to follow through against all odds.

•   •   •

CHAPTER EIGHT

Breakthrough, Time & Matter

Consider what God has done: Who can straighten what he has made crooked?
(Eccl. 7:13)

It is the ability to *generate scientific and technical* breakthroughs that most characterizes the third stage of Accelerated Thought. This is in contrast to the stunning personal, psychological and philosophical breakthroughs that mark the results, if not the intent, of the previous stage. Not only is thought vastly clarified and accelerated in its functioning through an elevated and energized consciousness, but thanks to this revolutionary state an accelerated rate of technological development also can result.

Leaps of thought that produce breakthroughs in advancing technical progress in a sense also speed up or compress time.[1] If we were able to measure history objectively in terms of technical development, beginning even before the discovery of fire and the invention of the wheel right up until recent discoveries in superconductivity and nuclear fusion, we would see that spectacular breakthroughs have so far been few and far between. Yet these have a tremendous impact on the rate and manner in which society is formed. Culture and material culture are in effect inseparable.

Dramatically increasing the frequency of discoveries and breakthroughs (the rate at which matter is formed and transformed) will even more dramatically influence human culture, attitudes and outlooks, freeing man's mind from matter-bound convention at an accelerating rate — a rate far too rapid to allow complacency to set in. There will be so much to discover, enjoy and wonder at that even the hardest cynic will open to the abundance of benefits and the flood of hopeful new prospects for the future. But the real cause for celebration will be the palpable lifting of matter's oppression from man's spirit, allowing him insights that

---

[1] See appendix.

before might have required a lifetime of grueling spiritual discipline to attain. It is the refinement of matter and its impact on the consciousness of mankind that brings about the contraction, abridgement and, ultimately, the elimination of time. As his mind opens, man's experience can include more and more of reality as extension in time contracts towards simultaneity.

An elevated consciousness will reveal to man that his experience of time is simply a function of the action of materiality on his mind. The coarser the influence, the more time (i.e., dislocated instances of cause and effect) and the less reality are experienced. The less we are dispersed in time the more we reveal truth until, ultimately, our experience of reality and truth become one and the same. When we live in the eternal present, time disappears and simultaneous, integrated cause and effect — "spiritual time" — takes its place.

Paradoxically, this kind of experiential compression does not imply the pressure, harassment and alienation of today's modern city life — an existence so subject to the material imperative that there never seems to be enough time to "keep up with the Joneses." On the contrary, innovation will come so fast and furiously that conventionality, entrenched in our institutions and embedded in our minds, will be unable to appropriate these within the system. The system will no longer be able to keep us in line through the classic device of allocating resources, since the material abundance derived from breakthrough innovation will eliminate lack and thus render the rationale for allocation obsolete. We will perceive that our well-being depends on understanding and not on ownership, power or status.

Salt became obsolete as England's "gold" standard once it became universally plentiful. As abundance grows in much the same way, fewer and fewer material possessions will be worth hoarding. Matter will become so malleable, so obedient to our will, that constraints of all kinds will progressively disappear and "new man," relieved of the morbid influence of greed and deprivation, will be free to pursue the development of his unique potential. The "more" with which man will have to contend will not be the pressure to accumulate material goods in order to stay fashionable and "in the running," but rather will be a rallying, vivifying confrontation with more possibilities, more security and more understanding. Finally, through genuine care and social support it will discourage[2] any recalcitrants from indulging in weakness and vice, at least to their former pathological extent. For total misfits, computer-simulated existences (already foreshadowed by developments in "virtual reality" [cyberspace] and artificial intelligence) could be used as havens (i.e., gilded prisons).

Difficulty & Stagnation

I still try to remember that there is another world—not so far off as most imagine — where ineffable bliss holds its inhabitants as permanent captives. (Paul Brunton)

To generate lucid thought sufficiently penetrating to produce a breakthrough, a new effort will be required. But before this phase can begin there comes a moment when, because of limitations inherent in subjectivity, the self-sustaining, plasma-like self-consciousness reaches its optimum dimensions, stops expanding, ceases to extract living meaning from the environment and begins to stagnate. It can no longer assimilate meaning from environmental impressions because of the dearth of such impressions compatible with the limited particularity of the subject's personal, subjective awareness.

This particularity which imposes such severe limits to the scope of awareness (limits invoked for us by the very word "subjective") is due to the narrowness of our subject's ideology, philosophy and contact with the world, as contrasted with the vastness of cosmic reality. Thus the limits of awareness which can be seen to have dynamically expanded to the limits of the subject's personal identity for the moment become more or less fixed at the frontiers of that identity.

Our subject is unable to read further meanings into the environment. What he lacks in consciousness, analogous to and compatible with cosmic reality, defines his "unknown." For truly to know something implies the ability to experience and reproduce within ourselves the pattern or quality of existence of which that "something" objectively consists. The character of each "something" is intimately and intricately connected with the forms and patterns of its immediately contiguous reality. Everything in the cosmos is interconnected. It is our inner experience of these points of correspondence that reveals the meaning of the parts by showing their functional and structural relationship to the

---

[2] See appendix.

whole. As the subject's consciousness arrives at the limits of its reach, the perception of such connections becomes diminished.

Overcoming Deflection

The truth is more important than the facts. (Frank Lloyd Wright)
At this point the subject begins to notice that the feeling of movement and growth — the growth of self as consciousness — has been a very rewarding aspect of the process. Once he learns experientially that under special circumstances it becomes possible to transform unfulfilled personal potentials into dynamically experienced inner realizations, he can hardly be satisfied with a static state of Being. He cannot help feeling cravings for the emotions of wonder and elation that accompanied the expansion of self-awareness.

Also, the slowing down and eventual cessation of the growth of self-awareness that results from the inability of consciousness to assimilate any more of the world into itself constitutes a challenge to the subject, considering the relative smoothness and facility of inner growth that followed his initial exertions. Suddenly, he finds himself facing a contradiction. On the one hand, there is the still palpable euphoria of reaching a substantially unified, dynamic awareness of himself and his values. On the other hand, our subject, embodying this awareness, finds himself confronted with discontinuity. This signals the gradual cessation of the process of inner development and his exclusion from a course that originally seemed to offer the promise of unlimited growth, joy and even eternity.

We are happy when for everything inside us there is a corresponding something outside us. (W. B. Yeats)
He now finds himself face to face with the inescapable fact of his own personal limitations. He has realized his potential in terms of personal growth, and there he stands.[3]

Owing to this stagnation, unintegrated outer reality, like the growth surrounding a deserted jungle village, begins to encroach and press upon the subject's psyche. Nature and the world are never at rest. They constantly generate new forms that bombard the psyche and impinge upon it, challenging and admonishing man to go on growing and urging him back into movement.

---

[3] See appendix.

Every time I close the door on Reality it comes in through the window.
(Ashleigh Brilliant)

They increasingly show our subject that the consciousness he has attained is as nothing when compared with the knowledge in the world that remains hidden.[4]

The unknown awaits revelation at the hands of a consciousness able to penetrate its veil of secrecy. Until the subject finds a way to mobilize himself for this task, the unknown will prey on his mind and weigh down consciousness with a growing awareness of its insufficiency and shrinking significance before the immensity of the cosmos. The risk of falling back into the dispersion and darkness of conventional reflective thought becomes more and more real as the subject begins to feel alienated from a world with which, subjectively, he felt already at one. Outward reality pressing on him in this way brings our subject back to the strategy he adopted at his original point of departure, but with a difference.

His confrontation with the unknown — with material forms that refuse to integrate with his Being — no longer stems from alienation and distraction. It is now the pressure of reality closing in on him that poses the challenge. Fortunately, he is newly armed for this confrontation with a highly integrated, self-contained, plasma-like, self-conscious presence specifically designed by nature for dealing with reality.

On pain of becoming overwhelmed[5] by the forms of relentlessly encroaching reality and of losing the advantage of his high-energy (albeit subjective) thought system, our subject must now renew his effort. He must again turn his attention outwards and concentrate on those aspects of the material world that are most significant to him, but which have, until now, resisted inclusion within his consciousness.

The change of quality in consciousness — subjective to objective — needed to break this deadlock implies that our subject's subjective experiencings, conscious as they are, must take as their underpinning a new, firmer, more substantial, more essential foundation. He must make a basic shift in the way he relates to himself. The intelligence programmed into his body through aeons of evolution, gradually must become his direct, experiential reference, replacing the representational imagery he has leaned upon until now. For his self-knowledge to gain in objectivity, he must relinquish his precarious subjective anchorage and turn to the objectivity prefigured in his essence.

---

[4] See appendix.
[5] See appendix

Without the ability to experience ourselves and reality directly through the deeper layers of our essence-mind or "body-mind," the closest we can come to deciphering cosmic reality programmed into our substance and structure is through the judicious use of intuition to help forge links deep within essence. Intuition, resonating with essence-truth, can afford us brief glimpses of the real world — glimpses which we then elaborate as best we can with the manipulative intellectual, emotional and kinesthetic skills at our disposal. We then express these discoveries as ideas, attitudes, art, objects, machines or devices.

Direct and complete contact with essence[6] — a condition we are said to have enjoyed in the Garden of Eden — implies that we relinquish the illusion of freedom and security gained through the fragmentation of our experience into its distracted intellectual, emotional and physical components. These components were always meant to function synergistically in a powerful, tightly knit, conscious unit. In principle, they could again do so if we could find the means to mobilize our various psychic constituents. Meanwhile, the fragmentation of our experience, corresponding to the experiential modalities of these components, grants us the license to form imaginary amalgams, the "Push-Me-Pull-You" entities we construe as everyday reality and which, by the grace of cosmic order, function admirably within the scope of the dimension we call "our world."

There is another world, but it is in this one. (Paul Eluard)

Most, if not all, major traditions agree that man is a microcosm — a small world — every part of which corresponds in some way to cosmic reality. The kind of introspection that leads to self-knowledge reveals these functions to us along with all the possible roles, ramifications and implications such functions can have in a working system. Finding those points of correspondence in the functioning of our consciousness and matching them experientially with their counterparts in the world implies that every part of our body must eventually participate in the process of consciousness, expanding our sense of self so that even in our bodily extremities we become "mind."

The insights gained in the second or "personal consciousness" phase on the way to Accelerated Thought (we could even call these insights "breakthroughs") were primarily personal insights — personal breakthroughs. It makes no difference how rigorously rational or scientific

---

[6] See appendix.

one's mind is, nor how objective and concrete the matter under examination. Passage through this phase is virtually indispensable. Yet, once an individual reaches a degree of involvement in his subject so great that it cuts him off from social approval and support, throwing him entirely upon his own resources for psychological sustenance (and usually long before any external practical result is achieved), a subjective result of astonishing proportions is attained.

This phenomenon of self-realization is so liberating and striking in its effect that the subject can easily be diverted from his purpose and forget his original goal. The discovery of the existence of a dimension beyond distracted, reflective consciousness can easily bring us to religion or to some brand of spiritual discipline under the tutelage of a teacher, guru or mentor. Notwithstanding many benefits, such a side trip can divert a seeker, even permanently, from his original quest and his confrontation with matter. Ghiselin makes reference to this phenomenon:

> *It is as if the mind delivered from preoccupation with particulars were given into secure possession of its whole substance and activity. This yielding to the oceanic consciousness may be a distracting delight, which . . . can divert the worker from formal achievement. In this extreme the experience verges upon the religious . . . More often it defines itself as no more than a sense of self-surrender to an inward necessity inherent in something larger than the ego and taking precedence over the established order.*[7]

Something decides to give precedence to spirit over matter, assuming as most do that there is a fundamental contradiction between the two — that our concern with one must necessarily be at the expense of the other, and that a human aim cannot possibly encompass both simultaneously.[8]

Under the special conditions envisaged by Project Mind for nurturing Accelerated Thought, the euphoric flights of spiritual and religious revelation and related misapprehensions contributing to the deflection of purpose in the creative process will be contained within a framework designed to keep our subject on track and maintain his perspective. He will be readied in advance for the psychological phenomena that tend to accompany the creative process, and will be given guidance while he is experiencing such phenomena.

> *Each of us must make his own true way, and when we do, that way will express the universal way. (Suzuki Roshi — Zen Mind, Beginner's Mind)*

---

[7] *The Creative Process,* Ghiselin, ed., 15.

[8] See appendix.

Our subject began by seeking new order in the phenomenal world; he ended up by establishing a new order within himself as an unexpected half-way point or way-station to his aim. His personal relationship to the environment has been revolutionized. But as far as the world at large is concerned, nothing visible has happened. His aim has not yet taken on any external, material form that can influence the reality impinging upon others.

To recapitulate, our subject's inner transformation was fueled by the force of attention retrieved from a profusion of institutionalized psychosocial mechanisms that normally dissipate energy and dilute consciousness. Once liberated and sufficiently energized, his new "personal" consciousness was able to maintain itself on the refined and easily consumed fuel of familiar, subjectively meaningful, partially digested, perceptual and conceptual inputs that made up his private world. Now that the accumulation of meaning has reached its maximum energy level, the process is ripe for a new and final high-energy phase requiring for its maintenance a "heavier" form of cognitive fuel[9] consisting of the "hard" material facts of reality (enigmatic and indigestible to a consciousness of less than scintillating brightness).

The Worst of Subjectivity — Society & Transcendence

The gulf between knowledge and truth is infinite. (Henry Miller)
Before showing how one makes the transition from a conscious state in which subjectivity is dominant to one in which objectivity plays a determinant role, it would be worthwhile to draw some general distinctions between subjectivity and objectivity, and to look at the impact subjectivity has on our distracted lives. This distinction is especially significant as it applies to our conventional, everyday, distracted awareness — the awareness we erroneously, if innocently, call "consciousness."

It is normally conceded that the so-called "soft" sciences (history, social sciences, humanities, etc.) and disciplines that depend upon concepts of a primarily aesthetic, experiential or relational nature, lack hard objective criteria that might allow them to exercise some precise influ-

---

[9] See appendix.

ence through the application of their "scientific" findings. They lack any firm factual foundation from which to start, nor have they reliable standards[10] with which to be guided, nor any precise, pre-defined objectives for which to strive. So anyone who chooses to innovate in these fields must use his own judgment and be his own arbiter about not only what goals he seeks to achieve, but also regarding the significance of the results he finally does achieve. How can any researcher in this field hope to break out of his own magic circle and escape the trap of subjectivity with no objectively determined signpost to lead him out of the woods?

Furthermore, even those who would wish to construct their view of life on some firm, factual, scientific basis discover they lack access to anything that might provide such a basis and that might correspond to objective knowledge. Whatever hard scientific knowledge we do have is relative and changes constantly with the times. The only "certainties" that remain, alas, are "death and taxes."

If there is some merit in the sophistication of modern industrial man, it is in his growing appreciation of the relativity of the "facts" he encounters and that everything is open to interpretation. Even in physics — the most precise and definitive of sciences — the very notion of matter changes continually. Having failed to isolate fundamental particles of matter that answer to any conventional criteria of materiality, physics is at present reduced to viewing matter as fluctuating fields of energy, or ripples induced by an "implicate order."[11] For some physicists, such notions come uncomfortably close to implying that a deity or consciousness is at the root of matter.

Cut off from the inner aesthetic certainties of early childhood and denied further access to the Biblical "Tree of Knowledge" (i.e., objective truth), we fall prey to our subjective fears and anxieties, unaware that in reality our feelings of vulnerability stem from our own enfeebled consciousness and our consequent inability to resolve or even face the existential dilemma of our matter-determined mortality.

The further removed we become from the primordial source of objective knowledge — knowledge of the world, of ourselves and of the reason we were created, deeply imprinted within our essence — the more superficial we become and the more relative and thus subjective our judgment. We tend to fall back on whatever subjective resources do

---

[10] See appendix.
[11] See Bohm, *Wholeness and the Implicate Order.*

remain at our disposal. And so for wisdom we substitute cleverness; for understanding, opinion;[12] and for intuition, idle hunches. Our dependence on such corrupted means leads us ever deeper into the spiral of perplexity and degradation.

Locked into subjectivity and left to our own devices, we mobilize whatever remains of our wits for the pursuit of our material comfort and survival. Perversely, our shell — our physical body — rather than truth, becomes the primary object of our concern.

Our relationship to the cosmos is corrupted accordingly. Any rigorously honest enquiry will reveal that we tend to learn, think and work primarily for the sake of our bodily sustenance and comfort. We work in order to eat. To most people, this state of affairs seems normal and healthy. Yet true expediency and self-interest dictate that we should eat in order to work. And it is indeed so for those to whom "work" implies sacred service and the pursuit of truth — as behooves creatures who conceive of themselves as cast in the image of G-d.[13]

Leisure is typically perceived as a merciful haven from work rather than, as it should be, re-creation, an opportunity to establish a new rhythm and get new perspectives on our work — work that bestows meaning on life and is our *raison d' être*. Caught behind the proverbial "eight-ball" of our subjectivity, we live this grotesque inversion, eating our way to the grave instead of working towards eternity.

Likewise, our educational and scientific research establishments (including almost all organized intellectual endeavors) end up having as their principal preoccupation not the quest for objective knowledge, but rather, as many a sociological study has pointed out, the pursuit of institutional self-perpetuation. Our institutions are served more than they serve. This becomes most evident when institutions seek any pretext at all to continue operating long after the functions for which they were created become obsolete.

Worst of all, the almost universal view of benumbed humanity that, ultimately, death is a good and natural thing, confirms our spiritual and intellectual bankruptcy. Our lack of horror is the main horror. In speaking of man's "invisible enemies," Haish-Min-Al, a spiritual entity in the esoteric work of Theon, exhorts:

---

[12] See appendix.

[13] The spelling "G-d" as used in this text is a convention used in certain traditions as a reminder that the Supreme Being is beyond human comprehension

Their main weapon is blind faith, false sentimentality and the tendency to suicide . . . which not only makes man bow with respect before this terrifying mortality, but also makes him salute it as though mortality were a supreme liberator, leading straight to heavenly, ethereal abodes.

Whoever teaches that retrogressive transformation or mortality is the predestined, legitimized end of man . . . is, therefore, the enemy of man. Of right, man is eternal, and the knowledge of the earth (from its centre to the limit of its aura), which is, in its entirety, his inheritance, will provide him with ample means of satisfaction, of well-being and of endless progress.

Moreover, it is precisely the too short duration of individual existence that keeps man in ignorance of the means of realization of happiness and well-being.[14]

With our values and those of society at large so fundamentally and extensively twisted, we find ourselves at the mercy of any and all public entities that happen to have a say in our physical comfort and well-being. Accordingly, we learn to conform to whatever society expects of us. We soon discover that all social and material advancement depends on our being socially accepted. Not surprisingly, we find it comforting to feel a part of something larger, stronger and more enduring than ourselves. Belonging is reduced to a vice, as Hoffer points out:

The effacement of individual separateness must be thorough. In every act, however trivial, the individual must by some ritual associate himself with the congregation, the tribe, the party, etcetera. His joys and sorrows, his pride and confidence must spring from the fortunes and capacities of the group rather than from his individual prospects and abilities. Above all, he must never feel alone. Though stranded on a desert island, he must still feel that he is under the eyes of the group. To be cast out from the group should be equivalent to being cut off from life.[15]

Seen in the light of consciousness and stripped of our social neuroses, no group cause — no pretext of any kind — can possibly have more meaning to us than the miracle of life and the cosmic role destiny has dealt us. Hoffer again:

To a man utterly without a sense of belonging, mere life is all that matters. It is the only reality in an eternity of nothingness, and he clings to it with shameless despair.

Dying and killing seem easy when they are a part of a ritual, ceremonial, dramatic performance or game. There is need for some kind of make-believe in order to face death unflinchingly. To our real, naked selves there is not a thing on earth or in heaven worth dying for.[16]

---

[14] Max Theon, *Visions of the Eternal Present* (Jerusalem: Argaman, 1991), 108-110.
[15] Hoffer, *The True Believer*, 61.
[16] Ibid., 60-64.

We succumb willingly to the illusion[17] of safety — of being cared for — that social approval provides. Not surprisingly, the injury to which we become most susceptible is social affront. A good reputation becomes our most valued asset, more dear to us than our essence, Being or integrity — often, more than life itself.

Branden calls this process "parasitism of consciousness:"

It must be emphasized that the social metaphysician's dependence on other men is not, fundamentally, material or financial; it is deeper than any practical or tangible consideration; the material forms of parasitism and exploitation that some men practice are merely one of its consequences.

The basic dependence of the social metaphysician is pyscho-epistemological; it is a parasitism of cognition, of judgment, of values—a wish to function within a context established by others, to live by the guidance of rules for which one does not bear ultimate intellectual responsibility—a parasitism of consciousness.

Since the social metaphysician's pseudo-self-esteem rests on his ability to deal with the-world-as-perceived-by-others, his fear of disapproval or condemnation is the fear of being pronounced inadequate to reality, unfit for existence, devoid of personal worth — a verdict he hears whenever he is "rejected."[18]

As we climb the social ladder — with all the incumbent comforts, amenities and privileges along the way — we tend to become secure, even smug. It is almost as though through this depraved form of integration we were unconsciously engaged in the process of becoming invulnerable — of achieving immortality.

As we ambitiously conspire to become a significant and integral part of society, we forget that "becoming a part" is more than a mere question of adherence. As we conform, of necessity we surrender pieces of our identity — our individuality — in small acts of downward-transcendent self-sacrifice. Eventually, the individual finds he is an insignificant cipher, a nonentity having little meaning or value beyond whatever mechanical function society assigns him. It is almost as if he were an organizational unit in a beehive or anthill. Jung sees it this way:

Our admiration for great organizations dwindles when once we become aware of the other side of the wonder: the tremendous piling up and accentuation of all that is primitive in man, and the unavoidable destruction of his individuality in the interests of the monstrosity that every great organization in fact is. The man of today, who resembles more or less the

---

[17] See appendix.
[18] Branden, *The Psychology of Self-Esteem*, 180.

*collective ideal, has made his heart into a den of murderers, as can easily be
proved by the analysis of his unconscious, even though he himself is not in
the least disturbed by it. And in so far as he is normally "adapted" to his
environment, it is true that the greatest infamy on the part of his group will
not disturb him, so long as the majority of his fellows steadfastly believe in
the exalted morality of their social organization.*[19]

Koestler describes in some detail the process of becoming lost in
something seemingly greater than ourselves. He justly reminds us that,
aside from common greed-generated violence, the self-assertive bestial-
ity of men expresses itself principally in the service and in the name of the
collective through the self-effacing, self-sacrificing, self-transcending,
altruistic, participatory emotions.[20]

In either case we must ask the deeper question: What is the "self" that
is asserted, either for purely selfish motives or selflessly, in the name of
the collective? Without the belief that there is well-defined essence-
individuality at our core waiting to be revealed, one could easily subscribe
to the Hobbesian belief that man is by nature savage and that it is mainly
society that restrains us or releases our inborn violence. Janov protests:

*One of the myths about humans is that underneath our placid exteriors we
are a seething cauldron of fury and violence kept in check solely by society.
When the checking system falters, man's innate violence erupts, resulting in
wars, holocausts. However, I am continuously struck by how unaggressive
and nonviolent people are when their so-called civilized fronts are removed.*[21]

The self-transcendence of which Jung and Koestler speak is downward oriented, whereby people, rather than rising above themselves
towards a higher form of integration, relinquish individual discriminatory
functions in favor of the perceptions and considerations of the prevailing
collective. The effect is more spectacular when we surrender ourselves to
participation in mobs and in wars, but the same process is everywhere,
quietly at work. And while Hoffer, Branden, Jung, Koestler and Janov go
as far as to recognize that society tends to bring out the worst in man, they
seem to ignore that the repressed individuality they lament was created to
overcome some aspect of material restriction in this world. Society can
perform many legitimate functions. But the point at which social associa-

---

[19] C. G. Jung, "Two Essays on Analytical Psychology," in *The Collected Works of C.
G. Jung* (London: R. F. C. Hull, new edition 1966), par. 240.

[20] Koestler, *The Act of Creation*, 299-300.

[21] Janov, *The Primal Scream*, 345.

tion truly becomes a harmful vice is the very point at which the individual and society lose sight of their real tasks and interests.

To the extent we allow ourselves to be absorbed in the framework of ready-made meanings we encounter in the world, we are matter, and subject to the vagaries of fate. To the extent that we are sufficiently active to absorb and transform our environment within the orbit of our personal meaning, we are mind, and connected to our destiny. To the extent that the world provides us with our meanings, we are distracted and subjective. To the extent that we bestow meaning to the world, we are conscious and objective.

This does not mean that we cannot accept and benefit from what the world offers us. It does mean that to be truly alive we must actively integrate what we encounter into our own thought systems — our own meanings — within the framework of a dynamic process of inner growth that weeds out contradictions and inconsistencies. Rand explains the process of integrating reality in terms of philosophy and experience:

> Philosophy does not replace a man's sense of life, which continues to function as the automatically integrated sum of his values. But philosophy sets the criteria of his emotional integrations according to a fully defined and consistent view of reality (if and to the extent that a philosophy is rational). Instead of deriving, subconsciously, an implicit metaphysics from his value-judgments, he now derives, conceptually, his value-judgments from an explicit metaphysics. His emotions proceed from his fully convinced judgments. The mind leads, the emotions follow.
>
> For many men, the process of transition never takes place: they make no attempt to integrate their knowledge, to acquire any conscious convictions, and are left at the mercy of their inarticulate sense of life as their only guide.[22]

Like Koestler and others, Rand tends to take for granted the conscious dimension — that in assimilating reality not only does one become successful in what is conventionally known as "life," but more important, one *becomes*. What we truly are, objectively, is our unique essence that distinguishes us from one another. It equips us to reveal some special piece of cosmic truth to which the essential uniqueness of other individuals is less favorably attuned. Like the seed that it is, essence must find its just expression, consciously, through the growth of Being. Paradoxically, through this process we do become absorbed and integrated within a larger reality. This reality is the objective world of living consciousness and not the illusory, matter-laden world of subjectivity and distraction.

---

[22] Rand, *Romantic Manifesto*, 29-30.

If we have virtually no contact with essence and refuse to recognize its existence, even ignoring the help of the various systems and disciplines that teach about essence, we could be said to have sold that birthright for a subjective[23] "mess of pottage." By "subjective" is meant the subjectivity of distraction, not that objective subjectivity which has at least some of its roots planted firmly in the outer layers of essence and can find expression, however restricted, through subjective consciousness. Estrangement from essence is the most fundamental form of alienation, and compromises our very humanity, for "humanity" implies at least some small, conscious expression, however subjective, of that cosmic essence that integrates the higher and the lower.

But conditions of social existence, overwhelmingly governed by the preeminence of matter, gnaw away at the little human dignity that reflective thought and the odd creative or intuitive insight allow us to salvage from our distracted state. The more we conform, the more we become a part and the more by default we allow society to define our identity, determine our needs, allocate the distribution of our energy and arrogate our initiative. It is grotesque that our exaggerated preoccupation with the physical side of our nature and our obsession with aging creates in us anxieties of a primarily social nature. In the process, we neglect profound questions[24] of life and death and feel little remorse for this evasion.

Fashionable theories and socially conditioned opinions become our expedient substitute for an objective awareness of life and the world around us. Inconsequential variations of style (any real dissension would quickly cost us our social station) distinguish us from our neighbors. This illusion of personal significance helps us ignore that we are locked out of lucid states of consciousness that could transform our lives. The very having of opinions provides us with the illusion of a unique personal identity, while the secure conviction of being a member in good standing provides us with a conscience-soothing substitute for our aborted quest for truth and personal integrity. From within this morass of socially cultivated subjectivity, all that remains to man of objectivity is the occasional glimmer of truth that rarely, accidentally filters up through intuition from the objective knowledge hidden deeply within his essence and hard-wired into the circuitry and structure of his substance.

---

[23] See appendix.
[24] See appendix.

As infants, we experience this mind-body and its hidden cosmic truths directly, until formal education and social intimidation distract us from its message and subjugate us to conventional standards. If anything of this spirit survives the brutally alienating ordeal of socialization, we may one day hear the far-off call of objective truth waiting to issue forth from essence. This truth and the essence which is its incarnation are our only real basis for authentic individuality. It is the pursuit of this truth, on both microcosmic and macrocosmic levels, that once again becomes the central concern of our subject as he prepares to pass from the second to the third and final phase of Accelerated Thought.

Certainty —The Key to Objective Consciousness

There is a victory yet for all justice and the true romance which the world exists to realize, will be the transformation of genius into practical power. (Ralph Waldo Emerson)

Grounded to some small extent in reality, our subject now approaches the experience of certainty — the firm, authentic, conscious certainty of his existence and unique identity. This includes the self-confidence to grapple more directly with the reality of his vulnerability, his mortality, and the incontrovertible fact that this vulnerability is attributable to matter in general and to the coarse material aspect of the human body in particular. Certainty, in embracing reality, manifests love of existence — both general, undifferentiated existence and our specific role in that existence. And love, in the end, is the negation of death.

Death and its harbingers — accident, deprivation, pain and disease — are perpetuated by our socially generated failure of courage and default of awareness. As a species, we wallow in a chronic stupor of ignorance, suspicion, superstition and fear, asleep to any possibilities not formally recognized or conventionally approved. We lack our subject's conscious conviction that absolutely nothing in the world can resist the force of intelligence when combined with the will to apply that intelligence without fear or reservation.

The most important aspect of our subject's newly-won certainty, conferring virtually unlimited hope and faith in the future, is the compellingly direct experience and cognition of the astounding fact that man, in his entirety, is intelligence — mind. The material aspect of the body, as necessary as it may be to provide a receptacle or cocoon while the intelligence within awaits its realization, nonetheless remains negligible. Until man realizes this intelligence, until he experiences himself fully and consciously as intelligence, the coarse, obscuring materiality of the body will continue to dominate consciousness through psychosocial mechanisms.

But now, our subject's consciousness (substantially relieved of this debilitating, subliminal psychic burden) can confidently scan the world while simultaneously exercising his highly-tuned intuition. Focusing on new issues he senses are important, our subject begins to seek a correspondence in form between what he feels intuitively could be true and whatever observation-based hypotheses he can formulate concerning what he actually finds in the outside world.

The chances of hitting upon a hypothesis that will completely and profoundly satisfy intuition are immeasurably better for our subject now that his intimate contact with himself — part and parcel of his hard-won personal consciousness — provides enhanced access to his own essential resources of cosmic knowledge. This new clarity of thought, which is just one of the functions of our subject's newly acquired inner coherence, is an expression, albeit incomplete, of essence itself. It enables him to gain insights and formulate new hypotheses about the world in completely new ways.

These insights are due not only to lucidity (which is only one of several attributes of consciousness), but, more importantly, to a sense of inner certainty communicating through feeling the promise of unlimited future possibilities.

This feeling of certainty — now the principal inherency of our subject's consciousness — will soon also be shown to be the prime mover of Accelerated Thought and a springboard to objective consciousness. Born of some direct experience of inner order and the sense of growing accord between thought and feeling accompanied by the actual witnessing of the dynamic and luminous workings of truth on even a limited scale, this certainty adds up to the unwavering conviction (the emotional equivalent of objective knowledge) that there are truly no limits to what can be known, felt or accomplished. We have it all but just don't know it.[25]

• • •

---

[25] See appendix.

CHAPTER NINE

Certainty, Truth & the Compulsion to Share

It takes courage for a man to listen to his own goodness and act on it. Do we dare to be ourselves? (Pablo Casals)

It is in the nature of things that when truth touches us, we find it compelling. It is the source of and guide to all that is or could be dear to us. Truth is the food of our Being. It is salvation in every possible form — but only to the extent we are able to recognize it. To distracted consciousness it remains hidden.

The price to be paid for certainty of vision is the compulsion, or cosmic obligation, to translate this vision into action, to invoke its benefits and confirm its validity in order to share it with others. This sense of obligation is communicated to the body through feeling even if the subjective side of our nature has no interest in altruism. Sharing — the channeling of abundance from higher and finer levels of materiality — is decreed by cosmic law through our divine human form and realized through the manifestation of the intelligence inherent to this form: Accelerated Thought.

To the extent that vision is complete and valid, it will also include a clear idea of how it must be realized. The absolute imperative that such a comprehensive vision represents means that, one way or another, we will single-mindedly seek out the means to realize the vision in its totality.

But to the extent that our level of Being is not sufficiently elaborated to encompass the vision, we will have to contend with the frustration and agitation of a real and desired possibility pressing us to act before we are ready to deal with the requirements and contingencies connected with action. This is one of the dangers that Project Mind can easily prevent.

As it develops, certainty increasingly lends a potency and incisiveness to thought which, for the most part, is totally foreign to us. Eventually, a point of intensity may be reached sufficient to trigger the process of Accelerated Thought.

Because of the unprecedented degree of his individuation (the result of refinement and specialization that has been going on since Creation), Accelerated Thought is uniquely[1] appropriate to modern, technological man. Without Accelerated Thought to enable us to break out of our "cosmic egg," we risk suffocation under the weight of the multiplicity of material forms we have created, and the concomitant physical and psychological deprivations these induce.

As certainty grows, fortifying our subject's efforts, intuition and keen observation work more closely together and intensify their task of finding and matching impressions under the ever-growing light of consciousness. This process soon generates insights about aspects of materiality observed in the outside world.

Matter & Objectivity

If you are willing to discipline yourself, the physical universe won't need to discipline you. (Leonard Orr)

It is important to keep in mind that the objects now seeking integration within the subject's plasma-like consciousness belong to the world of hard physical reality. Subjectively held philosophical, psychological, aesthetic and relational constructs still defy public verification, as witness the near impossibility of finding full ideological accord between even as few as two people. Respecting the social sensibilities that exist within any given culture or subculture, subjective entities[2] can be manipulated, abused or even disregarded, for the most part with impunity. Matter, on the other hand, belonging to the physical realm, commands respect, demands precise and rigorous accountability and is most unforgiving.

Matter resists attempts to deal with it using approximation. We are severely and instantly punished for any imprecision whenever we presume upon matter without fully respecting the laws governing the physical aspect of reality. When a bridge can no longer hold our weight, there is no appeal and no mercy.[3] We pay the consequences of our miscalculation in full, just as we are rewarded for our compliance with physical laws. In this realm the scofflaw is short-lived indeed.

Furthermore, the fine, intimate, inner material of thought, feeling and sensation (of which representations of reality are made) which can

[1] See appendix.
[2] See appendix.
[3] See appendix.

fuel subjective consciousness is more accessible to us for processing than is the foreign objective matter constituting the hard reality of the physical world. This personal representational material is stored in the various parts of our psychic apparatus and is called up for examination under the light of attention for possible inclusion into consciousness. It is available, preferentially, precisely because it is inside us. Thus, unlike entities on the outside, it can be accessed from all sides and through the middle. For the most part, we can touch phenomena in the outside world only superficially with our senses. Equally important is that as microcosms, we encompass (through our encoded essence) the full range of materiality existing in the cosmos. In principle, we can experience these materialities directly, with the help of external sensory inputs that awaken latent, essential, coded impressions and render them conscious and intelligible.

With the aid of the external senses, we are able to produce images and mental constructs of whatever physical realities we encounter. Unfortunately, we are still deprived of a wealth of data about "noumenal," "inner," or "higher" properties[4] of the object, substance or phenomenon under consideration. It is largely because of this that conventional science is denied objective knowledge. Unable to taste, feel or manifest consciousness, science's reductionist view of matter is condemned to repeated review as the secrets and substance of matter constantly recede under the probing scrutiny of ever more precise instruments and techniques.

Regardless of how thoroughly we inspect a part of physical reality or subject it to experiment, some information always eludes us. If the research in question is sufficiently rigorous, the missing data will eventually be shown to pertain to yet-undiscovered cosmic and natural laws[5] and levels of materiality. A holistic grasp of these laws and levels requires higher modes of consciousness. For similar reasons, objective reality resists even the plasma-like vigor of personal consciousness, at least until sufficient energy builds up for its transformation to the nascent state of objective consciousness now under consideration.

As already shown, subjectively conscious constructs offer only a partial representation of the reality they are meant to depict. In fact, only personally significant aspects of the construct are retained in consciousness. As a rule, these are restricted to intimately private appreciations of

---

[4] See appendix.
[5] See appendix.

an aesthetic or practical nature. The rest are, in effect, discarded.[6] These "discards" from consciousness are then filed in memory to be called up for use through associational cueing, subject to the efficiency or lack thereof of the filing and retrieval system concerned.

The virtue of subjective consciousness, in this context, is that something of reality (albeit a very minuscule, non-discarded remnant of objective reality) is actually integrated into consciousness. This raises the energy level and general efficiency of the mind in extracting meaning from the environment. The rich satisfactions of this elevating experience make it easier to accept that even that part of the vast unknown reality which is perceivable but excluded from consciousness is not known in any real sense of the word. Knowledge implies relation —our conscious relationship with the thing known. Biblically speaking, Adam "knew" Eve in enormously more aspects than our modern understanding of knowledge or sex would lead us to believe.

Most of us, trapped in everyday distracted awareness, find comfort in the illusion that the world we experience forms an authentic part of our knowledge. Little do we suspect that the perceptions are not ours at all — that they do not participate in any form of genuine consciousness. Except for the low grade of attention necessary for reflective, associative thought, as far as we are concerned there might just as well be no consciousness in which to participate. Images and concepts are mechanically filed in memory, retrieved and reflected upon according to some criterion of functional necessity.

The order in which these associations are called up from memory and what constitutes a cue is a question of conditioning and programming, education and experience. The little force of attention that conventionality allows us to retain is the energy by which this programming and our socialized functioning is accomplished. These forms and constructs constitute the substance that attention illuminates and manipulates but lacks the force to raise to its own energy level. Attention enfeebled by distraction lacks the force to feed itself and grow.

The requirements of life normally absorb our daily allotment of the energy of attention, rendering unlikely the efforts that might lead to

---

[6] As far as consciousness is concerned, this is something like killing a duck, eating the liver (if that is the part one likes), and then throwing away the remainder. This selectivity based on personal proclivity illustrates the weakness inherent in subjectivity. Here, what there is of consciousness is able to survive at the expense of excluding all that isn't immediately compatible with its process.

Accelerated Thought. We tend to exploit any surpluses we are fortunate enough to accumulate to better our circumstances, either by improving our personal programming or by running our existing programs more efficiently.

It never occurs to us that what we are at any given moment — our Being — is determined by the quality of our attention and not, as we seem to believe, by all that information and programming. We fail to grasp that, at our best, we are neither the seer nor the object seen — we are the seeing itself. We are neither matter nor energy but a process integrating the two. We are, in principle, living intelligence.

The special aspect of certainty that provides that new, all-important impulse to thought issues from our subject's experience of himself as living consciousness — as intelligence. Likewise, he is now sufficiently aware and confident to acknowledge fully and experience directly the material aspect of his nature and of the world. The chief implication of this conventionally uncomprehended[7] level of materiality is the vulnerability of the physical body, pointing unerringly towards mortality.[8]

Our subject finds himself confronted with the double challenge of redeeming[9] his life force from the ever-present threat of corporal mortality, and his consciousness from the confining limitations of subjectivity. Matter and energy, as we shall see shortly, are two sides of one coin: Accelerated Thought being a function of objective consciousness, with immortality being an attribute.

Formulating Hypotheses - Groping for Reality

Whether or not you can observe a thing depends on the theory you use. It is the theory which decides what can be observed. (Albert Einstein)
Normally, whenever we seek to understand or relate to something new to our experience, we tend to lean heavily on our aesthetic faculty in scanning our memory for forms encountered in the past. We hope to recognize parallels or similarities that might throw light on the nature and significance of the new phenomenon.

Having encountered an inner association or construct that we feel bears some similarity, we are free to speculate on the significance of this

---

[7] See appendix.
[8] See appendix.
[9] See appendix.

similarity. This matching process is repeated each time on a smaller scale — a scale restricted to the major class of things to which the first association belonged. We renew this effort within subclass after subclass until, having selected what we feel are the most likely attributes through the broadest use of our memory scanning system, we allow ourselves some hypothesis as to what it really represents and where it fits in the general scheme of things.

In other words, we consider all the ways in which it relates to the rest of what we "know" about the world. Some people are more efficient at this scanning and recognition process than others, just as some are more gifted than others in forming hypotheses. Those with improved access to the essence within themselves (thanks, perhaps, to grace, enlightened upbringing, intuition or spiritual practice[10]) have an important edge in this respect.

Once we have refined and developed an hypothesis as far as we are able, we begin to subject it to empirical testing in the kind of laboratory relevant to the field of our inquiry. This usually requires predicting how the object, substance or phenomenon under consideration will interact with "known" elements. The extent and degree of predictive accuracy revealed through experimentation determines the level of validity of the hypothesis and is called its predictive power. This is a slow, painstaking process. Anyone who has ever tried to formulate an original hypothesis or work out and execute an efficient experiment knows just how difficult and demanding this can be. Scientists must often resort to the sophisticated statistical manipulation of their data in order to claim "significance" for their findings.

Physicist Ernest Watson showed his insight into this problem by decrying the overemphasis of statistical analysis as a symptom of poor experimental design, or of a poorly conceived question. He felt that a well-designed, well-thought-out experiment should clearly answer a well-put question.[11]

Janov makes a similar point regarding the "soft" sciences:

Too often we in the social sciences have been content with statistical truths rather than human ones, piling up cases to "prove" our point when, it seems to me, scientific proof ultimately rests upon predictability — to make a cure happen, not simply to build theoretical rationales to explain later why someone improved in this therapy or that.[12]

---

[10] See appendix.
[11] See Jeffrey and Lilly, *John Lilly so far ...* , 31.
[12] Janov, *The Primal Scream*, 423.

Insight & Vision - Views of the Real World

The light of the righteous shines brightly. (Psalms 13:9)

Our subject, now at the very threshold of Accelerated Thought, finds himself applying a new, revolutionary approach to the formulation and verification of hypotheses, for he has gained enhanced access to the essential source of truth within himself. He has achieved exceptional clarity of thought, the impetus for which is provided by his new level of certainty concerning hopeful possibilities awaiting discovery.

There soon arises within him the first of many penetrating insights touching the constitution of physical reality. Just as intuitive insights bear within themselves some flavor of truth (it is the idea of truth that gives the very sense to the word "insight"), so the insight of our subject, unfolding within his brilliantly illuminated mind, projects an unprecedentedly clear and nicely elaborated vision of the phenomenon he has selected for consideration. Again, McClintock serves as our model:

> *From these reports one can get a sense of the unfolding of her theory as a hierarchy of hypotheses, each more abstract and further removed from the objects of perception than the one before, yet, in concert, providing an internal logic so compelling as to give anyone who grasps that logic the sense of being able to "see" the abstractions themselves. Witkin, who worked in the same building and who followed McClintock's workday by day, came to feel that she too, could "actually see genes turning on and off." In fact, a prodigious amount of cognitive processing intervened between the spots of pigment she could actually see on the corn plant and the controlling elements she ultimately came to write about. To invoke her own analogy, her "computer" was working full time — mediating between the spots, the patterns they formed, and her internal vision.*

> *For all of us, our concepts of the world build on what we see, as what we see builds on what we think. Where we know more, we see more. But for McClintock, this reciprocity between cognitive and visual seems always to have been more intimate than it is for most. As if without distinguishing between the two, she knew by seeing and saw by knowing. Especially illustrative is the story she tells of how she came to see the Neurospora chromosomes. Unwilling to accept her failure to see these minute objects under the microscope — she retreated to sit and meditate, beneath the eucalyptus trees. There she "worked on herself." When she felt she was ready, she returned to the microscope, and the chromosomes were now to be seen, not only by her, but thereafter, by others as well.*

> *If this were a story of insight arrived at by reflection, it would be more familiar. Its real force is as a story of eyesight, and of continuity between*

mind and eye that made McClintock's work so distinctive and, at the same time, so difficult to communicate in ordinary language.

Through years of intense and systematic observation and interpretation (she called it "integrating what you saw") McClintock had built a theoretical vision, a highly articulated image of the world within the cell. As she watched the corn plants grow, examined the patterns on the leaves and kernels, looked down the microscope at their chromosomal structure, she saw directly into that ordered world. The "Book of Nature" was to be read simultaneously by the eyes of the body and those of the mind. The spots McClintock saw on the kernels of corn were ciphers in a text that, because of her understanding of their genetic meaning, she could read directly. For her, the eyes of the body were the eyes of the mind.

Knowing that "everything was going to be all right," she found that, where before she had seen only disorder, now she could pick out the chromosomes easily. "I found that the more I worked with them the bigger and bigger [they] got, and when I was really working with them I wasn't outside, I was down there with them, and everything got big. I even was able to see the internal parts of the chromosomes — actually everything was there. It surprised me because I actually felt as if I were right down there and these were my friends." [13]

Such an elaborated vision is in its own right a ready-made, fully developed hypothesis. It so qualifies owing not to just one, but to many points of correspondence between the phenomenon selected for study and "known" phenomena. The wealth of correlation displayed is a function of the richness of the vision and its predictive potential. Tesla asserts:

It is absolutely immaterial to me whether I run my turbine in thought or test it in my shop. I even note if it is out of balance. There is no difference whatever, the results are the same. In this way I am able to rapidly develop and perfect a conception without touching anything. When I have gone so far as to embody in the invention every possible improvement I can think of and see no fault anywhere, I put into concrete form this final product of my brain. Invariably my device works as I conceived that it should, and the experiment comes out exactly as I planned it. In twenty years there has not been a single exception ...

and elsewhere:

As I uttered these inspiring words the idea came like a flash of lightning and in an instant the truth was revealed. I drew with a stick on the sand the diagrams shown six years later in my address before the American Institute of Electrical Engineers, and my companion understood them perfectly. The images I saw were wonderfully sharp and clear and had the solidity of metal

---

[13] Keller, *A Feeling For The Organism*, 117-148.

and stone, so much so that I told him: "See my motor here; watch me reverse it."

and again:

Ideas came in an uninterrupted stream and the only difficulty I had was to hold them fast. The pieces of apparatus I conceived were to me absolutely real and tangible in every detail, even to the minutest marks and signs of wear. I delighted in imagining the motors constantly running, for in this way they presented to the mind's eye a more fascinating sight.[14]

Remember, the development of the subject's personal consciousness required that the components of his subjective associational repertoire (actually the most personally meaningful of the associational material making up his private world) become energized and integrated within consciousness, thereby augmenting its light. Only luminescence of the intensity inherent in a well-developed personal consciousness manifesting the attribute of certainty is capable of generating sufficient force of insight and penetration of vision to reveal the complex elaboration of structure and richness of relation so characteristic of objective world phenomena.

Looked at in another way, the subject is here shown to be revealing meanings that, for lack of insight, were never before seen in the light of their significance and, for that reason, resisted integration within consciousness until now. When personal consciousness begins to expand and include within itself objective visions from the world of matter (visions immeasurably more comprehensive than those constituting subjective consciousness and the external forms and ideological and relational material that subjectivity embraces), we are moving into the realm of objective consciousness. No longer is the growth of consciousness restricted to the enhancement of subjectivity, spectacular as subjective consciousness is when compared with conventional distracted consciousness. From a certain moment, the quality of the experience changes such that to self-knowledge, knowledge of the world of matter as well as the world of form begins to be integrated.[15]

• • •

---

[14] Tesla, *My Inventions.*
[15] See appendix.

CHAPTER TEN

Materiality — Fine & Coarse

The best things in life are not only free, they are mostly invisible. (Thaddeus Golas)

Now, in penetrating the last major veil of obscurity (and revealing the full range and scale of cosmic materiality of which the matter of the body is only a limited aspect), our subject can begin more completely to experience and appreciate his relationship with the cosmos. This includes the lowest yet most fundamental level of materiality, conventionally called "physical reality," or, for most people, simply "reality."

His mind now beginning to encompass materiality on its finest levels, corresponding to the incredibly fine texture of objective consciousness, our subject can feel secure in allowing the matter of his body (which he now for the first time perceives as simply the coarse dimension or aspect of that intelligence) to commune directly with its own element. Peat considers this possibility:

> *The physics of the material universe can be understood in terms of the orders of its patterns, symmetries and relationships. Indeed it has even been suggested that the notion of elementary particles as fundamental building blocks should be replaced by that of fundamental symmetries. Could it be that "objective intelligence" and "creative ordering" are the generative principles that give rise to this underlying order of matter? In a similar sense the origin of mind may be discovered in the dynamic orderings that lie at a level of objective intelligence that is neither matter nor mind, but the source of both.[1]*

By corollary, to the extent that integration becomes increasingly possible on this most basic of levels, integration (already well advanced on the higher more "spiritualized," less "physical" levels) can also proceed toward completion.

---

[1] Peat, *Synchronicity*, 105.

The external conditions that allow us gradually to admit the full measure of the material coarseness and extreme vulnerability of our physical body also enable us to come to terms with our most fundamental restriction and most suppressed fear — death. We are at last granted the beginnings of psychological freedom from matter's paralyzing influence. Paradoxically[2] this freedom comes just when the mind, thanks to Accelerated Thought, masters the science of matter sufficiently to begin anticipating the gradual elimination of the physical basis of that same vulnerability, or what might casually be called the scientific remedy for mortality.

This mastery of matter through the process of Accelerated Thought, and the simultaneous transformation of subjective consciousness to objective consciousness, involves new, symmetrical changes in the way our subject experiences the world and himself as the two merge and integrate. Each accretion of awareness concerning the significance of some world phenomenon, as in subjective consciousness, is accompanied by a corresponding realization of self. But this time the "self" begins to take on an objective, absolute aspect. Something in us is formed with each new awareness; something concrete and enduring is realized.

So far, subjective and objective consciousness have been described as two entirely separate stages in the development of Accelerated Thought. Schematically this portrayal is legitimate, since objective consciousness depends on the energy of subjective consciousness for its development. Nevertheless, in practice this process is unlikely to proceed in a smooth, consecutive manner.

Because of the idiosyncrasies of subjectivity, each person starts from a somewhat different point and directs his attention towards that which to him is personally most significant, using whatever methods of concentration he favors. Personal awareness of given specifities, even at the early developmental stages of subjective consciousness, can, if they generate sufficient energy, lead to powerful, premature insights of an objective or quasi-objective nature. This has advantages and disadvantages, which make for bumpy going, somewhat characteristic of the way everyday life unfolds. Thus, awarenesses generated by Accelerated Thought have both a subjective and an objective dimension.

Correspondingly, experiencing these new awarenesses while they integrate into the flame of consciousness has, besides the quality of

---

[2] See appendix.

certainty already discussed, a pronounced aspect of what could be called "pleasure." Just as various combustive processes tend to give off unequal amounts of light and heat, the flame of consciousness, owing to its imperfection and incompleteness, produces the feeling of pleasure,[3] albeit sublime and potent.

Ideally, this pleasure — along with the certainty of vision from which it stems — binds the subject to his aim and provides the motive to drive Accelerated Thought. To the degree that it remains harnessed to the subject's purpose, this force leads ultimately to the mastery of matter in all its forms and degrees of subtlety in the world and in ourselves.

Subjective & Objective Meaning

In the way of righteousness there is life; along that path is immortality. (Proverbs 12:28)

The development of consciousness through the process of Accelerated Thought is generated by a search for meaning. The discovery of meaning (or, more correctly, our becoming aware of meaning in the cosmos) has been shown to have two principal effects:

1. The first could be termed "subjective," whereby experiencing the discovery of new possibilities and the prospect for their realization fills us with pleasure and elation. These in turn tend to promote exhilarating sensations of hope and faith.

2. The other, more mature manifestation could be termed "objective," whereby the substance of discovery (i.e., the energy of awareness flowing through newly established connections with reality that constitute the discovery's meaning), rather than just influencing our state, is completely absorbed by consciousness and becomes an illuminated integral part of our Being.

Objective consciousness means that the world becomes an integral part of our presence. To the extent that at the point of our contact with the world we have become a unified awareness — pure intelligence — we need no longer be limited to an awareness of ourselves as entities (not even as conscious entities).

McClintock again exemplifies the process in question:

---

[3] See appendix.

She spoke of the "real affection" one gets for the pieces that "go together:" "As you look at these things, they become part of you. And you forget yourself. The main thing about it is you forget yourself." A hundred years ago, Ralph Waldo Emerson wrote: "I become a transparent eyeball; I am nothing; I see all." McClintock says it more simply: "I'm not there!" The self-conscious "I" simply disappears. Throughout history, artists and poets, lovers and mystics have known and written about the "knowing" that comes from loss of self—from the state of subjective fusion with the object of knowledge. Scientists have known it, too. Einstein once wrote: "The state of feeling that makes one capable of such achievements is akin to that of the religious worshipper or one who is in love." Scientists often pride themselves on their capacity to distance subject from object, but much of the richest lore comes from a joining of one to the other, from a turning of object into subject.[4]

During the process of discovery, because of old habits of reflection, the occasional separation of what we are from what we see we are likely to become (a perception performed for the purposes of comparison) is plainly inevitable. Normally, the part of ourselves still dominated by our distorted relation to matter is experienced as a distinct entity, quite separate from our observing part. This phenomenon within consciousness is analogous to alienation from oneself in distraction. In Schachtel's words:

By making some quality or circumstance, real or exaggerated or imagined, the focal point of a reified identity, I look upon myself as though I were a thing (res) and the quality or circumstance were a fixed attribute of this thing or object. But the "I" that feels that I am this or that, in doing so, distances itself from the very same reified object attribute which it experiences as determining its identity.[5]

This contradiction,[6] inherent in what is commonly called the "duality" of life, is already somewhat mitigated by the very experience of discovery that includes the hope and anticipation of soon being relieved of contradiction. We hope to reveal one more degree of intelligence within ourselves to be redeemed from that realm which, until now, we perceived as physical.

---

4 Keller, *A Feeling For The Organism*, 117-18.
5 Ernest G. Schachtel, "*On Alienated Concepts of Identity*," in: *The American Journal of Psychoanalysis*, (November 1961).
6 See appendix.

Truth as Touchstone —
Becoming Free of Matter —
Induced Pathology

Some people want to achieve immortality through their work or their descendants. I intend to achieve immortality by not dying. (Woody Allen)

More concretely, when some important problem is solved or some secret of nature is revealed through the insight provided by Accelerated Thought, matter has a little less of a hold on us. It restricts us a little less in our movements and in what we are able to produce through our inventive ingenuity. This is the whole difference between conventional science and the effects of breakthroughs that predominate when the mind is freed to work at its "natural," accelerated rhythm.

The more revolutionary the initial discoveries of Project Mind, and the more new possibilities (inconceivable by conventional standards) revealed, the more men will come to believe in the likelihood of a world free of suffering and binding constraints. These possibilities point unerringly in the direction of our liberation from the tyranny of matter that limits the scope of human action, relentlessly cripples the spirit and ultimately ravages the body.

It is precisely this increasingly convincing vision of immortality and associated utopian possibilities that releases the energy that moves Accelerated Thought. Small visions lead to larger ones until the plasma-like flame of our subject's subjective consciousness begins to transform into a controlled fusion-type reaction, which is the first stable phenomenon of objective consciousness. Until this point, repeated flashes of insight into the objective world emerged from the state of subjective consciousness and served to spur our subject on. Now, thought clears and accelerates considerably to an entirely new energy level, enabling our subject to penetrate into nature's secrets in a more constant and systematic way.

Penetrating insight, in forming hypotheses of ever-increasing elaboration and predictive power propelled by hope, faith and certainty generated during the progressive expansion of subjective plasma-like consciousness, is only the precursor to a kind of meta-insight consisting of rapid, far-reaching extrapolation. It is possible only to a mind harboring Accelerated Thought in its maturing stages — a mind illuminated with the fusion-like brilliance of objective consciousness.

Just as the feeling of certainty accompanying the penetrating insights of subjective consciousness produced well-articulated hypotheses revealing modest quantities of multilayered truth that got the fusion process of objective consciousness under way, this truth, at the core of the fusion-reaction-like objective consciousness, aligns with and confirms the corresponding truth of selected hypotheses. This enables the subject to carry these hypotheses as though they were concretely proven reality, which, as far as he is concerned, they are.

This is the payoff of a consciousness that encompasses all the levels of materiality of any given aspect of reality. Having some measure of objective truth, however small, as his touchstone (this truth manifesting in a mind created to accommodate multilevelled functioning and to encompass the cosmic laws and realities that actually formed it), our subject can enjoy an unobstructed view of the way before him. Whenever in doubt, our subject need only return to the experience of this truth as his growing, unfailing reference. This reference is an inner cosmic compass, deeply rooted in essence, guiding him to the actualization of his destiny.

But it is inevitable, even at this advanced stage of the process, that after a lifetime of conditioning to distraction, part of the subject's psyche not yet integrated within consciousness will remain vulnerable to the forces of conventionality and will continue to be identified with matter. In his weaker moments, this disposition will emerge and engulf the flame of consciousness, temporarily usurping its prerogatives. What he experiences at the core of consciousness as a pure sense of existence and as being increasingly one with the cosmos degrades to a sense of physical separateness and ego-satisfaction under the influence of conventional distraction. What in consciousness becomes pure ecstasy, to the matter-dominated ego becomes the corrupt satisfaction of having and knowing more than others. This by-product of his efforts, most prevalent at the early stages of Accelerated Thought, could be considered to be smoke[7] generated by periodically stifled combustion owing to the premature imposition of incompatibly coarse fuel upon the flame of awareness.

As the process advances and becomes more self-supporting, less smoke is produced and the ego and its illicit pleasures are revealed for the now unnecessary, matter-based illusions they really are. Meanwhile it should be noted that this tricky, arcane, ambiguous and often "smoky" process of developing a heightened sense of reality (totally incomprehen-

---

[7] See appendix.

sible to one's family, friends and society at large) can amount to a perilous escapade, especially at the early stages.

The Pitfalls & Perils of Commitment

Commit to the Lord in whatever you do. (Proverbs 16:3)
From the beginning, such an adventure implies the total involvement of the subject. No partial commitment could possibly initiate or sustain Accelerated Thought. Our subject's new consciousness is his new reality. For this he is gambling his future. Whenever challenged, he will fiercely and with all the means at his disposal defend what, as an ego, he experiences as his new identity.

Nor will the people he encounters during his daily life hesitate to challenge whichever of his assertions happen to conflict with their own distraction-inspired, matter-subjugated ideas. For even in the face of our subject's ardor and conviction, how could they possibly suspect the true nature of the mind confronting them or the metamorphosis it is undergoing? Our subject's psyche, continuously mutating, is ill-prepared[8] for repeated onslaughts of this kind. Even if his new state had already acquired some degree of stability, he could still offer no truly tangible evidence of his extraordinary condition, nor any concrete, verifiable proof with which to confirm and share the validity of his private vision and reality. Branden recognizes this need to share and objectify ourselves:

> In the course of a man's life, his values, goals and ambitions are first conceived in his mind, i.e., they exist as data of consciousness, and then — to the extent that his life is successful — are translated into action and objective reality; they become part of the "out there," of the world that he perceives. They achieve expression and reality in material form. Man desires a form of objective self-awareness and, in fact, needs this experience.
>
> Since man is the motor of his own actions, since his concept of himself, of the person he has created, plays a cardinal role in his motivation — he desires and needs the fullest possible experience of the reality and objectivity of that person, of his self.[9]

And yet not to share the truth, bliss and passion with which he is bursting is almost unthinkable. After all, from where he stands how could

---

[8] See appendix.
[9] Branden, *Psychology of Self-Esteem*, 200.

others refuse to see what now, to him, is so decidedly and luminously true? Hoffer recognizes this drive, even in those who have only an intimation of truth:

> Proselytizing is more a passionate search for something not yet found than a desire to bestow upon the world something we already have. It is a search for a final and irrefutable demonstration that our absolute truth is indeed the one and only truth.[10]

This predicament can be most unsettling to a tenderfoot consciousness still vacillating in its struggle for stability and ascendancy. While the acquiescence of others willing to share some new awareness will reassure one in his enterprise and assuage and release him momentarily from its hold, their refusal to accept his truth can lead him to an overwhelming ego-based sense of isolation and solitude that is perilous to the balance of his psyche and general well-being.

Without a specialized environment such as Project Mind, the subject would need someone beside him during his mind-adventure, to reassure, comfort and encourage him in his quest for truth and vitality.

Mind Processes & the Energy of Anticipation

Above all else, guard your heart, for it is the wellspring of life. (Proverbs 4:23) The time has come to consider a little more closely the content of thought and feeling. A grasp of the inner mechanics of these functions will explain more clearly just why and how it is possible for one's mode of integration with the world to be completely transformed and to have transformational implications for the world itself.

Although the relative importance of the functions of thinking, feeling and bodily sensation can be debated, one could say without much controversy that one tends to begin any initiative by isolating the idea or ideas that seem best to lend themselves to the situation at hand or, alternatively, that seem to be invoked by the situation. At the next step, the individual tends to ask himself how he feels about the intellectual orientation he has assumed. Only when he is emotionally reconciled with his own conceptualization is the body linked into the circuit for whatever action[11] feeling will judiciously permit.

---

[10] Hoffer, *True Believer*, 102.
[11] See appendix.

There must be feedback loops between thought and feeling and between feeling and action (i.e., the body's motor functions) since if an idea is insufficiently adapted to one's sensibilities it is sent back "upstairs" for adjustment. Inevitably, the process is complex and rapid to the point that one can actually experience oneself as feeling one's way through thought and action. Nevertheless, it should be remembered that emotion is an evaluative process while that which provides the construct for evaluation is the intellect, through the expedient of thought. Thought can consist of various levels and degrees of completion of ideation.

Feeling, in its turn (and, to a degree, in parallel with its exchanges with thought), speaks to the body through the intermediary of bodily sensation. It communicates its approbation in the case of something the body already wants to do (which includes the whole domain of natural and acquired bodily desires and drives), or its dictate in the more likely event of bodily resistance. The message of resistance is fed back both to feeling and often (at least to some extent) to thought. This is done in a process of negotiation that will ultimately determine to what degree thought will be implemented. Please note that it is the thought and not the feeling that is implemented. Feeling provides approbation implying the release of energy needed for the task at hand. This includes the modulation of the effort according to how the action progresses (i.e., the moment-by-moment requirements dictated by inner and outer circumstances).

As already implied, the energy of anticipation, released through the mechanism of feeling, is a function of vision coming through the intellect — vision that reveals imminent threats or desirable prospects for the organism as a whole. This form of revelation is taken by feeling and is communicated to the body as an imminent reality.

Thus anticipation, based on vision, is the mechanism for releasing energy. But from where is this energy released? Where is the reservoir and what is its nature? At this point, all that need be said is that the very substance of the cosmos, including "empty" space itself, contains many levels of energy accessible to man in varying degrees. Our ability to plug into cosmic reservoirs of energy is a function of our ability to release the energy that separates one level of materiality from another. This implies the increasing ability to participate in reality with the whole of our Being. For this, a modification in our whole mode of functioning is required, beginning with a change in our way of looking at things — of interpreting reality — and then the effort to adapt inwardly (feelings and body) to this new reality. If we know with absolute certainty that everything our heart and soul desires — everything that man has ever dreamed of — depends on a given act, we will be able, for the brief moment necessary for that act, to summon superhuman abilities.

•   •   •

CHAPTER ELEVEN

Dynamics of Thought, Feeling & Action

As for conforming outwardly, and living your life inwardly, I do not think much of that. (Henry David Thoreau)

God will not have his work made manifest by cowards. (Ralph Waldo Emerson)

To modern man, new things usually begin with new thoughts, which give new meanings to old perceptions and thus transform them. Thought — fresh thought — is the primary function. Depending on the inner makeup of the individual and the life challenges he meets, the ordering of the functions can take on various configurations. Action or feeling can assume primacy under special circumstances, and even habitually in certain people. Nevertheless, in modern man, for whom the transformation of the physical world through technological innovation (as a social expression of the prevalent philosophy of science) represents an increasingly dominant human orientation and way of life, the intellect and its ability to formulate, express, manipulate and apply ideas is prime.

By now it also should be evident that the more tightly integrated are the intellect, feeling and bodily sensation (through increasingly compact and finely enmeshed feedback loops), the more coherent the individual is likely to be in his thought, the more fluid in his feeling and the more concerted in action. This general clarity of perception and response to the world, suggesting a coordinated, balanced and yet dynamically changing relationship to reality, implies a state of heightened awareness.[1] It also implies that there are different levels, grades or strata of reality to which one can become attuned, provided one has the corresponding inner integration and balance. The energy necessary to achieve this level of activity can be released to the organism through the feeling function as alluded to above in the description of the process of intellectual discovery.

---

[1] See appendix.

Inner & Outer Integration —
Assimilating Reality

I have chosen the way of truth; I have set my heart on your laws. (Psalms 119:30)
Energy is released to the organism from a higher dimension when it passes from a less integrated, less efficient mode of functioning to one that is more economical of the life energies generated by the various human metabolic processes. When these are functionally more tightly and more organically integrated, a new degree of receptiveness results. The problem is how to trigger a change of equilibrium so that increased sensitivity will transform into a stable new way of being. How does one become a new kind of receptacle for receiving higher energies — a new kind of creature requiring a new kind of food? How does one generate enough psychic pressure so that the old habitual way of being loses its hold long enough for a new rhythm, waiting at the threshold of perception, to take hold and permanently bind the functions of the organism more closely together, increasing their efficiency and their ability to vibrate with a higher reality?

It was just suggested that thought and feeling must be in accord for appropriate action to be released and that, in parallel, feeling (with bodily sensation) weighs the appropriateness or the desirability of an idea-input for implementation by the organism. Something in the interface between the functional centers (characterizable as wavelength, vibration and texture of materiality) establishes resonance and compatibility between these centers, as defined by their contents evoked or rendered active by a given set of circumstances. Feeling is our inner psychic-equilibrium testing-tool. It is our means for verifying if we feel right and in tune with our current view of the world in the light of new input. Our sanity and survival depend on this sense of equilibrium.

A new idea, perhaps a new perspective on reality, represents a challenge to these feelings of stability, suggesting that the old reality and the old equilibrium are inadequate and ought to be modified. Head and heart are thus divided and put temporarily out of phase. The forms of sensibility that previously enabled thought and feeling to conform to one another are now forced to seek a new accommodation incorporating the new intruding idea, thus somewhat modifying the feeling of self in order to conform to the new idea. This new idea plainly represents a challenge to the organism as a whole, which must adapt or reject the newly perceived aspect of reality. Thus, in adapting a new idea or perception, the individual is obliged to alter his world view along with his feelings about the world and about himself. These are the kinds of change that lead to transformation.

Likewise, thought and feeling can sometimes have remarkable correspondence and affinity leading to outer transformation. Such an alliance would have to be inspired and sustained by a strong intuition about some aspect of reality as yet unsupported by evidence readily visible in the outside world. To resolve the dissonance, a new way of looking at things (such as a new theory, a new method of observation or analysis) will be needed to reveal supportive evidence in the world. If not, the dissonant pressure could mount unbearably until the subject would be forced to renounce his intuitive certainty — something that could seriously compromise his sense of self, defined by the links joining thought, feeling and (through intuition) body-essence. When we betray ourselves in this way, we tend to lose faith not only in what is "possible," but more cogently, what is "possible for me."

Even should he succeed in producing the conciliatory evidence necessary for inner harmony, our subject will still have to face the challenge of the socially generated dissonance that comes from skepticism, if his theory or the material embodiment of his theory are insufficiently convincing.

Alternatively, and for obvious reasons more often, the prevailing sense of self wins over and the new idea is rejected as being incompatible with "reality." The challenge of the new world view represented by a new idea is repulsed as invalid, untenable. Something in its texture or vibrational frequency as expressed by its embodiment within the intellectual apparatus does not induce accommodation in the feeling center. So the head relinquishes the intrusive, mental embodiment of that alien "reality" (i.e., the idea) as a "foreign body" and once more accommodates feeling in its lower layers. Meanwhile, it continues in its higher layers[2] to scan the "environment" for notions that could represent solid challenges to the status quo in the future — if indeed the individual can maintain a belief in the possibility of real change long enough for feeling to lend the energy necessary for such scanning. This will be the case only to the extent that the individual is a seeker of truth.

---

[2] See appendix.

The same continuum, "exploration — evaluation — commitment," that exists from intellect through feeling down to bodily action exists also within the layers of each of these sentient centers. It is through these layers within each of these centers that communication between centers can take place cybernetically in the form of feedback loops. For the intellect to bring an idea all the way down to the feeling level, a certain effort of assimilation or digestion is first necessary. The highest part of the intellect — those layers furthest from and least committed to the integral workings of the individual as an organism — are the freest and most flexible. With relative impunity to themselves and the organism, they can taste virtually any idea by temporarily accommodating (i.e., assuming the form of) that idea, regardless of how foreign or potentially damaging that idea might be to the organism. Intellect's lack of commitment *vis à vis* the organism is the source of its freedom of action, but also accounts for its lack of direct influence over the organism as a whole.

If by some miracle we could suddenly feel, with all our Being, the full meaning and implication of every thought and perception passing through the "higher," more flexible layers of mind, we would undoubtedly go mad. It would carry the impact of an LSD trip amplified many, many times. In an instant, our body would be compelled to fulfill the requirements of a hundred different commitments. Our frustrated mechanism of feeling would be shredded by an overload of contradictions it was never meant to contain.

Before it will commit the body to action, feeling requires from the intellect certain input standards of quality, consistency and coherence. It requires the discrimination of thought characteristic of a critical mind — a mind with some degree of integrated intention, whereby thought is well anchored in the world of experience. Feeling needs the reassurance that it will be able to "sell" to the body some new slant on reality and the action that this implies.

Thus the bottom layers of the intellectual apparatus have less freedom and flexibility, since they have to maintain responsible contact with the rest of the organism through feeling. One of the more important and interesting features distinguishing the psychological makeup of one individual from another is how contact is maintained between thought and the "feel" one has about oneself and the world.

The nature of this interface plus the quality of feeling the individual maintains are major items determining his capacity for Accelerated

Thought. As alluded to earlier, it is this feeling that, in defining his sense of reality, dictates the visions of reality that inhabit the bottom layers of his mind. This visualization goes hand in hand with feeling to define the sanity or mental stability of the individual who, through imagery, conceptualization, etc., copes with the world in accordance with his sense of reality. The flexibility of the upper layers of intellect serve faithfully to interpret, shape and explain his personal sense of reality back to the world in terms more or less comprehensible to those "significant others" he encounters in life. More important, they serve to weigh the forms he encounters in the world and to consider the suitability of such forms for retention, adoption and, perhaps, integration within consciousness.

The passive side of this functional mode shows what happens when the initial impulse comes from without — such as from society. As conventions, fashions and other aspects of the external environment change, they are first assimilated by the more nimble outer layers of mind and communicated downward (and inward) with concomitant and progressively larger modifications in our sense of reality as the lower, less flexible and more grounded levels are reached. This form of inner reality-adjustment, or conformity, imposed more or less vigorously from without (or, in terms of layers, from above) is usually accomplished with little obstruction or difficulty while the organism strives for a sense of inner and outer balance.

Social Opposition & the Budding Deviant

The reasonable man adapts himself to the world; the unreasonable one persists in trying to adapt the world to himself. Therefore all progress depends on the unreasonable man. (George Bernard Shaw)

Any resistance felt by the individual (and some people do tend to adjust to life's pressures more slowly than others) causes inner dissonance and tensions to build up. This is outer reality's (or, in most cases, society's) way of dictating terms to the individual, who is largely defined by his inner sense of things. How we feel inside — our physical, emotional and intellectual perception of our situation — defines our sense of reality. Roughly speaking, it is through this mechanism and the pressures that outer or social reality exert on our psyche that we are made to conform to our environment. Not conforming to the essentials of outer reality cuts us off from the world, normally with disastrous consequences for our experiential, psychic and biological equilibrium. Survival, after all, implies sufficient coherence to live off one's environment without an excess of stress. Then again we have, in principle, the freedom — each according to his virtue — to decide what will constitute our environmental reality: fashion and the opinions of others, or our truth (what we perceive through our own independent thought and vision). Speaking through John Galt, Ayn Rand says:

> "A rational process is a moral process. You may make an error at any step of it, with nothing to protect you but your own severity, or you may try to cheat, to fake the evidence and evade the effort of the quest — but if devotion to truth is the hallmark of morality, then there is no greater, nobler, more heroic form of devotion than the act of a man who assumes the responsibility of thinking.
>
> "Non-thinking is an act of annihilation, a wish to negate existence, an attempt to wipe out reality. But existence exists; reality is not to be wiped out, it will merely wipe out the wiper. By refusing to say 'it is,' you are refusing to say 'I am.'
>
> "To the extent to which a man is rational, life is the premise directing his actions. To the extent to which he is irrational, the premise directing his actions is death."[3]

McClintock — always true to the evidence she encounters — takes the idea of rationality and existence a step further by adding the notion of expanding consciousness, implied in what she calls "other" ways of knowing:

> That there are valid ways of knowing other than those conventionally espoused by science is a conviction of long standing for McClintock. It derives from a lifetime of experiences that science tells us little about, experiences that she herself could no more set aside than she could discard the anomalous pattern on a single kernel of corn. Perhaps it is this fidelity to her own experience that allows her to be more open than most other scientists about her unconventional beliefs.[4]

However we express knowing, it is contact with reality on as many levels as possible that allows us to survive and prevail. It is fundamentally important for any individual wishing to subject himself to the buffeting and stress of dissonance (which eventually arises when one begins seriously to adopt an innovative and thus deviant view of reality) to have significant sources of stamina and stability within himself and in his immediate surroundings. These sources derive from anchorage in reality. Jung is skeptical about the reader's ability to grasp this idea:

---

[3] Ayn Rand, *Atlas Shrugged* (New York: Signet Books, 1960), 943-45.

[4] Keller, *A Feeling For The Organism*, 201-2.

Resistance to the organized mass can be affected only by the man who is well organized in his individuality as the mass itself. I fully realize that this proposition must sound well-nigh unintelligible to the man of today.[5]

One could easily and erroneously surmise that to the extent an individual succeeds in finding within himself the inner resources for creating a new internal order in the face of (and probably in defiance of) conventionality, he will necessarily also have the inner substance needed to bear all the stresses involved. But the process of Accelerated Thought involves several distinct stages, and the nature and locus of the forces acting within the subject vary accordingly. Different people with differing personalities, psychic structure and habits will tend to cope better with some stages of the process than with others.

For those willing to recognize both their possibilities and their limitations (temporary as these limitations may be) the exceptional conditions offered by Project Mind will furnish vital support to the subject — surrogate strength — whenever a weakness or flaw in his psychological makeup threatens to compromise his creative efforts or throw him off balance. Project Mind also will offer him shelter from the more gratuitous forms of psychological violence that characterize society's treatment of original thinkers.

Commitment, Integration & Transformation

Conceit is the finest armor a man can wear. (Jerome K. Jerome)

When he just begins thinking about a problem that touches him, our subject is still an integral part of social reality — a reality that itself is far from consistent or coherent. Criticism of this society, implied by his preoccupation with his chosen problem, is probably shared by a segment of that society itself (although any criticism of the status quo beyond a certain point is perceived by society as a potential threat). Likewise, within a given social subgroup — electrical engineers for instance — the problem that concerns our subject may, to a greater or lesser degree, concern many other such engineers who share much the same idea universe, paradigms and interests. He could legitimately claim a sense of camaraderie with those "significant others" of his selected reference group who are concerned with the progress and general standing of their

---

[5] C. G. Jung, *The Undiscovered Self*, translated by R. F. C. Hull (N.Y.: Mentor, Nal Penguin Inc., 1958), 72.

intellectual or professional subgroups within the context of society at large.

Even at this stage, however, our subject, in subtle ways, already differs from his like-thinking colleagues. Under the surface, he already begins to have a certain single-mindedness — a degree of interest and commitment — that sets him apart and that significantly deviates from the norm, among even the most dedicated of his colleagues. He still retains "social acceptablity." And yet his prolonged and intensive preoccupation with his work — and probably some rather esoteric aspect of his work at that — begins to raise eyebrows among his colleagues, not to mention his friends and family, who for him, in his preoccupation, have almost ceased to exist. Depending on the social role and orientation of the observing individual, the irregularities attributed to our subject will vary. To his professional subgroup, for instance, he will be seen to be deviating from an unwritten work code that requires members of a given profession or team to respect certain limits to competition — to not rock the professional boat.

Note well that no one could reasonably begrudge another member of his society singular success stemming from the choice of some specialty or research direction, nor could one fault another for diligence of effort. On the contrary, these things tend to preserve and promote the interests of the group as a whole, even if sometimes at the expense of individual members. His friends and family also will indulge and even encourage singular devotion to some specific preoccupation at the cost of a certain amount of neglect or discomfort to themselves, but with the tacit understanding that — win, lose or draw — things will return to normal within a reasonable interval. For the sake of harmony, custom allows deviant individuals some leeway — a kind of grace — that acts as a buffer to dampen the shocks that ruffle and even threaten the collective, in the sagacious expectation that the pressure to conform will usually prevail over the determination of the individual.

Where is the line drawn? In the eyes of the subject's entourage he has gone too far when they begin to feel that they no longer constitute a reference group for him. This happens when he loses interest in those around him and in those things that, in their eyes, should interest him. Depending on the individual, this apparently spontaneous apathy towards any social grouping — each in its own way a representative and guardian of conventionality and the status quo — can be interpreted as anything from eccentricity (at best) through snobbery and disdain to insanity (at worst).

Objectively speaking (to the degree one can be objective) our subject has begun, if ever so slightly, to answer to the description of the revolutionary by focusing on the specifics of his choosing. He may do this even to the actual neglect of routine and group maintenance concerns. Once he passes a certain point, group members will suspect that whatever he wishes to accomplish will necessarily prove to be more disruptive than integrative. This is already prefigured in the "pretentiousness" of the individual in squandering himself — a social resource — in a quest of things that depend, to too exclusive an extent, on his own private, unshared perceptions. At this first stage on the path to Accelerated Thought our subject has begun to "march to a different drummer," and his entourage has begun to take notice.

While at the earliest stages in particular, depending on the nature of the relationship, those around our subject will accord him varying degrees of indulgence for his nonconformity. The most casual contacts will not notice anything at all unusual. If he persists, eventually he will cross the line and his new commitment (created at the expense of conventionally approved loyalties) will become a social fact. A general consensus about the need for sanctions will emerge. Sanctions are likely to include the denial of routine expressions of tacit approval implied in simple salutations, signs of solidarity and recognition, etc. — in short, the "cold shoulder." Family members may try to send him the message by subtly, or not so subtly, withholding affection.

Until this point, the motor behind our subject's effort has been his interest in the furtive vision of some highly appealing new possibility. If his sense of resolve, independence and personal integrity is strong, he may be able to forgo seeking social approval for his notions and maintain a low profile. Nevertheless, at some point social dissonance will become a nuisance and even a source of real, pressing concern. McClintock bears witness:

> *Individuals who have a strong conviction of being right as McClintock had expected to be listened to. In the long run, that conviction served her extremely well; it provided the protection she needed in order to continue her work. But in the short run, it could only have exacerbated the shock. She tends to make light of it now, but at the same time she admits that the 1951 symposium "really knocked" her. "It was just a surprise that I couldn't*

communicate; it was a surprise that I was being ridiculed, or being told I was really mad." [6]

Provided he doesn't compromise himself by returning to the fold and, assuming he avoids having a nervous breakdown by finding some source of succor and support, he may find a new equilibrium. Once consensus labels him "deviant" and he accepts the challenge of this new role, social pressure is no longer an impediment. On the contrary, once he reconciles himself to being socially beyond the pale, society has unwittingly forced him into full commitment to his new direction and into the second stage of Accelerated Thought — objective consciousness.

I live in a world of my own, but visitors are always welcome. (Ashleigh Brilliant)

McClintock again provides the example:

As her isolation reached into her intellectual and professional lives, it deepened and took on new dimensions. Her efforts to talk about her work during the 1950's were in vain, and the principal consequence was that she stopped talking.

She withdrew further into her work, protected more and more by her "inner knowledge" that she was on the "right track," but at the same time becoming increasingly wary about confronting potentially hostile audiences, and even about visits from unsympathetic colleagues. Her lab remained open to anyone who genuinely wanted to listen or even just to talk, but she had always had a quick sharp tongue and now used it to protect herself whenever she felt the need. [7]

Fusion, Will & Objectivity

We are what we pretend to be, so we must be careful about what we pretend to be. (Kurt Vonnegut, Jr.)

Any doubts our subject may have entertained until now — any substantial foothold conventionality may have maintained in his psyche — he now perceives as expressions of weakness and vestiges of self-indulgence belonging to the past. Thus, thanks to social isolation, what had been a strongly held theory representing anything from a powerful preoccupation to a mild obsession becomes his new staff of life. Any corners of his psyche that have not yet yielded to the new way of thinking (the new psychic order imposed by his new conceptual framework) must now of necessity admit this mental "virus." This is the secret of binding commitment.

---

[6] Keller, A *Feeling For The Organism*, 140.
[7] Ibid., 142.

Clearly, not everyone has what it takes to "go the distance," and each of us has limits as to how much pressure he can take. While some of us can handle different kinds of "heat" better than others, each of us tends to allow himself to be compromised a little differently. It is a rare bird indeed whose integrity survives this far into the obstacle course we call "life." Few of us ever get very close to this kind of autonomy.

The function of feeling, deprived of sustenance normally provided through the misleading reassurance of social stroking, must change loyalties now and find new, non-conventional prospects for survival.

The intellect, first through the upper more flexible layers, and later through the lower, more determining layers, has, with the connivance of feeling, created a predicament that constitutes a challenge to the organism as a whole. This is a challenge that the intellect, by its very structure, can neither perceive fully nor meet. With its proverbial back against the wall, feeling (which until now had in only a limited way helped the intellect explore ideas through certain vibrational affinities) is now forced to open itself in an unprecedented way. To an unanticipated extent, feeling must now accept ideas that have become the new and only mechanism through which any reassurance concerning future possible survival might flow into it. Rand explains emotion through the character of John Galt:

> "Your emotions are estimates of that which furthers your life or threatens it, lightning calculators giving you a sum of your profit or loss. You have no choice about your capacity to feel that something is good for you or evil, but what you will consider good or evil, what will give you joy or pain, what you will love or hate, desire or fear, depends on your standard of value. Emotions are inherent in your nature, but their content is dictated by your mind." [8]

The danger here is clear. Once the individual's feelings become his main reference, he risks giving any half-baked notion or hypothesis the weight of truth and assumes himself infallible. (Project Mind will provide environmental antidotes to megalomania.)

Assuming a balanced psyche, our subject is on the way to being transformed into another kind of being. No longer will he be sustained by conventional psychic nourishment (including "stroking") normally provided through the intermediary of social mechanisms but, at least to some extent and for a certain period, he will be maintained by a new food [9] made digestible through his new, self-imposed psychic order. Different kinds of beings are distinguishable partly in that their natures require particular

[8] Rand, *Atlas Shrugged*, 947.
[9] See appendix.

kinds of food and modalities of social and aesthetic sustenance. Well worth considering is the idea that man's nature can change, that he can become a different kind of being — one sustained differently, who experiences life completely differently from conventional man (an idea contained in the esoteric roots of many traditions).

Our subject has now arrived at and is totally committed to a tightly integrated inner functioning whereby he has considerably elaborated a personal hypothesis into a functional ideology. This hypothesis is now completely determining for the idea universe with which it is concerned. By extension, it has important implications for all other aspects of our subject's life. The incursion of this influence into the rest of his life is mainly caused by the social dislocation resulting from his creation of an idea or paradigm from which others have been excluded. The subject's ideology will unavoidably carry disagreeable and unflattering implications, for that is the nature of innovation and revolutionary thinking.

In this context it should be emphasized that Project Mind, in providing a supportive environment, does not in any way rob creators of their fervor or individuality. Rather it puts them at the heart of a revolutionary movement that supports their fledgling vision system, enhances their commitment and validates their rebellion. They are included precisely because of their uniqueness and not for their sameness or ideational submission. They are encouraged to the utmost to be themselves.

Once the balance is tilted in the favor of the individual — from the moment he makes the irrevocable decision to go it alone — the already initiated process of inner integration intensifies considerably. The energy of loyalty and commitment, formerly draining into the body politic, is now dedicated to the binding of mind and feeling, consigning the organism and its future action to one self-selected direction. Directions of any kind require commitment or else we wouldn't need courage to assume the risk of action. Action always has consequences. By corollary, the indulgences[10] common to an ordinary life of dispersed energies no longer make any sense or exercise any attraction for our subject.

For the moment, our subject doesn't require new input from the external environment. This stage, analogous to digestion, is mostly limited to the concerns of inner transformation — the objectification of inner substance that previously formed the nucleus of subjective con-

---

[10] See appendix.

sciousness. What in conscious appreciation he felt to be true, with fewer and fewer reservations he now "knows" to be true. The feeling function begins to be integrated within thought. At the growing point of overlap (reflecting the extent of the integration), he thinks what he feels and he feels what he thinks; there is no separation. Within this process of fusion, "mind" itself (in the sense of a faculty capable of objectively knowing reality) begins to become real. Feeling commits the body, determining its fate. Thus, to the extent the integration proceeds, thought commands the body directly.

This state of affairs — this increasingly absolute confidence — is incomprehensible to ordinary mind. Just as ordinary mind (what we normally call "thought" or "intellect") and ordinary feeling (what we normally call "feeling" or "emotion") are manifestations of restricted mind, so higher feeling (what we call subjective consciousness) is a restriction of higher thought (objective consciousness). The empowering of higher thought begins releasing this restriction, eliminating the distinction and most of what little remains of distraction.

When thought dominates feeling, what we think is what we feel, and this in turn conditions action. This kind of committed conviction is sometimes called "will." To do anything of significance — to extend a well-defined influence in the world — requires will. This is "will," taken in the strong or esoteric sense, implying the implementation of a plan towards a given aim whereby results are foreseen completely from beginning to end.[11] It is only here through the efficient expression of essential aim, that one can begin to measure objectively the cosmic place or role of one essence compared to another.

Until subjective consciousness began to manifest, our subject had no special claim to individuality beyond the normal limits of whatever particular, individualized tint of distracted consciousness was permitted by his social environment. Whenever some idea or perception began to make some undue call on feeling, inviting an above-normal degree of commitment, feeling weighed the possible consequences of action and either rejected the idea on some ground discovered during the weighing, or deferred the idea for further elaboration and scrutiny. Under subjective consciousness our subject gained a firm sense of identity and a high degree of emotional certainty about what he wished to accomplish, and some degree of conviction concerning his chances of success. However,

---

[11] See appendix.

once feeling is committed to the process of integration, the normal process is completely reversed. Now the mind's contents (one's personal thesis) are taken to represent objective reality, and the impressions received from the environment (outer reality) are reinterpreted and reordered according to internal dictate (inner reality). In saying "I know" in this unequivocal way, he puts his life on the line. He also knows the gamble is worthwhile.

> *To punish me for my contempt for authority, fate made me authority myself.*
> *(Albert Einstein)*

The new vision derived from this process will eventually be tested for validity in the world. If valid, it will enter the culture of mankind as a binding new reality, displacing its conventional counterpart just as a new invention renders old ones obsolete.

Extrapolation & Objective Consciousness

I love those who love me, and those who seek me find me. (Proverbs 8:17)

Once internal integration goes as far as it can, the subject's mind will be ripe to touch a new frontier of uncertainty — the unknown. His main thrust becomes extrapolation — the exploration of the implications and possibilities of his new frame of reference — his new truth. It is through extrapolation that the greatest amount of energy is released into the process of Accelerated Thought. Now, armed with his own unwavering truth and free to explore its far-reaching implications, our subject begins to see the inevitability of concrete, indisputable benefits to be derived from developments based on this new, higher form of thought. Seeing the inevitability of the fulfillment of one's inner potential — one could even say destiny — and all this attributable to the development and newly-found efficacy of one's own mind, one's confidence tends to soar.

This process begins to feed upon itself in a chain reaction. Once the subject's hypothesis, carried as a certainty, brings in a wave of energy with the discovery of the inevitability of rewards (intrinsic and extrinsic), this energy of anticipation — the first quasi-tangible evidence of his newly-found potency — reinvested in extrapolative thought operates with compounded intensity. The process of Accelerated Thought is firmly established. Even without enduring tangible rewards such as broad social recognition or some physical embodiment of his vision — say an invention — the vision itself, including the modest but consistent confirmation he gets from his environment validating this vision, is the promissory note he gets on a life about to be materially transformed. In other words, the vision brings with it the energy for its own actualization in the best tradition of self-fulfilling prophecies.

Armed with this new consciousness incorporating his truth, the adventure of life truly begins. Everything our subject encounters now — everything that comes into his purview — is reprocessed, divested of its old conventional meaning and incorporated as fuel into the fusion reaction of his burning new reality. The certainty of this reality gives an incisive quality to his vision of the future as he confidently and faultlessly extrapolates in his new light of reality from what is now known to what must materialize in the future. Each new extrapolation, each new realization, each vision of future inevitability feeds our subject's consciousness as it grows in intensity and dimensionality. It does so in the measure of the reality it encompasses. Time for our subject becomes less a succession of random events and more a lawfully ordered pattern of cause and effect as he gradually begins to perceive how everything is connected.

In this mode of extrapolative thought, hypotheses based on the subject's truth are formulated and projected for their implications and connectiveness to the various branches of his truth. They are instantaneously modified, accepted or rejected, generating still more energy with each successful matching of patterns. At this rhythm and energy level, repeated success is virtually guaranteed.

Our subject is no longer constrained by the requirements of experimentation — the painstaking process of defining the experiment, then setting up an experimental situation and then struggling through the motions of the experiment itself. Such experimentation is normally plagued with all the vagaries and vicissitudes of the mundane world that complicate and obscure resulting data. These data must then be tabulated and subjected to statistical or other analyses to determine their significance or lack thereof. Nor does he have to wait weeks, months or years, not even counting the preparatory burden of arduous (and mostly irrelevant) study to hit upon a promising hypothesis — hypotheses being the basis of all experimentation. He avoids the usually substantial financial cost of doing experiments within the budgetary limits afforded by his status and general circumstances. In other words, by the grace of this newly acquired vision, he is freed from the limitations of mundane thought and action. He can now contrive more in moments than he could before in years. He has only to concentrate on some aspect of the world that seems to have promising possibilities in connection with his central truth — aspects with which he has some connection or insight — and the process of Accelerated Thought locks in.

Through the initially perceived connections, illumination flows from the core of the mind to the aspect at hand, bestowing light upon it and making it visible to the mind's eye by reflection. However, if true and not only apparent relation exists between the central truth and the aspect at hand (between the mind's searing white-hot core and the distant and as yet cold mental associations concerning the aspect in question), light increasingly energizes it to the point that it also begins to glow from inside with the light of meaning through its compatibility with the conscious core. It becomes infused with meaning, causing it in turn to reveal its relationship to those aspects with which it is associated in reality.

Idea Universes, Meaning & Connectedness

Give me understanding, and I will keep your law and obey it with all my heart. (Psalms 119:34)

Every possible idea, thought, association, etc. belongs to some idea universe or cluster of ideas that have shared meanings and certain correspondences with reality. Pivotal ideas will belong to more than one idea universe at a time. But to the pedestrian capability of ordinary mind, keeping even a small number of ideas within the spotlight of common distracted awareness is a precarious juggling act and has to be repeated again and again until we glean a glimmer of meaning connecting them. This is the problematic limitation inherent in reflective thought. The light of awareness by reflection outlines the general form of ideas under consideration, revealing almost nothing of satellite or related ideas. This spotlight of attention is constantly moving. Each hard-earned glimmer of meaning (if no spectacular consciousness-raising connections are encountered) is consigned to memory. The memory collects observations permitting their comparison and evaluation in a subsequent operation, perhaps to be matched up in the unconscious in an isolated instance of "Eureka-style" creativity.

It would be necessary to work at this rate for a very long time — perhaps an eternity — to reveal all the interconnectedness of existence. It's a little like exploring a city map with a microscope. Our perspective is just too limited. Even with an excellent memory we have to abstract all the substance out before we can make any use of the map at all. Using this process of abstraction, we tend to distill out all the vitality and sense of completeness or wholesomeness. We thereby lose the world of reality we were trying to comprehend and are left with sterile concepts and theories leading us slowly and painstakingly back to their referents. We need — and were meant to have — a broader view. For this we need an integrated mind capable of directly perceiving relatedness in the world. No one says this better than Thoreau:

> *I have been to the lumber-yard, and the carpenter's shop, and the tannery, and the lampblack factory, and the turpentine clearing; but when at length I saw the tops of the pines waving and reflecting the light at a distance high over the rest of the forest, I realized that the former were not the highest use of the pine. It is not their bones or hide or tallow that I love most. It is the living spirit of the tree, not its spirit of turpentine, with which I sympathize, and which heals my cuts. It is as immortal as I am, and perchance will go to as high a heaven, there to tower above me still.*[12]

Accordingly, Accelerated Thought takes us in the opposite direction. It begins with ideas, just as does reflective thought. However, as the process gains momentum, the connectedness-to-ideas ratio increases dramatically. In other words, instead of manipulating many ideas in the hope of extracting a little meaning (i.e., connectedness) here and there, we now are increasingly confronted by a wealth of connectedness[13] wherever we look. At first the connectedness comes to us by way of mental constructs. But soon, thanks to a mind increasingly integrated on its thinking, feeling and motor levels, we begin to see connectedness in the world as thinking, feeling and doing become an integral, instantaneous part of a single coherent process. In doing all this simultaneously, not only do we become integrated, but our view of the world does so as well.

When a concept is evoked it is no longer just an idea with evocative potential — an associative label — but a whole galaxy of meaning-rich consciousness. This is the true expression of intelligence — the immediate and direct perception of meaning. This whole idea-universe is "handled" with the agility of the embedded skill it has become, and with manipulative virtuosity evocative of that which is quickly attained in virtual reality (cyberspace) simulators. But by placing virtual reality within the mind, simulation will come as close to reality as it ever will. Accelerated Thought will indisputably prove the enormous advantage conscious thought has over mechanical and mechanically enhanced thought. And if

---

[12] Thoreau, "The Maine Woods," *Walden and Other Writings*, 398-9.
[13] See appendix.

"the image of G-d" within us is a machine design, it is without doubt the design of the ultimate machine.

Mind-Bodies & Immortality

Everybody considers dying important but as yet death is no festival. (Nietzsche)
Enlightenment means at some point literally becoming light. (Dane Rudhyar)
The ability to extract meaning from life requires connectedness on various levels. It implies functional efficiency, energy conservation and a generally heightened vitality and sense of existence. The perception of meaning bestows connectedness, and yet meaning depends on those same connections. Meaning is that existential glue that can give us the fine, coherent, inner substance and structure capable of replacing the physical body as a receptacle of life-intelligence. Connection is the secret of immortality.

Intellectually, connections reveal meaning; subjectively, connection and meaning are the same. The confirmation of the validity of our meaning awaits the acid test of application in the world — the objective court of reality. When connections are made structure appears, allowing energy to flow where before there was only inert potential. Between two parts in ourselves where there was formerly the obscurity of opaque but living flesh, emerges Mind. "Mind" implies order, coherence, lucidity and bodily sensations of vibrancy and well-being.

The pathways thus created must conform to cosmic law which dictates the requirements of life. Otherwise, through the adoption of illusory meanings, we will be creating distorted connections only partially supported by truth. We find this kind of non-viable connection in the anatomy of certain abnormal fetuses. For a distorted mind-body, de-crystallization is analogous but much more painful than the self-effacement of false personality in spiritual practice. With such distortions the mind-body will be unable to face the "light of day" when, finally, death rips away the supportive infrastructure of our physical body.

We establish basic motor and sensory connections with relative ease. This is a "given" from the efforts of childhood — a gift bestowed through the dictates of instinct meeting the demands of life. But intellectual connectedness, and to some extent the connectedness of other functions required for everyday social integration, depend so much more on individual motivations, tendencies, gifts and inclinations, and is the object of the extended and usually painful process of socialization.

In order to live even the most ordinary life, a certain modicum of connectedness is necessary, as is a minimum level of contextual coherence. But the nature of this connectedness and the concomitant flavor of the meanings we attribute to existence are very much conditioned by society. On the one hand, society provides us with ready-made meanings and interpretations we call culture. On the other hand, it exacts a payment from us in terms of restrictions it places on our connectedness.

In gradually discovering that the cosmos is harmoniously and universally interconnected, we also discover that the cosmos is coherent and accessible to understanding. We begin to see that existence is the way it is simply because it could not possibly be any other way — that life is ordered by the very nature of the matters and energies of which reality is made, according to Truth. In Emerson's words:

> *Motion or change, and identity or rest, are the first and second secrets of nature: Motion and Rest. The whole code of her laws may be written on the thumbnail or the signet of a ring. The whirling bubble on the surface of a brook, admits us to the secrets of the mechanics of the sky. Every shell on the beach is the key to it. A little water made to rotate in a cup explains the formation of the simpler shells; the addition of matter from year to year, arrives at last at the most complex forms; and yet so poor is nature with all her craft, that, from the beginning to the end of the universe, she has but one stuff — but one stuff with its two ends, to serve up her dream-like variety. Compound it how she will, star, sand, fire, water, tree, man, it is still one stuff, and betrays the same properties.*[14]

More important, having discovered that interconnectedness bestows meaning and that meaning renders networks of true relationship conscious, we tentatively begin to experience the ultimate and inevitable realization that the cosmos itself is conscious, and that we as individuals, through the reactivation of the unique cosmic imprint upon our essence, have our role to play in completing conscious cosmic manifestation. The degree of the primacy of our personal truth and our courage to pursue it will determine to what degree we will fill that role. There are even those who say that it is for this role we choose, in a higher world, to be born into the obscurity of this one. Rand, through her hero, John Galt, gives us an intimation of a harmonious, conscious existence:

> *"In that world, you'll be able to rise in the morning with the spirit you had known in your childhood: that spirit of eagerness, adventure and certainty which comes from dealing with a rational universe. No child is afraid of nature; it is your fear of man that will vanish, the fear that has stunted your*

---

[14] Ralph Waldo Emerson, *Essays: First and Second Series* (New York: Vintage Books, 1990), 317.

soul, the fear you acquired in your early encounters with the incomprehensible, the unpredictable, the contradictory, the arbitrary, the hidden, the faked, the irrational in men. You will live in a world of responsible beings, who will be as consistent and reliable as facts; the guarantee of their character will be a system of existence where objective reality is the standard and the judge. Your virtues will be given protection, your vices and weaknesses will not. What you'll receive from men will not be alms, or pity, or mercy, or forgiveness of sins, but a single value: justice. And when you'll look at men and at yourself, you will feel, not disgust, suspicion and guilt, but a single constant: respect." [15]

To arrive at such an existence, again through Galt, she advises:

"Do not let your fire go out, spark by irreplaceable spark, in the hopeless swamps of the approximate, the not-quite, the not-yet, the not-at-all. Do not let the hero in your soul perish, in lonely frustration for the life you deserved, but have never been able to reach. Check your road and the nature of your battle. The world you desired can be won, it exists, it is real, it is possible, it's yours." [16]

Robbins challenges us:

Instead of shrinking, the hero moves ever toward life. There is no small heroism in the full and open enjoyment of material things. The accumulation of material things is shallow and vain, but to have a genuine relationship with such things is to have a relationship with life and, by extension, a relationship with the divine.

To physically overcome death — is that not the goal? — we must think unthinkable thoughts and ask unanswerable questions. Yet we must not lose ourselves in abstract vapors of philosophy. Death has his concrete allies, we must enlist ours.[17]

Unlocking all of nature's secrets — the multi-dimensional secrets of matter and energy — will not only bring unlimited, universal prosperity and peace, but will assuredly lead to physical and ultimately to spiritual immortality.

So that your days and the days of your children may be many in the land that the Lord swore to give your forefathers, as many as the days that the heavens are above the earth. (Deuteronomy 11:21)

Those who share the vision of Project Mind and wish to explore opportunities for participation should write to Project Mind at the address on page 195.

• • •

---

[15] Rand, *Atlas Shrugged*, 992.

[16] Ibid., 993.

[17] Tom Robbins, *Jitterbug Perfume* (N.Y.: Bantam Books, 1985), 373.

CHAPTER TWELVE

Questions & Answers

One should expect a book proposing a revolutionary approach to life predicated upon new modes of consciousness to invite misapprehension and skepticism.

Some readers can entertain the belief that a real basis for hope may still be found in man's psyche, and that man — and by extension existence — may yet be shown to be fundamentally good. Such readers are also more apt to give a fair hearing to a new theory as long as it does not blatantly contradict itself or egregiously insult common sense or offend human dignity. The following questions and answers cover the key ideas presented in this book.

Q. What are the main qualifications required of candidates for participation in Project Mind and how will they be screened?

A. Candidates will be selected according to several criteria: independence of spirit, matter-related aspiration and strength of character, among others.

1. Independence of Spirit

It is vain to expect breakthrough thinking from those who from childhood have surrendered the freedom of thought and aspiration that springs from individuality to the "group think" of society in general, and professional and other reference groups in particular. The desire to innovate must be intimately linked with one's love of life and the freedom to pursue one's unique destiny regardless of what others think. This freedom is nipped in the bud in all but the rarest of individuals.

The earmarks of such individualists are quite unmistakable. The fact of our recognition of their hidden virtue and potential to humanity is enough to gain their appreciation; the offer of assistance to pursue that which their heart most desires, enough to win their cooperation and loyalty.

2. Matter-Related Aspiration

Although all things, including human goals and aspirations, are ultimately connected with questions of matter, only sufficiently independent and spirited individuals will have the necessary spunk and temerity to have tied their intense love of life to the need to affront the matter aspect of existence with any degree of directness. After all, is not the transformation of matter the vocation of Project Mind? Accordingly, the candidate's attitudes and aspirations towards matter will be of cardinal importance in screening for participation. While specific approaches will not be given at the outset, it is likely that certain disciplines will be encompassed to complement work already in progress. The main concern is whether there exists an adequate pool of available individuals who in fact satisfy the first two criteria for participation. However, if man was meant to succeed as the bearer of consciousness in the cosmos, there must be.

3. Strength of Character

Independence of spirit covers this criterion to a degree, although not completely. For instance, an individual could very well be a deeply intuitive, original, non-conformist inventor and at the same time be incapacitated by bitterness and resentment, immersed in self-pity or worse. This is by no means to say that such people are forever lost to Accelerated Thought. It may very well turn out that Project Mind will have to resort to the retrieval of genius driven to desperation by a deaf, blind and unfeeling world, in spite of the intense initial outlay this may entail.

It is hoped that a nucleus of qualified individuals can be found who have had the good luck or ingenuity to survive the ordeal of civilization as we know it without developing serious character flaws, incapacities or failings that might hinder their ability to function as required by Project Mind and by their own creative aspirations.

Q. Are the vast majority of scientists who, by your standards of creativity, fail to qualify for participation in Project Mind, to be thought of as dross and unfit to help build the "brave new world" you envision? And even if you succeed in focusing and integrating the mind processes of a few select individuals, how can the resulting discoveries amount to anything more than a mere "drop in the bucket"?

A. The principal criterion for participation in Project Mind is an overriding desire to enter a state of Accelerated Thought in the tenacious pursuit of objective knowledge — truth. Thus it is to a considerable extent a self-selecting criterion. Those who eschew this path for whatever reasons are by no means written off, but remain recruits-in-potential.

Few people are by nature pioneers. But this does not mean that they will not eventually join the effort. They have yet to be convinced of the desirability of this direction. Such conviction will come with the emergence of tangible results from Project Mind. The activity of Accelerated Thought will gain sufficient credence to spread beyond the boundaries of Project Mind; ultimately, to encompass all thought.

Q. What is so special about the conditions of Project Mind that will enable creative people to change the quality of their thought sufficiently to produce scientific breakthroughs?

A. The psychological environment provided by Project Mind will be unique and unprecedented. On the one hand, it will embody a recognition of the grandeur of the immense, even divine potential of mind that is overlooked by modern technological society. On the other hand, it credits man with having the innate creative capacity to technically transform matter and energy. This capacity has been envisioned to an extent by traditions and religions, but mainly in spiritual and allegorical terms. This kind of mastery has yet to be envisioned by modern science in any explicit manner at all.

These conditions will grant individuals having real vision and a reasonable level of practical command over the elements of their chosen domain due credit for their most intimate pretensions — pretensions that would be spurned by the world, if revealed. Such conditions, once established, will recognize and take into account what these pretentious aims (and the effort to maintain them) have cost these individuals in terms of personal courage and suffering. Project Mind will encourage them to delve into their minds more deeply than they ever dared before in the pursuit of their destiny. These conditions will also include a built-in understanding of the dangers attendant to such mind-adventuring, and the measures to be taken to steer the adventurer clear of certain stumbling blocks, and help him over the rough spots.

Q. Without divulging too many details concerning the mechanisms of Project Mind, specifically what special conditions will your "subjects" — the pioneers of Accelerated Thought — be offered that are so unique?

A. Some aspects of the environment of Project Mind will be unique, others less so. The combination will be uniquely tailored to the needs of individuals seeking to transform the world through the results of Accelerated Thought.

1. First and foremost Project Mind, recognizing the deepest psychological needs of these pioneers as well as their potential, is the only entity truly capable of defending the dignity of these valiant individuals. Every contact subjects have with the personnel of Project Mind will reflect that dignity.

2. Subjects will be provided with self-contained living quarters offering complete privacy, solitude and total comfort enabling them to concentrate on their chosen problems without fear of intrusion or interruption. All necessities will be provided to relieve subjects, to the greatest degree possible, of the bother and distraction of life's chores — big and small.

3. To the degree possible, Project Mind will underwrite the financial obligations of subjects during the course of their participation. This is meant to facilitate the subjects' participation in Project Mind and alleviate the distraction of their financial responsibility towards others.

4. Project Mind will have an in-house, on-line, computerized information retrieval system second to none in the world. Subjects will be able to locate sources of strategic information from the quasi totality of the world's technical literature within moments after the need arises. Complete texts, when necessary, will be delivered within a brief interval.

5. To assist visualization and computation, access will be provided to the latest and most powerful computer equipment and software including virtual reality and neural networks. Workstations, personal computers, programs, peripherals and other equipment will be provided as required.

6. Subjects will have rapid access to a broad spectrum of in-house personnel specially trained to deal with blocks, stress, disorientation and other conditions related to intense creativity. General guidance will also be available. Several experts with the required philosophical sophistication, experience, empathy, impartiality, wisdom and dedication are being selected now.

7. Daily conditions of existence will be regulated as closely as possible to subjects' needs.

8. Subjects' progress will be closely monitored. Everything possible will be done to enhance their effectiveness and well-being.

9. Appropriate resident medical staff will provide first aid — both physical and psychological.

10. Project Mind will do everything possible to realize commercial gain for subjects from their discoveries. The object will be to release them definitively from financial worry and enable them to give their lives over to breakthrough-oriented creativity either within or independent of Project Mind.

    While environmental elements are crucial for encouraging and nurturing creativity, it cannot be overemphasized that the key factor for success is the will and motivation of the individual. Only the most intrepid "meaning-adventurers" merit the opportunity which the exclusive conditions of Project Mind represent.

Q. You claim that matter is what keeps us down. Yet you also claim that it represents a challenge, and that in overcoming it we will be liberated. Is matter a curse or a boon?

A. Our relationship with matter is dual. We must consider matter a boon, as the matrix within which we must struggle and thanks to which we may eventually prevail. At the same time — if only temporarily — it represents a curse, for it weighs upon the spirit, cuts us off from higher reality and is suffocating for the majority of humanity.

   The equity of the cosmos that justifies the suffering and apparent injustice of human existence can be found in the realization that once matter is vanquished the spirits of all living men will be liberated, and the spirits of all those who ever lived will be revealed to exist and will play their proper, blissful roles in cosmic eternity. Those pioneers of Accelerated Thought who eventually bring about that revelation will, as their special reward, be granted the experience of that same great existence with one additional degree of perspective. That bonus — available only from the incarnate condition — is the perspective of benefactors.

Q. You seem to condemn the material aspect of reality on the basis of man's excessive attachment to material possessions. But matter is one thing and material things, which represent formed matter, another. Why don't you condemn form rather than matter?

A. It is indeed form that gives meaning, value and "intelligence" to matter, and we are easily hypnotized by form. In fact our slavery to matter becomes more and more established with the elaboration of form in matter, as our preoccupation with style and fashion make grotesquely clear.

Of all the raw materials that appear in nature, there are relatively few that interest men as such. Certain rare stones and metals are coveted for their beauty, plants and animals are valued for their flesh, earth and water for subsistence and power. But the vast majority of materials, whether natural or artificial, assume value only for the forms they take on — intelligence embodied in matter.

While we may well be fascinated with the forms that technology subsumes, it is the physical embodiment of technology that we covet. We may worship the beauty of great works of art, but it is the physical originals that the money pursues. We may have some appreciation for fine and gentle souls, but mainly we wish to possess those of physical beauty, fame or fortune.

Yet as matter accumulates intelligence, it loses its material aspect and assumes the characteristics of a higher world — the world of form. As form in matter becomes more readily manipulated and reproduced, material goods reach a stage where they begin to cost less rather than more (modern electronics is a case in point), leading to the devaluation of matter. Matter — the embodiment of death and restriction in our world — is not to be condemned, but refined and conquered through intelligent human endeavor.

Q. Science, as you point out, is constantly redefining matter which is proving to be more and more ephemeral. How can you make unequivocal distinctions between form and matter?

A. Any given level of consciousness in man manifests a precise level of materiality defining his contact with reality and his place in the cosmos. Thus in contradistinction to the intellectual abstraction of science, consciousness experientially defines materiality and form. As long as the distinction between levels of consciousness is maintained, there will be no confusion as to the materiality under consideration. The evanescence of matter being encountered by modern science represents concrete experiential realities for certain states of consciousness.

Q.   You claim that through Accelerated Thought we will be given more and better inventions, and yet you also claim that society is corrupted through constant novelty. Is innovation to be our salvation or our ruination?

A.   Innovation plainly cuts both ways, at least under our current conditions of existence. Breakthroughs — the revelation of key pieces of new knowledge — offer us new possibilities which we tend to harness in the service of short term comforts and the expense of our common, long-term interests. As the world-wide appetite for comfort-oriented technology and distraction-promoting gadgetry expands, a smaller and smaller proportion of our resources is allocated to the kind of pure research that might favor our redemption. The "pure" research that does survive is increasingly selected for its potential application to problems defined by our ever-narrowing perception of what is "useful." Tragically, what is considered useful is conditioned at least as much by military needs as by those which spring from our inner corruption. New knowledge, and breakthrough knowledge in particular, is necessary if we are to break out of our restricted perception of reality and human potential. Such knowledge is absolutely essential if we are to remove the material basis of that restriction. Project Mind will show that this is both possible and desirable.

Q.   Since you as the author and creator of Project Mind do not even pretend to objective consciousness nor embody Accelerated Thought, how do you come to recommend such risky, mind-altering adventures to others?

A.   Sir Edmund Hillary, the first to climb Mount Everest, said that one climbs mountains "because they are there." The challenge posed by matter along with all the restrictions related to matter — death in particular — is likewise "there." And while mountain climbing poses little threat to the status quo of conventionality, the kind of original, breakthrough thinking that could materially transform our lives and society as a whole, namely Accelerated Thought, does. Accordingly, those individuals who by their relatively uncorrupted natures are drawn to this challenge are, for the most part, sociologically and psychologically prevented from embarking on the adventure of Accelerated Thought for which they thirst, and for whose material results the world is in dire need.

I have not invented the challenge of matter, nor the phenomenon of Accelerated Thought, nor the need for its results. As the author of Project Mind, both as a book and as an enterprise, I simply try to envisage environmental conditions providing shelter from pernicious social forces where individuals so inclined can detoxify their minds and spirits from the deleterious forces of distraction and pursue cherished trains of thought that would otherwise remain throttled.

As for the risks, not only does the concept of Project Mind make provision for proper "grounding" as a counterpart to the release of mind from the pressure cooker of distraction, but rigorous screening is being designed to weed out applicants who are unsuitable. Project Mind regards individuals with a leaning towards Accelerated Thought as humanity's most precious resource. They hold the possibility of alleviating incalculable physical, psychological and spiritual suffering through Project Mind.

It should be painfully obvious that the ability to envisage all that is laid out in this book, and much more that is not, derives from more than just idle speculation. Detailed as they may seem, the psychological descriptions are in fact general descriptions — intimations gleaned from the author's own experience without benefit of a "Project Mind" type of environment. To the extent that the author is deficient in the exercise of creative vision, he will be called to account in the supreme court of reality, just as others will be called upon to make up for his insufficiencies.

Q. Given all you are prepared to do for participants in Project Mind, is there not a risk of indulging delusions of grandeur in certain individuals?

A. The risk is very real. Exploring the unknown through intense creative effort is by definition hazardous. In principle, balanced individuals in a favorable environment should be able to get through the "rough spots" without mishap, and every aspect of Project Mind is designed to this end. Yet we probably all have the spores of megalomania lurking in us somewhere, and messianic complexes are not uncommon in creative people.

For this reason and others, the "psychological management" of Project Mind will be fully attentive to symptoms of distress and well equipped for contingencies.

Q. Assuming for the sake of argument that physical possessions do have a more or less corrupting influence on man's spirit and that abundance will somehow defeat material greed, how is this to affect man's avidity for territory, power, attention, adulation, glory, honor, love, sex, privilege and other non-material objects of man's desire? Might not the capacities bestowed upon man by highly advanced technology only exacerbate his competitive drive as far as these are concerned?

A. The principal evil of the universal phenomenon of alienation is that we reduce the miracle of man and his attributes to the status of objects — things to be possessed. To recognize our neighbor as pure process, and his physical body as merely a casing to contain this process, requires the conscious vision we presently lack.

To become weaned of the cannibalistic vice of relating to our neighbors as anything lower than the potential expression of pure intelligence, we will have to begin to see the concrete proof of that potential through the expanding impact of Accelerated Thought on our lives and minds. Nothing less will induce remorse in us for the habit of considering others, their bodies, their time, their attention, their esteem, their love or any other aspect of their existence as the means to our happiness or comfort. Eventually we will see that even their intelligence will be fully valued — not when it brings us some kind of benefit, but rather when we enter into direct relationship with that intelligence through the conscious exercise of our own.

As for power and territory, the moment the insignificance of matter begins to be revealed these will be abandoned as the means for mitigating aims as swiftly as speculators today abandon a failing currency.

Why covet territory when technology will render the vast uninhabitable areas of our world (and undoubtedly, in time, those of other worlds as well) veritable gardens of Eden? How much physical space is necessary for those who see excess of all kinds as a universal sign of obtuseness and deficiency, and who, for their fulfillment, seek only to increase the common pool of consciousness and understanding? What limits need we fear concerning metaphysical space, substance and energy?

Q. Does not the claim that our bodies are potentially incredible mind reservoirs invite the argument that "dumb" animals, that evidently do not suffer from distraction, are in reality highly intelligent beings?

A. And intelligent they are, not in the sense of calculation or intellectual reasoning, but in the sense of harmony and integration. Nature as a whole, in fact, is one enormous intelligence providing the matter and form to complete the cosmos. Animals have full access to the instinct which is the truth of their essences and they achieve "technical" accomplishments, many of which still defy scientific understanding. Furthermore, animals pursue their purposes with single-minded devotion. Through our representation of them through myth, legend and parable, they offer man enviable moral examples.

The cosmic form we call "man" — made in the image of G-d's name — fails to merge with that natural harmony from which he emerged. He is forced by the special, separative quality of human, goal-defined intelligence to seek for himself the naturally harmonious, flowing nourishment of life-energy that comes only when one is integrally connected to the cosmic energy that gave him birth.

Q. You claim that, over the centuries, man's sensibilities have been steadily in decline under the influence of material deprivation, bringing him into his present state of distraction. Given the lamentable state of the world, this argument theoretically has many compelling aspects. Yet what direct evidence have we of this decline?

A. One interesting indication to be found on the "seam" between the physical and the spiritual concerns human dietary habits. Consciousness, and more particularly, objective consciousness, implies a continuity between outer and inner reality. Ingested food crosses this frontier between the outer and the inner in a most direct and explicit way, yet our awareness of this transition is normally little more than vestigial. Feeding is certainly far from the sacrament that it could be.

Evidence that we once had an awareness of the inner qualities of food — their consequences in the process of nourishing our spirit — can be found in various religious dietary laws and taboos. Some nations refuse to eat pig and crustaceans; others, horses, cats, dogs, rats, human flesh, etc. While some argue that these scruples can be found to have some medical basis, it seems clear that considerations of spiritual purity are primary. If, in fact, the kinds of foods we eat have implications for our spiritual health — for our consciousness — either through the experience they induce in us by their very taste or through their biological action (or both), we must recognize that we have lost not only sensibility for feeling these effects but also (and this is more grave), the inner capacity to derive conscious benefits from these ritual indications. Are we so spiritually ill that we are beyond help from the practice of this form of alimentary hygiene?

Q. Isn't it possible that satisfying the vices and crude desires of mankind through what you so glibly call "abundance" will, like scratching a mosquito bite, only inflame these weaknesses rather than calm them? Since there is, in principle, no limit to depravity, how will you deal with misfits and criminals who will only be encouraged in their vile ways?

A. Putting aside for a moment the question of criminal and psychotic pathologies, mankind as a whole is suffering from a severe kind of neurosis that I call "distraction," characterized by a consciousness saturated with fantasy and illusion. This modality of existence becomes increasingly confirmed until the individual becomes totally incapable of taking notice of his objective situation even when those initiated in the matter try to bring the situation to his attention.

It is like a stiff muscle turning into a knot or "charley horse." It can become so established, so inextricable, that its release passes totally out of our control, no longer accessible to our enfeebled capacity for loosening up and unwinding on our own. In this sense our psyche becomes distraction-bound and we take it for our normal waking consciousness and emotional balance. In others we call it personality.

Thus our psyche has need of the spiritual equivalent of an externally applied massage or, in some cases, local anesthetic, to escape its self-imposed prison of illusion and gain some small foothold in reality. How else could we possibly rediscover the healthy animal we were in childhood and the sense of wonder this vital state entailed? How else will we discover the expansive visionary processes of thought and feeling which would have been ours had this healthy, incipient state of growth not been so dreadfully compromised and curtailed by our connivance with the shamefully untoward conditions of outward existence surrounding us?

Depending on the extent of the pathology and the relative inextricability of the psychological knot into which we have tied ourselves, differing measures of intervention are called for. Classic examples of treatment include various forms of meditation, yoga, Tai Chi, reflexology, acupressure, psychotherapy, psychoanalysis, hypnosis, group dynamics, drugs, etc. These methods have varying degrees of efficacy, but require the kind of interest and motivation which is beyond the average person who is rarely even aware that anything is wrong. Under ever-prevailing stressful life conditions the battle is long and never really won, even for those who apply themselves assiduously to the discipline and purpose of becoming free.

Only by removing the root cause and motor behind our abnormal living conditions will we be able to find the shelter that will allow us to let down our guard and experiment with new ways of being. The cause, of course, is lack and competition stemming from limitation and restriction — the essence of matter. In an environment of unlimited abundance, however, people can psychologically "breathe" easily enough to think about what they really want and need. They no longer need to focus solely on what has always been dictated to them by the physical needs of their body and further aggravated by the twisted values imposed by societies perversely feeding upon man's acquisitive tendencies, weakness and corruption.

Should anyone cling to crime and perversity for whatever reason, the technical means will be made available to harmlessly indulge 'most any fantasy. Pathological intentions could be acted out (and perhaps exhausted through satiation and healed) in a synthetic world of virtual reality. The rest of us would have no trouble steering clear of harm's way. But what motivation could lead someone to harm others who have completely ceased to be sources of resentment and jealousy? What basis for deviation will remain?

Q. The remaking of society seems to imply major institutional dislocations, social disorder and even chaos. Assuming for the moment that Project Mind will induce sweeping changes in man's thinking and conduct, is there any way to assume a smooth, non-catastrophic transition to the utopia in which you believe?

A.   Early on, abundance can act as a balm to relieve the stress of deprivation so that people's psyche can begin healing. Then, with the alleviation of the social pressures that legitimize artificial needs and the pursuit of their satisfaction, people will be able to start taking stock of their real needs, and not just superficially. While abundance does not automatically bestow consciousness, it does weaken external and internal sources of distraction so that the individual can gain insight into his situation. He can then take steps to rectify unwholesome habits of thought and feeling, and his relations with others.

Changes of this nature can only reduce the friction of invidious comparison and increase the humane basis of social order and cohesion. With the withering of the social and psychological underpinnings of predatory attitudes and behavior, society will become what it was meant to be — a crucible for sharing complementarities. Change in the sense of eliminating dysfunction can hardly be a source of dislocation and disorder. The fact that we'll all be changing together in a way that reinforces mutual interest will eliminate the many ills and stresses that normally derive from social maladaptation and isolation.

The problem is how to get the ball rolling, how to catalyze the initial reaction in the absence of such supportive conditions. This is the job of Project Mind and the pioneers of Accelerated Thought.

Q.   I think I understand what you mean by distraction. Personally, I find my powers of concentration are good; further I do not feel at all distracted. How can I verify the truth of my situation?

A.   Distraction as the catch-all term to succinctly express the deleterious effect of external conditions of existence on our psyche goes beyond merely denoting the immediately distracting effect of life's interests and concerns which, like the media, constantly vie for our attention. It refers to the consequences of surrendering our vitality and love of life (which governs the vividness with which we are able to perceive and experience reality) to personalities, groups, and forces in general. In return for our surrender, these offer us shelter from the full brunt of awareness of the horror of non-being (death) constantly threatening us, and from the whole scale of lesser restrictions upon our being that derive from the matter aspect of reality.

It is easy to overlook this permanent state of existential amnesia for the very fact of its permanence, and for the paucity of the memories of anything sufficiently vital in our existence to contradict and reveal it for what it really is. It takes isolated occurrences of "peak" experiences to shock us into the animation that bears the possibilities of a higher existence. But true to our unwritten pact with conventionality and existential mediocrity, we quickly conclude that these rare episodes are exceptional, and our usual distracted state, normal. Everything around us is structured to confirm this illusion. The very idea that normal consciousness could be pathological and peak experience normal seems absurd. Again we become the willing stooges of moribund banality.

Very few people have the initiative or volition to test their powers of attention to the limit and discover the extent of restriction to which their spirit is subject. The growing few who gravitate to spiritual systems find they are required to discover their limits and extend them through various exercises. This favors the gradual attainment of self-knowledge which, even if insufficient, is still of a kind inaccessible through conventional, reflective thought and observation.

It appears that for the mass of humanity the only circumstance that will alert them to this state of restriction of spirit we are calling "distraction" will be the attenuation and eventually the elimination of lack, which is the root cause of this distraction and of our infatuation with the rind of reality — matter.

Q. How does the phenomenon of reflective thought affect the way a person may perceive his role in life?

A. While it is true that we are destined from above to receive, our own essential purpose as created beings is to give — to extend higher influence to this world through the channel of our Being. We can, of course, try to pursue receiving directly. But in doing so, we will in effect be seeking a state of being, and perhaps the higher influence that will induce that state of being. To anticipate and seek a better existence is legitimate. It can be a help to know that we are not what we could be. But our purpose must not be to change or to be better, for otherwise our actions (however altruistic they may seem on the surface) will at heart be selfish and for ourselves alone.

The exercise of purpose implies the extension of an influence over some aspect of the universe, if only the digging of a ditch. Influence implies the betterment of the conditions of our neighbor's existence and, by extension, our own. So how do we fall into the trap of seeking such goals as self-development, self-fulfillment, etc.?

Our ability to reflect, to intellectualize, makes it possible to make an abstraction out of how we feel and what we become when some purpose is achieved. As with masturbation, we tend to fixate on the result. That the achievement of purpose is relegated to fantasy (or, in more corrupt cases, abrogated altogether) only aggravates the problem.

Reflection is a two-edged sword. It can corrupt us and seduce us away from a healthy involvement in purposeful activity, or it can enable us to take stock of our situation and notice the lack of meaning that only purpose can give. We can learn that pain and pleasure are not goals but indicators as to whether we are properly integrating with reality — whether we are satisfying the requirements of our nature and fulfilling our potential.

These requirements, and that potential, demand that we invest our natural vitality in useful work that suits our nature. Properly invested, our share of energy grows along with our capacity for work and for distinguishing what kinds of endeavor most suit us. Improperly invested — for instance in the direct pursuit of happiness — that capacity diminishes and our natural vitality becomes depleted. We become increasingly dependent upon external sources of energy, props, fantasy and illusion to get us through the day.

Q. What is the meaning of a desire to exert an influence in the world?

A. Moment by moment we receive the gift of life that streams into and through us. This life usually comes to us in ways too subtle for us to distinguish. The energy which consists of our mostly invisible cosmic environment is none other than the light of reality pressing relentlessly against us, urging us to awaken to consciousness. This is the essence of influence.

But in emulation of this energy, we aspire in our own way to exercise an influence in the world. The efficacy of this influence, if indeed it is benign, will be a function of consciousness — the subtlety and intricacy of the perceptions and understandings that guide our actions. To disrupt intelligence is easy. We need simply act in a coarse, undiscriminating manner. Unconscious of the wider implications of our actions, we abuse the energy lent to us by nature. Instead of acting as a channel in the service of vision and giving form to higher reality in the world, we use this energy to add to the conventional image of reality by stressing the already vastly overemphasized role and importance of matter. In our opacity, we act as a screen blocking the light of reality and preclude the awareness of the very existence of anything higher than what, in our distraction, we can conceive of.

In principle, we are able to creatively transmit higher influence and transform our world thanks to our indivisible double nature. Through our essence this enables us to receive, and through our essential form, enables us to give. This double nature of our essence is the motor of life, expressed at every level of our being that functions coherently. It is evident first and foremost at the physical level, where "receiving in order to give" is expressed by the biological exchange of materials, fluids and gases between our body and the environment. Through inner striving and integration with higher reality, analogical structures carry out parallel processes on finer levels of materiality thanks to this same double nature. The further removed these finer processes become from the coarse physical level, the less mechanical they become and the more we experience them and our essential desire to give. These processes, together with our desire to receive, enable us to convey influence.

Q. There are those who see real influence and grace in the genuinely altruistic acts of people like Mother Theresa and Albert Schweitzer. Such acts multiplied through the good will of a growing number of individuals around the world are seen by many to be the key for alleviating human suffering and bringing peace into the world. What is wrong with this approach?

A. Nothing is wrong with true charity. On the contrary, the unadulterated desire to bring a new, merciful action into the world is exactly what this book is about. But each of us who seeks to represent a beneficial influence must decide on the level at which he will intervene. A truly innovative intellectual contribution can, in principle, exert a universal influence as opposed to "activist" altruism whose results tend to remain local. It is a self-evident truth that the greatest leverage to be had in alleviating human suffering — physical and existential — is in the transformation of matter. For this reason it offers the greatest challenge and requires the greatest leap into the unknown.

The direct "person to person" kind of helping, because of the complexity of human nature and the many booby traps of the ego waiting to snare us, requires tremendous purity of intention and perseverance. Personal comfort and security must be sacrificed without regret. In short, almost superhuman qualities and efforts are required to alleviate, or more often just to briefly lighten, suffering on the most minuscule of scales. We cannot but stand in awe before the virtue and the faith of those who assume such burdens.

Those who feel this call must pursue it. The degree of their success and sense of fulfillment will in time indicate whether it was truly for this they were born. But if rather than exhilaration and exaltation they experience tedium and discouragement, it may be because they did not go far enough in asking themselves what it is they really wished to do in this world.

Q. You seem to blame all of man's ills on the external conditions of his existence. Yet if there is even a grain of truth in theories such as astrology and reincarnation, we are born with tendencies and predispositions which prejudice us towards excesses in some things and deficiencies in others. Is not the root of our imbalance to be found in these inborn predilections?

A. The "imbalance" that characterizes our nature at birth, including physical form, temperament, talents and tendencies, represents our specific essence. It assigns us our role in the historical body of humanity, or in what is sometimes called "primordial" or "universal" man. This special mix of attributes represents a potentially stable constellation of traits — a viable personality of harmonious proportions. Given favorable conditions for their development, the functional components of our essence (like the expression of our genetic DNA) would faithfully render us as we were meant to be. As it happens, the modern family, educational system and professional marketplace, which now and throughout history have constituted the matrix or "womb" for our development, have offered less than ideal conditions for the gestation of our personalities.

The artificial, distorted, neurotic, imbalanced, false personalities we tend to develop are reflections of the abnormal conditions of existence in which we find ourselves, and not the mere amplification of that essential "imbalance" that gives each of us the characteristic color which inherently is ours. A fetus gestating in similarly abnormal uterine conditions would emerge monstrously deformed.

Q. Where do you stand on reincarnation?

A. The notion of reincarnation can be psychologically useful. It can help us adapt to the notion of higher worlds and alternative realities. At its best, it portrays the soul in an odyssey, seeking its soul mate and its destiny. More often, the idea of reincarnation lends itself to abuse, escapism and destructive fantasy.

   If prior incarnations have brought me to where I am now, and it is only through this incarnation that I can act, perhaps my efforts would be better placed investigating the purpose of this incarnation directly — within this body — rather than risking misinterpreting the gist of prior lives. (Then again, if all else seems to fail, no avenue should be left untried.)

Q. Project Mind seems to be a kind of synthesis between spiritual endeavor and science. But in "conventional" spirituality, notions such as "non-doing," "non-desire," "self-effacement," "submission" and "dying to oneself" are central. Where do they fit into your system?

A. Having moments of losing one's sense of separation — the sense of belonging to the oneness of everything — is only the first step on the way to consciousness. This stage in classical spirituality involves the "non-doings" of abstention, fasting, renunciation, purification, ritual and negative precepts in general. These certainly apply to outward acts. But also, and more importantly, they apply to inner ones in the sense of not giving way to arbitrary impulses of thought, feeling and movement. To the degree that the individual thus becomes free of the bonds of distraction (that is, to the degree that he starts to "be" in any real sense of the word), he can tentatively begin with authentic "doings" — should he come to feel any such essence-impulse within himself.

   The "non-doings" of Accelerated Thought, to the extent that it could be said to include such elements, do not include explicit techniques for stilling or emptying the mind or even for relaxation. Instead, it uses desire as a lever for funneling the individual's energy to a focal point of concentration sharp enough to pierce the veil of distraction. This focus is an early precursor of will, which grows with the consolidation of our fractionated desires.

   Distraction consists of a chaos of inner "doings" controlled by the chaotic vagaries of external circumstances. Thus the "non-doing" of Project Mind is initiated by an intensely focused "doing." This "doing," consisting of intense reflection driven by the individual's deepest creative urges and most persistent desires (precursors of will), allows him to work simultaneously through the two processes — "doing" and "non-doing" — that lead to objectivity. The individual need not await a seemingly endless chain of "non-doings" to lead him to a glimmering of personal purpose some time in the remote future. He has the advantage of knowing very early approximately where he wants to go. Each small success clarifies and reinforces his purpose and his will.

It is only natural that in immature individuals this goal or desire tends to be expressed through ego. But as distraction-inspired illusions fall away, the desires in question find more essential expression and become more unified, more meaningful and more generative of consciousness.

Lastly, but most important (and most difficult for ordinary mind to grasp), is that the pioneers of Accelerated Thought, in resisting seeing the "emperor's clothes" while they were still little children, achieved the greatest non-doing of all — the principal non-doing upon which the only real hope for our world resides. This heroic act is the noble non-doing of our essence attaching itself against all odds to life. It lays the foundation for manifesting independence of spirit and even true individuality later in life.

Q. If Accelerated Thought involves primarily a change in the quality of consciousness at the expense of distraction, why can't deep meditation or even hypnosis serve the same purpose?

A. "Stilling the mind" is definitely a pathway to self-knowledge and beyond. However, everything in the world, in our habits and in our personalities, is fashioned through the generalized action of distraction to perturb and obstruct us in such efforts. We can, up to a point, require ourselves to be still and withdraw our attention from the thoughts, feelings and sensations that distract us from self-observation and direct experience. But we do so against almost all our inclinations. And although there are ineffable, spiritual compensations for climbing inner mountains, even those of us most enamored of this kind of challenge and the virtue it brings soon find our enthusiasm dampened if we have to do it all day, every day.

Remember, freedom of any kind does not come cheap. And salvation from physical and spiritual restriction (and even from spiritual restriction alone) means weaning oneself from all one's illusions and self-indulgent habits of mind, feeling and body — a program that is often said to take "many lifetimes." Where is this incredibly intense and devoted motivation to come from if not from our deepest, most intrinsic, most fundamental desire — the desire to live? And how are we to awaken this essential desire so hopelessly encrusted with a thousand, petty, superficial desires if not by eliminating the oppressive weight that engenders and perpetuates them?

Spiritual efforts of "non-desire" such as meditation attempt to lift this ponderous weight directly. And while encountering the sheer difficulty can undoubtedly bring about the loss of some illusions concerning one's own motivations and virtues, this process, liberating as it can be, is not equal to the weight that keeps down all of humanity, nor could it reasonably be expected to be.

Hypnosis does have the element of channeled intention and can produce quite remarkable phenomena beyond the reach of everyday willpower. It can even give some access to material deeply buried in memory or in our unconscious. But to all this there are very definite limits. It is well known, for instance, that repressed material is difficult and sometimes impossible to get at. Our lack of contact with the repressed contents of our subconscious (contact ruptured in childhood through self-betrayal and compromise) amounts to the most basic of denials — the denial of our own perception of reality. Such short-circuiting of our spirit at a tender age followed by a lifetime of compromises stacked one upon another constitutes a bulwark of repression that will resist the assault of far more "will" than can be mobilized by hypnotic suggestion, regardless of how talented the practitioner.

Q. How does Project Mind compensate for distraction?

A. Project Mind takes hold of the other end of the stick. It does not take as its starting point attempts to weaken or purify the corruption so ensconced in our efforts related to the non-desire which is the principle behind meditation and relaxation techniques. Instead, it focuses on our most essential desire, the desire to live — to be. It recognizes that while each of us gives expression to this most basic and universal of desires through a multiplicity of paltry, often perverted and conflicting desires (depending on how much, during our formative years, we have allowed our direct contact with life to be compromised), we have other desires secretly nurtured in our heart of hearts that more closely reflect our real, individual, essential attachment to life.

Project Mind recognizes that very few such desires ever become sufficiently delineated to concern themselves directly with the dilemma of matter as the prime source of restriction and suffering in life. Even among those who do have desires and ambitions directed at the fashioning, modification or transformation of matter in the everyday sense, very few ever make such a desire the *raison d'être* of their lives. But for those who do harbor such desires and aspire to give them concrete expression, Project Mind proposes conditions which will give free reign to these intense desires and make possible their expression through the process of Accelerated Thought.

Instead of struggling to become free (purified) of all the parasitic desires and habits we develop through a lifetime of distraction (in hope of eventually revealing our true essential inclinations), Accelerated Thought permits the rectified assimilation of these parasites into the conscious current of the individual's already directed intention. Here they are purified by the "fire" of essence-desire rather than by the "water" of non-desire. Only the most fervent pursuit of truth (for the reality we reveal becomes part of our own reality) can allow us to return to direct experience and the essential, pristine vitality of infancy.

Q. What is the difference between "peak" experience and "Eureka" experience?

A. While these terms are used somewhat loosely, and sometimes even interchangeably, peak experience is a general term taking in a broad spectrum of feelings resulting from temporary contact with higher reality or involving a new level of awareness. It is often a response to beauty, is usually restricted to aesthetics and symbolism, and remains implicit.

Eureka, a limited case of peak experience, is a response to a specific discovery in the realm of form or matter which allows for some sort of application in our world. It involves not only a higher feeling function, but also some aspect of higher thought. The explicitness and practical implications usually add an extra dimension of force and future promise to the Eureka experience.

While classical peak experience can lead to enlightenment, subjective consciousness and release from unnecessary suffering, only Eureka in its extended form — Accelerated Thought — can lead to objective consciousness and immortality.

Q. The psychological system implied by Project Mind puts heavy emphasis on focusing and on cognitive closure, and seems to treat the process of opening and Accelerated Thought as natural consequences of the special kind of concentration proposed. But in exploring the unknown, are not questions more important than answers?

A. We live in a time of compromise, uncertainty and relativity. We are less and less willing to commit ourselves to any clear-cut direction or any explicit ideology. Our age of reason abhors certainty, extremes and perspectives drawn in black and white. It is increasingly an age of questions rather than answers. And our questions, rather than leading to solutions and then to a new higher level of questioning, tend to turn on themselves, raising only more of the same old questions. In fact, interrogation and vagueness are beginning to surpass mere fashion and are taking on some of the earmarks of established culture. In more and more circles, the expression of personal opinions on any subject other than perhaps the weather, is tacitly considered to be in poor taste.

Individuals who persist in affirmation can find themselves *personae non grata*. Not only have we largely lost our bearings in reality, leaving us adrift on the tides of public opinion, but we are becoming effete and ineffectual as individuals in our social complicity to avoid making waves that might cause us the slightest embarrassment or discomfort — or that might cause us to be challenged in any way. Even the act of protest today leaves little room for individualism. The media, which dictate rigid terms to those who wish to be heard, favor monolithic, consensus-winning "sound bites."

To be "in question" is a necessary and valuable mode not only for arriving at answers, but also as a means of opening our minds and enlarging our perspectives. But questioning, like anything else, turns to vice when through passivity it skirts issues and avoids responsibility for action for which answers in this material world are still necessary.

Q. Although several years of spiritual practice have significantly improved the quality of my life and changed the way I see things, the intensity of what I experience is a far cry from what it was earlier on. I am beginning to recognize the need for some form of conscious engagement with the substance of outer life as a means of inducing a more intense inner struggle and to elicit higher energy levels than those with which I have been content until now. How can I identify the ground upon which I can best make my stand? How can I discover the mission and task that will consume me with interest without losing the degree of Being accumulated so far in my regular meditative withdrawals from the distractions of life?

A. If you are in the fortunate position of being alerted to the reality of distraction by having struggled with it, you are likewise fortunate to recognize the need to mobilize all your faculties around a task that suits your nature so that your encounter with reality and your struggle with the forces of distraction that veil it may be greatly intensified.

Even if someone could indicate to you what that task is — a highly unlikely possibility — it is far from certain that this would work to your advantage, for this is the work of adolescence (seldom taken to term). Through precocious, intuitive knowledge we must plot our own course and give form to our neophyte sense of Being-obligation. It is largely in the process of discovering our task that we are granted the certainty that it truly is our assignation — our destined calling. This certainty is the hallmark of authentic adulthood. All anyone can really do for you is to refer you back to yourself and invoke the urgency and sacred nature of your search.

Remember, your life is an open book. You have a rich history of thoughts, feelings, observations and experiences that like a puzzle contain confused elements reflecting what you are and what you want. Meditate deeply on these. Try to rank things in order of their importance and see what kind of picture emerges. Although this kind of analysis tends initially to reveal intellectual rather than experiential knowledge of oneself, if taken seriously it cannot fail to confront us with contradictions within our own value systems. Anyone with the minimum of conscience to seek coherence from his own desires cannot fail to be touched to the quick by discrepancies and galvanized to the task of getting at the root of his incongruity. This process will unfailingly lead you towards the discovery of your true inclinations — your uniquely individualized life theme.

However shallow and immature its preliminary expressions, you still must be guided by the theme of your unique, personal ambition. Later, the experiential elaboration of the components of this theme will produce a more impartial vision of yourself. However surprising this new vision may turn out to be, it will bear familiar aspects, as though somehow, somewhere within you it was always known. Struggle and experience, lived as adventure, will clarify understandings that still lack. Thanks to your spiritual practice, you are already partly aware of what is required for this elaboration. What you lack is your essential theme. This theme will give your inner work a direction in the world of action and add new dimensions of meaning and incentive to your efforts.

As extra protection (thanks also to your spiritual practice) you can fall back upon Being as the best possible solvent for pretension that is not well-grounded in essence. The difference between conventional ambition and individual essence-calling is distinct. The former embroils you in the pursuit of values governed by distraction — values which can never touch you deeply and which alienate you from your inner self. The latter constantly reminds you of your most intimate desire and, through action, binds your body and spirit ever more tightly in the pursuit of its realization and yours (since you and this desire are essentially one and the same).

Q. How do thought and feeling participate in transforming our sense of reality?

A. Whenever we perceive an increase in our possibilities that stems either from some new idea that helps us realize potentials, or from some corresponding change in outward conditions facilitating the realization of these potentials, our energy increases. Nature grants us a kind of encouragement to carry on in that same direction.

Ideas show us what must be done and how. Through discovering their correspondences with reality, they show us how different aspects of reality are related. They increase the scope and clarity of our vision in preparation for action. Action is the manipulation of aspects of the outside world in line with some inner model or theory. We seek coherent theories as guides to action. The more coherent and the more encompassing the theory, the more promising the results in its implementation. The closer the theory's component ideas correspond to reality, the more likely its successful implementation.

Energy is released because we become convinced that success is imminent. We see what is to come. In confident anticipation we begin to taste the attainment of a goal even before it is reached. What is imminent becomes our reality. We suddenly feel free of the restriction of an old reality.

Q. You make a clear distinction between subjective and objective consciousness, claiming that the former concerns the expression of more superficial levels of essence, and the latter, deeper levels. But you also claim that the outer layers of essence express levels of being common to all men, producing a communion of consciousness, while the heart of essence is the seat of what makes us unique and thus distinct from others, which also seems to imply separation and subjectivity. Does objectivity point to the truth that we all share, or to that which separates us? Can you clarify these apparently contradictory uses of the concepts of subjectivity and objectivity?

A. This is not so much a contradiction as a paradox — some might call it a koan. In the objective sense each of us is unique. Not even two leaves or two snowflakes are exactly alike. Thus our connection with one another in the level of objective consciousness we can attain is not through our commonalities (as with subjective consciousness), but through our complementarities. We must eventually discover that, despite the peaceful communion of shared experience that subjective consciousness grants, our ultimate salvation derives from our essential differences and our interdependence that can be fully revealed only through objective consciousness.

Q. The question of death seems to be at the core of your understanding of life. In what ways has mankind been conditioned by his awareness of death?

A. From the moment man could distinguish good from bad, he has found himself constrained to recognize life as the good and death as the bad. The awareness of death, or rather the anxieties spawned by that awareness, sent mankind, as a species, along two separate avenues.

Through submission and supplication, some sought to reunite their spirits with the primal source of life from which all of existence springs. Others pursued the conquest of nature, and the limitations it imposed, through the aggressive use of their wits and ingenuity. These two orientations — religion and science — provide the most fundamental keys for understanding human purpose and aspiration, and reflect two modalities of response to life hardwired into our nervous system. These neurological systems, called "parasympathetic" and "sympathetic," respectively, provide what Koestler calls our "integrative" and "self-assertive" modes of responding to situations.

Through both tendencies we strive to derive a sense of unity and coherence from existence. But each is insufficient on its own. While the predominance of one over the other leads to the impasse of imbalance, simplistic notions of balance and synthesis only befog the issue. Systems and solutions based on such notions, tantalizing as they seem, have always failed to create paradise on earth. The implacable fact is that such systems, however ingenious, fail to generate the potent forces necessary for their own sustenance and advancement.

Far beyond the priming stage, where the need for external sources of energy can be justified, such systems sustain themselves on the fruits of energy sources external to their own processes. Spiritual students feed on the energy of their teachers, while there are never enough students to give a determinant boost to the teacher. Such schools gradually lose the force of the impulse that launched them and limp along for years, decades and sometimes centuries before eventually disappearing. Science is compromised by consenting to serve ends other than the pursuit of truth and life. Individual scientists seek comfort and status while the scientific establishment, unable to support or justify itself through scientific ideal, allows itself to be used cynically by an expedient industry and by the military.

To all appearances, our integrative path is blocked, preventing us from returning to our life-giving origins, while our self-assertive course of thinking our way out of death's stranglehold is condemned to emasculation and depletion.

This is the riddle of existence ensconced in man. This is the riddle man was created to solve.

Q. There are those who say that death is just a process and does not oppose life, that life is eternal, irresistible and indestructible. Death of intermediary forms is said to be part of a transformatory process which serves to reveal life. So why the adversary attitude towards matter and death?

A. Life is indeed eternal. But Creation, with a capital or small "c," is the elaboration of form within matter to the point where the blend becomes sufficiently refined and intelligent to reveal and accommodate life eternally. The search for that total compatibility between matter and life, through form, is the role of man as a partner in Creation.

Accepting the spiritual suffering of "little deaths" — the effacement of egoistic characteristics — is done in the name of that larger life in which the aspect of essence concerned finds its rectified expression through Being or awareness. Following the dissolution of such an ego-blockage or "knot" in our Being, we awaken to a new, freer, more essential expression of our particularity — one connecting us to rather than separating us from others.

Physical death, on the other hand (at least as far as this world is concerned), is the ultimate relinquishing of particularity and, with it, the privilege of exercising an influence in matter. To be recalled "into the light" may be a welcome relief to those whose lives have become tiresome, exhausted, aimless or hopeless. But for those whose life's theme has been a prelude to action — vital action connected to salvation — death is the annihilation of the exquisite vibrancy of an objectively hopeful life.

The place where words and thoughts fail us most, including the words of our greatest poets, is in evoking the preciousness of life. The deprivation that death represents is felt most keenly by little children who, through their innocence and openness, taste the sweetness and wonder of life fully and directly. It is felt this way in a very few adults who poignantly return to their childlike attachment to life through their individualist striving towards meaning and, still more important, through the purposeful expression of that meaning.

To go into the bliss of the next world may be the ultimate consolation for failure in this one. But the process of making possible the significant expression of that higher world now is to help realize the purpose of Creation and confirm the eternal validity of the particularity of the individuals concerned. Unity does have its eternal expression in multiplicity through archetypal particularities as hinted at through the 12 months of the year, the 12 sons of Jacob, the 12 tribes of Israel, the 12 signs of the zodiac, etc.

Q. Essence-desire is to be found deep inside all mankind. What makes it possible for some of us to establish contact with that desire and feel it mobilizing our inner resources in the service of our predestined goal, while others of us — acquired tastes and artificial needs notwithstanding — remain essentially aimless?

A. Five principal factors determine over a lifetime to what degree we contact our inner reality — that desire which essentially we are:

1. The degree to which in early childhood our vitality and direct innocent perception of reality is subjected to the spiritual violence inherent in familial and social requirements to conform:

    Convention is society's way of getting us to bulk-process reality so that in the absence of genuine commonality of interest based on inner development we will at least have some synthetic basis for social cohesion. What is important to the child is his immediate experience of the world and his unique personal way of exploring how the outside world is connected with his inner experiencings. But this rhythm of self-realization is far too slow and costly for the needs of modern society, so it short-circuits the process by telling the child what he "should" know and feel.

    The defenseless child has little option but to conform and obey, and quickly learns that in order to survive he must fit in. His inner references are replaced with protocols. Instead of independence of spirit erected on a firm foundation of direct, "hands-on," "on-line," "real time" experiential processing of reality, his sense of self is grafted upon skills concerned with "playing the game" and "getting along." The knowledge required for this game of life is knowledge about things — manipulative knowledge — not directly apprehended, experiential knowledge.

2. The degree to which the child resolves to survive the assaults of conformity upon his spirit:

    It is not impossible for the child to resist some of this corrosive influence. Fantasy is undoubtedly the most common shelter, although hyperdependence, hypochondria and mental illness also provide refuge. What the child dares to fantasize is a function of the encouragement he receives from "significant others," usually parents, to see life as an arena for the pursuit of his dreams. However, most of us keep our inner and outer worlds separate and never seriously consider the possibility of realizing our fantasies.

3. The degree to which parents support the child's right to individuality and self-determination:

    Even a highly conformist parent can harbor rancor towards the steamroller aspect of society and want a more dignified existence for his child. The nonconformist, though, has a better chance of influencing his child by providing a maverick example.

4. The degree to which the world of conventional values disappoints them:

    Very often success eludes us in our pursuit of socially sanctioned goals. In the face of conventional failure, some people retrench and fall back on inner values. In a sense they are reborn to the possibility of discovering for themselves what they really want.

    Disappointment can also come with success. On achieving their conventional ambitions, some people find they are unsatisfied and then embark on a search for meaning.

5. The degree to which the individual as an adult falls under influences that nurture his spirit and encourage his search:

    There are significant quantities of "higher" ideas and, better still, individuals embodying such ideas, circulating in a kind of underground. This "underground" is strange because it is not hidden, at least not physically. One simply has to have an inkling of what is going on and keep one's eyes open in order to perceive that there are those among us going about their business while at the same time engaged in something quite distinct from everyday pursuits. Nor is this underground organized in any ordinary sense of the word. Rather, those so engaged recognize one another with relative ease by the fact that their quests, regardless of details, are related through higher principles and forces. Since they are aware of the distraction which envelops them, they struggle to be vigilant.

Not surprisingly, they recognize others engaged in the same struggle.

It is possible to connect with such people and seek their help and guidance. Failing that, the related literature also represents an enriching source of conscious influence and can help you find that special note with which you resonate. It may even bring you in contact with others whose destiny is related to yours.

Q. Candidates for participation in Project Mind are portrayed as having hit upon some question or hypothesis that represents the object of their essential desire. What about those of us who might aspire to candidacy and have a strong urge to discover our specific direction and destiny, but have only the vaguest idea as to the essence of what we want?

A. Begin by listing on paper your values and strongest desires. Be as detailed and specific as you can, with a view to defining yourself with the greatest accuracy. In trying to establish a hierarchy of all that is most important to you, you will encounter contradictions and questions. You will discover that you are far less coherent in your desires than you imagined.

In your effort to make sense of your contradictions and discover your truth, you will have embarked — in whatever measure — on the adventure upon which Project Mind is based. If you persist and sufficiently overcome the inner manifestations of distraction, the light of truth will begin to grow in you.

When your search has reached the point at which you are ripe for Project Mind and the disciplined cultivation of Accelerated Thought, you will know.

Q. The main thrust of Project Mind is to create spectacular scientific and technological breakthroughs. But who will exploit these? How can they be kept from falling into the wrong hands?

A. Project Mind, by flooding the market with radical innovations, will break the stranglehold of those who presently control technology. Those who are involved in production for reasons of pure greed will lose interest once they see that their social privilege and material advantage are condemned by the prospect of universal prosperity. Industry will be left to the truly industrious. This new breed of industrialist (individuals who will enjoy their work for its own sake and who will recognize the objective privilege of participating in the process of releasing humanity from matter's tyranny), will be drawn to the business sector.

The key word here is breakthrough. Less than spectacular technological advances lack the ability to undermine the existing system and its current cartels and monopolies. They also lack the ability to spark hope in the mass of humanity and signal the arrival of a new age.

Q. How will these breakthroughs be developed and brought to market? How will their benefits be made available universally and equitably?

A. Initially, the existing system with all its shortcomings will appropriate breakthroughs as it has always done. Corporations, most expediently placed to do so, will rush to make fortunes on the time-honored premise that even a minor breakthrough is a freak, a windfall to be exploited for their own benefit. But as breakthrough opportunities multiply, monopolies based on older technologies will be broken at a pace that those with vested interests will find disconcerting. So many research establishments and businesses will be scrambling to innovate that the net effect will be liberating. The question will no longer be: who will control what technology? It will become: what wonders will be appear next?

The agility and flexibility of smaller, more agile companies will begin to pay off as it becomes increasingly difficult to operate from technologically entrenched positions of power. The impulse to share and cross-fertilize findings will be irresistible. The advantages of information hoarding and secrecy will evaporate.

Success will increasingly favor those who deliver technological options to end users, while the word "success" changes meaning daily. The growing ability to produce what one needs at home will gradually eliminate the need for ponderous distribution systems. Nanotechnology and molecular engineering, increasingly becoming credible options, are offering prospects of home-grown cars, appliances and anything else we are likely to need. Similarly, food indistinguishable from natural products will be synthesized at will.

Even before benefits are disseminated, breakthrough proliferation will signal real hope to the genuinely deprived while the rest of us will pause to reassess our values and priorities.

Q.   If the vision inherent in Accelerated Thought is so penetrating that it leads to objective consciousness, why will it be necessary to have so many candidates and why must Project Mind be so large and costly? Would not one such superior mind, invested with Accelerated Thought, be able to envisage and invent all that man requires?

A.   In principle, one person embodying objective consciousness would eventually be able to elucidate the objective knowledge of all things. Part of the problem is that this state of being, even under the auspices of Project Mind, takes time to become established in us.

While Accelerated Thought represents an expanded state of the Eureka experience and permits penetrating insights and visions, it does not become permanent all at once. The mind makes forays of gradually increasing duration into this intensive mode of functioning. In fact, one of the roles of Project Mind will be to apportion these inroads into the perilous unknown so that the subject will not become immediately consumed by the fire generated in him by the perception of imminent, unlimited possibilities. For while a small part of him will indeed have undergone a transformation, the rest of him will, at least initially, have quite mundane reactions to this contact with higher reality, including the impulse to rush in and prematurely submit to an intensity of experiencing to which one must adjust progressively. Part of us wishes to run before we have mastered walking.

These exciting and rewarding forays logically begin where our interest, knowledge and commitment are greatest. As the scope of our conscious involvement with the matter of this world expands, more and more of our body's mass participates in its higher and transformed role as mind. Little by little it will be able to sustain incrementally longer sojourns into the realms of higher reality.

So although one highly exceptional pioneer suffering a minimum of setbacks and given enough time might theoretically cover all the territory, eventually, a number of such pioneers could do so more quickly. Furthermore, as the mind's true potential becomes recognized, entities such as Project Mind can be expected to proliferate throughout science and industry, rapidly propagating scientific breakthroughs and their technological expressions. The main and most urgent purpose of Projects Mind's initial embodiment will be to bring about that recognition and spread hope.

While it could be said that the seed of macroscopic, universal man has spawned us all, we mortals, in our individuality, must largely be content to aim for the realization of our microcosmic individuality. Such realization remains exceedingly rare. Yet it is the real possibility of completing this realization and the possibility of sharing it with each other which will enable us to attain to the universal and the eternal.

Q. How long will it take the world to feel the effects of Project Mind from the moment it goes operational?

A. While the total mastery of matter may take as long as 40 years, it will be necessary to concretely prove the validity of Project Mind and Accelerated Thought within five years. The short-term impact of the breakthroughs made during this period must suffice to send an unmistakable message to the world that the age of greed has ended. Excessive retentiveness will be universally regarded not with envy, but rather with the same jaundiced eye as smoking, sexism and racism are now in some quarters in the West. This message of hope will defuse political tensions and relieve ecological stress as mankind prepares itself to enter the Age of Mind.

Q. Won't a perfect world be boring?

A. When contemplating a world of material and social perfection, we tend to forget that most of existence is metaphysical. The far-off vision of absolute perfection — the ideal of G-d — will hold our interest. Is unending ecstasy boring? Is G-d bored?

Q. If Project Mind is so all-important, why have you waited for so late in life to get things started, and specifically what do you expect to gain?

A. Distraction is a formidable enemy. And while I have been true to the spirit of Project Mind from the age of four, it has taken over 40 years to acquire the understanding and confidence necessary for this first disclosure. Claiming to have discovered the key to the cosmic riddle is a pretension that risks provoking incredulity in most, and worse in many. My use of a pen name is a measure taken to buffer the onslaught of pique to be expected from some quarters.

Adolescence is ideally the time to find and formulate the assignation of our essence — the mission of our soul. Majority is the time for realization — for action. Under distraction's regime childhood is trammeled and true adolescence rarely even approached. The subjects of Project Mind (the pioneers of Accelerated Thought) having substantially sustained their adolescence have the best shot at realizing their essential purpose and thus themselves. Those like myself dedicated to providing conditions for such realizations will benefit firsthand from the resulting world transformation as well as from the satisfaction of knowing and doing what was necessary for it to happen. We will try to be worthy of our charges and grow with them.

Q. There exist many dedicated and accomplished teachers in a wide variety of spiritual schools and disciplines whose knowledge of man's inner life in all likelihood substantially surpasses your own. If they haven't been able to solve the ills of mankind, how are we to believe that you or I could do what they could not?

A. Spiritual systems and schools today are primarily extensions, relics or atavisms of ancient teachings that pursued "pure consciousness" — a euphemism for attachment to G-d. In those times men were more self-possessed, more in touch with themselves. Their perceptual, emotional and spiritual acuities were much finer than ours. Even in the absence of modern scientific findings there was a much stronger and clearer feeling for the inner meaning and structure of existence.

While the earliest sources of such knowledge are clouded in the obscurity of our historic origins, we do have legends concerning ancient schools bearing secret knowledge. But side by side with the unquestionably superior wisdom and sensibilities of the ancients, especially among the uninitiated, there existed considerable superstition and fear based largely on the lack of empirical knowledge. This lack characterized all epochs up to our modern scientific age. Men gradually began to rely less upon direct intuitive knowledge and gained confidence in the "rational," "scientific," "intellectual," "positivistic" approach which increasingly gave them control over their immediate physical circumstances and well-being.

But pre-scientific fear and superstition stemming from ignorance of the outer, phenomenal world has gradually sunk into the largely subconscious noumenal world of inner experience. In our newly-found Cartesian arrogance, we have lost contact with this world. Given the vacuum left through this spiritual abdication, the residue of such superstition has been able to invade and corrupt most of what we know of religion and spirituality today.

In the face of this disquieting development, certain individuals were able to tap into sources of hidden secret knowledge transmitted by various means from the past. Picking up the thread, they somewhat reconstituted ancient modes of spiritual work and experience. The spiritual activities evident today are the proliferating branches of this periodic revival common in many if not most cultures. Some of these activities take their inspiration from closer to the root than others. But virtually all — from the most authentic to the least — place themselves not only experientially but also philosophically in opposition to the current of modern civilization and its increasingly distracting nature.

Although these systems or schools are normally in favor of the spiritualization of matter, none to my knowledge have succeeded. Nor to any serious extent have they even considered the issue of the physical transformation of matter — a domain they have abandoned to the external sciences. Even the ancient discipline of alchemy, which on the surface did address itself to such matters, is said by authoritative sources to have been a purely spiritual endeavor, seeking inner transformation exclusively and using the laboratory paraphernalia and the "transmutation of metals" largely as camouflage against the aggressively superstitious church and civil authorities of the period.

Since the spiritual disciples feel themselves indifferent or unequal to the challenge of engaging external matter directly, and science in its servitude to conventionality is unable to make full use of man's creative intelligence (which is the domain of the spirit), the field is left wide open to anyone who has some appreciation of the problem and who, for whatever reason, desires to try to fill the vacuum.

As for my personal qualifications, time will tell.

•　•　•

Readers are invited to submit their own questions and comments to:

Project Mind
P.O. Box 1603
Ormond Beach, FL 32175-1603
U.S.A.

APPENDIX

Note:

Because this Appendix comprises *selected* references only, the numbering within it is not continuous. The numbers are sequential, however, and match the footnote numbers throughout the text. Each number is preceded by the chapter number in which the footnote is located. For convenience, these references are divided by chapters. The first reference is for Chapter 3; none are needed for Chapters 1 or 2.

— Chapter 3 —

3-2. However "successful," a man who is not fully realized — who does not give expression to his infinite potential — must be considered to some degree alienated. Yet it would serve no useful purpose to complain throughout this text that humanity is alienated. The emphasis is on man's possibilities, not his failings. While the notion of distraction and the corrupt conditions of our existence are often noted, it is not so much to evoke the very real fact of our alienation from ourselves and reality, but to remind us that our experience of ourselves and reality, regardless of how rich it may appear at any given moment, is dull and insipid compared with what it could be. In this respect, as in many others, our potential remains to be fully realized.

The term "alienation" points to the separative consequences of distraction. For those who have difficulty grasping the experiential or psychological sense of distraction, more intimacy with the notion of alienation will undoubtedly help. Recommended reading is *Man Alone: Alienation in Modern Society*, edited with an introduction by Eric and Mary Josephson (New York: Dell, 1969). One would do well to focus on the following works quoted therein: Ernest G. Schachtel, "On Alienated Concepts of Identity," in *The American Journal of Psychoanalysis*, November 1961; Erich Fromm, *The Sane Society* (U.S.: Holt, Rinehart and Winston, Inc., 1955); Marya Mannes, *More in Anger* (J.P. Lippincott Co., 1958); Murray B. Levin *The Alienated Voter* (New York: Holt, Rinehart and Winston, Inc., 1960).

For many of the social aspects of distraction read the chapter entitled "Consensus Trance The Sleep of Everyday Life" in Charles T. Tart's *Waking*

Up—Overcoming the Obstacles to Human Potential (Boston: New Science Library, 1986), 85-106.

3-3. *If something can go wrong, it will. (Murphy's Law)*
If it is not perfect, watch out! (David's Bylaw)

In the world of daily striving (i.e., "the best laid schemes of mice and men" [Burns]), the distance between theory and practice is a matter of record. In the realm of cause and effect which we inhabit, the further in time and space "causes" are removed from their "effects," the less relation cause and effect is seen to have.

We do not seem to notice the validity of this universal law, and tend to explain our failures as "flukes," "bad luck," "miscalculations" or "flawed theory." We try again with what we presume to have learned from our experience. We proceed as if things could correspond to such theories — as if conditions were logical, benign and generally working in our favor and that all anyone really had to do to succeed was to try harder. We fail to appreciate the immense complexity of human life and the diversity of forces and influences that bear upon every event making up the content of each moment. This, basically, is why it is so much easier to destroy than to build.

The further removed from our starting point our goals are, in terms of time, space and substance, the more events will impinge upon and influence the forces we set in motion. Very quickly, the meanings and directions of our words and actions are deflected by misunderstandings, conflicts of interest, and all kinds of random forces which breed exponentially through space and time and impinge upon our poor battered schemes. We watch helpless and frustrated at the deviation of these schemes after their release from our control. Often, we end up cursing the ineptness and stupidity of others who inadvertently thwart our designs.

We can try to "ride herd" on our schemes to track their progress and bring them back on course, but we soon discover that the factors influencing the fate of our efforts are more numerous than we imagined. Had we the slightest inkling of the extent of confusion that reigns around us, we might not attempt anything at all. Only nature can afford to send out millions of seeds for a single anticipated result.

Then how is it, we may ask, that the world muddles along and things seem to get done? Experience and common sense, instinct and fear, alert us to the danger of betting on the future. So, pragmatically, we learn to lower our sights and restrict ourselves to tedious step-by-step courses where effects are somewhat less removed in time and space from their causes. This strategy reduces us to a less risky but correspondingly duller existence, the kind we attribute to the mass of humanity.

How then does one account for the success of those who take long-term risks and actually do prevail? Dismissing at the outset freak cases of pure luck and the not-so-rare cases of criminality, we are faced with the limits of skill and foresight — the bane of managers everywhere. The main idea behind management is the analysis and handling of the aspects of a venture in order to reduce the risks of which we are speaking to the extent economically feasible. Sometimes a small advantage in this respect can provide a significant edge over one's competitors. What we fail to realize is that gaining an advantage does not necessarily mean that the envisaged goal has been reached in a form even approximating the one originally conceived.

Accordingly, we define success conventionally — not as creative accomplishment but as financial gain: the making of money. Kierkegaard observed:

> *In the end, therefore, money will be the one thing people will desire, which is moreover only representative, an abstraction. Nowadays a young man hardly envies anyone his gifts, his art, the love of a beautiful girl, or his fame; he only envies him his money. Give me money, he will say, and I am saved. But the young man will not run riot, he will not deserve what repentance repays. He would die with nothing to reproach himself with, and under the impression that if only he had had the money he might really have lived and might even had achieved something great.* (Kierkegaard, *The Present Age*, 40-1.)

Thus money becomes an end in itself rather than what it should be: the generalized means to the attainment of an end. Spender concurs:

> *Men willed it to be so, and the pitheads, slag-heaps and the ghastly disregard of anything but the pursuit of wealth, are a symbol of modern man's mind. In other words, the world which we create — the world of slums and telegrams and newspapers — is a kind of language of our inner wishes and thoughts. Although this is so, it is obviously a language which has got outside our control. It is a confused language, an irresponsible, senile gibberish.* (Spender, "The making of a poem," 118-19.)

However gratifying the results we attain, they rarely bear much resemblance to the original intention. It is our conniving side that leads us to explain the chain of events that brought us some good fortune as the anticipated, logical, even inevitable result of our foresight and careful planning. Who among us is not guilty of sharing in this conspiracy of hiding from others the full range and extent of our failures and of rationalizing our successes with after-the-fact "foresight?" We garnish these "successes" with tales illustrating our intuition, skill and mental prowess, thereby perpetuating the myth that at least the more talented among us have things well under control. This is not to say that talent, vision and careful attention to detail don't improve our chances of getting along in the world. But they are meant to underscore the vast complexity of converging, diverging, intersecting and crisscrossing influences that make attaining any precise aim, at least by conventional means, virtually impossible.

It is natural for our feelings to rebel against this kind of reasoning, regardless of the painful experiential confirmation of this state of affairs we continually witness. It is natural not only because of some deep-seated attachment to our illusions about ourselves, but rather because this feeling has its roots firmly planted in a universal, unconscious, well-based, common-sense conviction that life ought to be a lot simpler and more rational than experience indicates — if not for us, at least for some people, somewhere. This conviction — part of the legacy of our "collective unconscious" — springs from intuitive contact with primal knowledge programmed deeply within human essence, and varies little worldwide despite vast cultural disparities. This same essence is the source of certain fairy tales and works of art that whisper to us of the possibility of creating conditions that we, in our somnambulate existence, try to hypnotize ourselves into believing already prevail. According to Jewish myth, we are created with complete Torah knowledge. But before birth, an angel makes us forget by pressing just above our upper lip, which also causes the indentation there.

In the obscure world of matter, of one thing we can be sure. Just as nature ensures the extension and refinement of its mineral, plant, animal and human forms through a variety of highly complex evolutionary mechanisms, other related but higher cosmic mechanisms guarantee the extension and refinement of noetic (i.e., pertaining to meaning) forms towards an ultimate intelligence that will inevitably banish restriction, lack and death.

3-4. The term "matter" refers to the substance of which any given material is composed. On the molecular level the form inherent to matter is organic to matter, inseparable from it. This is distinct from whatever superimposed pattern happens to shape matter into what we normally call "things" or "objects." Both kinds of form can enhance matter's utility.

Matter subsuming the form of life is the limit case where it seems nothing is superimposed or superfluous. Any significant interruption between form and substance causes the phenomenon of life (i.e., the functioning we associate with life) to disappear at the point of interruption. Systemic death is just such a generalized separation occurring between the matter of our bodies and the form inherent in it. We, ourselves, are essential forms whose every element contributes functionally and structurally in some way (poorly understood for the most part) to what we are, both individually and collectively, as human beings.

In relation to energy, matter itself is form in that matter restricts its energy to its limits. Like matter, energy can take on many aspects and manifest on many levels. What appears as energy on a lower level manifests as matter in relation to the still finer energy of a higher level. These distinctions will be referred to as levels of materiality, which in turn will be shown to correspond to states of consciousness. These states of consciousness and the corresponding levels of materiality are yet little recognized by modern science.

3-5. For those who maintain that it is not matter that divides mankind and creates conflict but man himself, it should be remembered that man, especially in the way he deals with reality, both forms and is formed by his environment. He depends on it, is inseparable from it, and could even be said to form a continuum with it. When it changes, he changes. When he modifies something in it, he himself is compelled to adapt and change. To what degree man is subject to the influence of the matter of which his world is made (one could even say at its mercy) and to what degree man has already mastered matter and freed himself from that influence is a question worth asking and very central to the theme of this book. We could likewise ask, in terms of man's knowledge of matter and of himself, what is his evolutionary potential and how far along is he in realizing it? Munk offers us a biblical perspective on matter:

> *The Torah begins with an affirmation of creation* ex nihilo *... because on this affirmation is based the faith in a unique and omnipotent Creator Who is not Himself bound to matter, but Who has created the world with a definite purpose. If God had been confronted with pre-existing matter, then He would necessarily have been limited and the world of His making would not have been a free and perfect creation. With such matter God could only have made a world which would be relatively good but still nonetheless imperfect. All physical ills, all moral depravity, would then have their origin in the imperfection of the primal matter, of the raw materials, and God himself would have been incapable of delivering us from them. Under such circumstances man could be no more master of his body than God could be master of matter. Freedom would disappear from the world; a blind and disheartening necessity would rule over the earth together with its God and its humanity. This is the fallacious doctrine that is still fundamental to every heathen conception of life.* (Rabbi Elie Munk, *The Call of the Torah*, translated from the French by E.S. Maser [Jerusalem - New York: Feldheim Publishers, 1980]), 12.)

All that is created (i.e., all that is *ex nihilo*), including souls, spirits and especially our "selves," by virtue of having been differentiated from the sacred source of all creation (the G-d-head of pure spirit) consists of finer or coarser matter, depending on its place in the great cosmic hierarchy. And while man contains sparks of divinity and has the potential to accommodate infinitely more than just sparks, literally he is, in essence, matter. If that matter, through lack, attracts us to divine energy, it is the form of that matter — the "image of G-d" in which it is cast — that makes possible the reconciliation of the antipodes of energy and matter. It is through this divine human form that we are invited to resolve the paradox of existence and matter.

Thus it is not unreasonable to assert that until man has mastered matter including that of which his own body is made (at least to the extent that he no longer need suffer physical deprivation or insecurity), he must be considered to be substantially under matter's limiting influence. This subjugation finds expression through man's passions, appetites, vices and foibles. Gurdjieff sees lack and deprivation as inherent to cosmic reality:

And as in general, on none of the planets of our great Universe does there or can there exist enough of everything required for everybody's equal external welfare, irrespective of what are called "objective-merits," the result there is that the prosperity of one is always built on the adversity of many.

It is just this exclusive regard for their own personal welfare that has gradually crystallized in them the already quite particularly unprecedented and peculiar properties of their psyche which I cited, as for instance "cunning," "contempt," "hate," "servility," "lying," "flattery," and so on, which in their turn, on the one hand are factors for an outer manifestation unbecoming to three-brained beings, and on the other hand are the cause of the gradual destruction of all those inner possibilities of theirs, placed in them by Great Nature, of becoming particles of the whole of the "Reasonable Whole." (G. I. Gurdjieff, *All and Everything* [U.K.: Routledge & Kegan Paul, 1973], 383.)

One could very well speculate that the pinch of deprivation may be a cosmic mechanism, part of a total cosmic plan to constrain us to wake up and come to terms with the paradox of the human condition rooted in the paradox of the cosmos, and solve its puzzle.

3-6. The question of desire and renunciation is masterfully treated by Tom Robbins in a passage which ends on a note that is central to the theme of this book:

"A storm is building," said Alobar. "There is one thing we have not, and it is that thing we are obliged to desire." "And that is?" Kudra buttoned her vest against the first blown drops of gelid rain.

"Some influence over the unknown tribunal that sentences us to die against our wishes. A reform of that law that decrees death a certain consequence of birth." (Robbins, *Jitterbug Perfume*, 105-116).

Paul Brunton likewise rails against the escapism that seems to go hand in hand with philosophies of renunciation:

I discovered in the end that the yogi is afraid of action and consequently indifferent to the troubles of the world and unconcerned about mankind's well-being; that his society and presence does not radically change human character for the better, as is claimed, but merely lulls its worst qualities into semi-quiescence to spring up again, however, at the first release from his immediate influence (Paul Brunton, *Reflections on My Life and Writings* [New York: Larson Publications, 1987], 8:115).

Jacob Needleman puts it simply:

It is necessary to experience desire more consciously, not turn away from it toward some high but bloodless and finally, illusory ideal religious image! (Jacob Needleman, *Money and the Meaning of Life* [New York: Doubleday, 1991].

3-10. Feeling helplessly vulnerable is a legacy of our childhood. When the strengths and privileges of adulthood fail to suffice, and we find ourselves overwhelmed by the challenges life throws at us, we tend to regress to that childish inner attitude that calls out for parental help and protection. In return we offer unquestioning childlike obedience — a seemingly small price to pay once our adult prerogatives and resources have let us down.

Certain sociological and psychological dispositions and political circumstances can bring us to surrender our physical liberty and independence to a demagogue whose empty promises we deceive ourselves into believing. More common is the custom of putting our fate in the hands of various groups, each affiliation assuring us of some brand of security in return for a given measure of servitude and self-effacement. To a very few affiliations that ostensibly offer us physical security (the military representing the limit case) we grant the right to place our lives in jeopardy, even send us to our physical death. Most armies today still go as far as legitimizing the tactic of "sacrifice," whereby a certain number of soldiers may be sent to their certain death (for instance as decoys) to provide a tactical advantage elsewhere in battle.

These various and sundry forms of regression and surrender — some would say idolatry — must eventually be seen for what they are: not merely failures of courage but abdications of consciousness, of the awareness of being alive. To the extent that we escape from threatening realities by accepting illusory solutions, we also compel ourselves to accept illusion as reality. Since consciousness means "consciousness of reality," we must realize that when we sacrifice unpleasant realities to illusion, whatever little consciousness we do have is sacrificed to the comfort the illusion provides. Branden says it thus:

> *Consciousness is man's tool for perceiving and identifying the facts of reality. It is an organ of integration. To focus is to set the integrative process in purposeful motion — by setting the appropriate goal: awareness. Nonfocus is non-integration. Evasion is willful disintegration, the act of subverting the proper function of consciousness, of setting the cognitive function in reverse and reducing the contents of one's mind to disconnected, unintegrated fragments that are forbidden to confront one another.*
>
> *Man's life and well-being depend upon his maintaining a proper cognitive contact with reality — and this requires a full mental focus, maintained as a way of life.* (Branden, *Psychology of Self-Esteem*, 45.)

3-12. Alvin Toffler, in his book *Future Shock*, largely underestimates man's adaptive capacity. (I would love to be able to think of society or even individual man as capable of being shocked out of complacency for longer than it takes to find a fast fix and soothing escapist balm.) Dislocation and discontent are soon swamped by the larger movements of inertia and apathy. We adapt passively despite ourselves. As our insulation from reality grows thicker, we become impervious to larger and larger shocks. Leonard expresses it this way:

> *We are so numbed, so inured to feelings that the creators of current movies and television dramas must resort to the most extreme tactics to make any sort of*

impression on us — the shotgun blast in the face, the thud of a pistol butt on the back of the neck. So horror and terror and torture become staples in our family fare, rated "G," safe for children, perhaps their safest way of learning not to feel. (Leonard, *The Transformation*, 156.)

Death is the ultimate shock. It rips away the carnal insulation keeping what there is of our sensibilities intact, mercilessly exposing us to the unthinkable. On the other hand, we do know from the literature and from life that sudden changes in life circumstances — good or for bad — can trigger what is psychologically known as "anomie," whereby people lose their bearings in reality and as a result sometimes even commit suicide. Such people tend to define themselves generally in terms of externals, of their environmental circumstances and of how others consider them. They become severely stressed when a change in their individual fates causes their relationship to society to change abruptly. The more everyone is affected by changes, the more we feel consoled and cushioned from the blow, especially those of us who have completely surrendered our individuality to the collective. Then again, society can't protect us forever. Any change tends to throw us back on our own inner resources as Leonard notes:

If numbness offers no real sanctuary, awakening promises shock and vertigo. Added to the Gift that Civilization has bequeathed us is the intolerable pain of the gap between what we could be and what we are. We all feel that now, but some fail to recognize it for what it is, and try to find something or someone to use as a scapegoat for what exists in them. I am under no illusions. When I curse the old culture, I curse that culture in me. When I hope for Transformation, I hope that I may be transformed. And sometimes it is hard to hope. (Ibid., 158-9.)

Those of us who can mobilize our wits to confront the challenge of change are ourselves changed in the process. This kind of self-mobilization, this rising to the challenge, unfailingly provides an enhanced sense of existence since a successfully met challenge requires us to function at least for a time at a higher energy level. It requires us to somewhat reorganize our inner way of responding, including our attitudes towards ourselves and towards life. But how far-reaching are these inner changes and what kind of changes in a man's life could galvanize him to the limits of his potential?

3-14. There are few events more ridiculous or hypocritical than modern funerals. Under the pretext of "honoring the dead," the corpse, a now obsolete and discarded receptacle, is treated as though just asleep. It is placed in a sumptuous casket, often costing thousands of dollars, and is promptly buried in the ground where it can benefit no one. Out of consideration to the fancied comfort of the corpse, the casket is lowered ever so carefully into the earth. The slightest jiggling would jar the nerves of the onlookers, so the gathering is often dispersed, even before the coffin is lowered. They are spared the sound of earth and stones striking the casket: anything to cushion shock and deaden awareness. The need for this charade is pitiful, but serves to remind us that the gap between the living and the dead in terms of courage, awareness and all-around contact with reality is constantly shrinking.

— Chapter 4 —

4-2. The beatific abandon of ego-identity, so popular in the East and in some current spiritual attitudes, breeds the kind of weakness, passivity and lack of discrimination that amounts to an evolutionary dead end. One of the more common and worrying effects of such volatile states, especially when induced by drugs or guru-worship, is heightened suggestibility — the enhancement of the already marked tendency to see pattern and meaning in too facile a manner. This often leads to the most bizarre and delusory theories.

4-6. The following thought-provoking comments of Jung prepare the reader for the notion that the cosmos is composed of interconnecting layers of reality of vastly varying levels of materiality, and that body and soul — apparently irreconcilable, at least from the body's point of view — are material precipitates of something finer yet:

> It was universally believed in the Middle Ages as well as in the Graeco-Roman world that the soul is a substance. Indeed, mankind as a whole has held this belief from its earliest beginnings, and it was left for the second half of the nineteenth century to develop a "psychology" without the soul. Under the influence of scientific materialism, everything that could not be seen with the eyes or touched with the hands was held in doubt; such things were even laughed at because of their supposed affinity with metaphysics. Nothing was considered "scientific" or admitted to be true unless it could be perceived by the senses or traced back to physical causes. This radical change of view did not begin with philosophical materialism, for the way was being prepared long before. When the spiritual catastrophe of the Reformation put an end to the Gothic Age with its impetuous yearning for the heights, its geographical confinement, and its restricted view of the world, the vertical outlook of the European mind was forthwith intersected by the horizontal outlook of modern times. Consciousness ceased to grow upward, and grew instead in breadth of view, as well as in knowledge of the terrestrial globe (Carl Gustav Jung, *Modern Man in Search of a Soul*, translated by W. S. Dell and C. F. Baynes [New York: H.B.J., 1933], 172).

That which is finer is more alive, Jung reminds us in this passage, and thus it represents energy in relation to that which is materially coarser. If we aspire to a less restricted understanding of existence, we must learn to acquire the perspective of that which is finer — to become one with it through our inner capacities. He hints at a direction for inner searching. But first we must become convinced of the organized existence of higher levels of reality:

> This instance may serve to show that the idea of an autonomous spirit whose existence is taken for granted has not died out everywhere in Europe or become a mere fossil left over from the Middle Ages.
> If we keep this in mind, we can perhaps summon up the courage to consider the

possibility of a "psychology with the psyche" — that is, of a field of study based on the assumption of an autonomous psyche. We need not be alarmed at the unpopularity of such an undertaking, for to postulate mind is no more fantastic than to postulate matter. Since we have literally no idea of the way in which what is psychic can arise from physical elements, and yet cannot deny the reality of psychic events, we are free to frame our assumptions the other way about for once, and to hold that the psyche arises from a spiritual principle which is as inaccessible to our understanding as matter. To be sure, this will not be a modern psychology, for to be modern is to deny such a possibility. For better or worse, therefore, we must turn back to the teachings of our forefathers, for they it was who made such assumptions. The ancient view held that spirit was essentially the life of the body, the life-breath, or a kind of life-force which assumed spatial and corporeal form at birth or after conception, and left the dying body again after the final breath. The spirit in itself was considered as a being without extension, and because it existed before taking corporeal form and afterwards as well, it was considered as timeless and hence immortal. (Ibid., 180-1.)

4-8. Eventually, there arises in the mind of every thinking person the question of how it is that man, of divine origin, finds himself bound and restricted by matter. Cosmology is the study of how pure, spiritual, infinite essence descends, creating worlds, time and beings. Each religion and tradition has its own version — its own cosmology. And while all these doctrines vary somewhat, they all agree that man (and existence as a whole) originates in a higher, refined, non-material plane — in unity. The hope they offer for overcoming the suffering that stems from separation, restriction, constraint and limitation is to be sought in the study of how matter coalesces and crystallizes from spirit, and in the struggle to understand the secret of why and how all this is in man's own best interest.

4-9. We are recognizing that our resources have been badly misman-aged. We have flagrantly ignored our collective dependence on environmen-tal matter. Ecological forces are beginning to venge themselves on us, no longer only at a regional level, but increasingly on a planetary scale (e.g., global heating, ozone layer depletion and general air, water and land pollu-tion).

One hazard we seldom think about — perhaps because it comes into play only at intervals tens of thousands of years apart — is the cataclysm of asteroid impact. A moderately sized mass of one cubic mile packs the wallop of thousands of H-bombs, enough to eliminate mammalian life and induce an ice age. Pole shift is another catastrophe that some researchers consider almost imminent. Thus even if mankind were capable of keeping its balance indefinitely, we would still not have unlimited time to develop all the means necessary to assure our survival.

4-10. The question remains as to whether the cards are cosmically stacked against this possibility. Could it be that inherent in the relationship between intelligence and matter there exists a checks and balances system preventing mankind from exploiting or abusing matter beyond a certain point by confronting him with an inevitably resulting pathology on the various levels of his life? Doesn't our conventional, pretentious and superficial form of intelligence repeatedly and unfailingly venge itself upon us through the all-too-"human" phenomena of mutual intolerance, conflict and strife whenever the extant multiplicity of interests and points of view diverge sufficiently from one another and from the requirements of material reality to reach an inevitable point of irreconcilability? Is not the Tower of Babel our living reality?

4-11. The nation that at one time most personified this promise is Brazil. During the 1960s a country displaying more optimism concerning its technical, industrial and social future would be hard to imagine. Brazil perceived itself to be in the throes of unstoppable expansion and was confident of becoming the bread basket of the world. The population was proud of its Brazilian identity and the huge potential of its enormous, fertile, resource-rich territory. Thanks to an unshakable confidence in the forces of progress, its realization seemed to be just around the corner. Social, racial and political tolerance were the watchwords of the day.

It was almost impossible to provoke anger in a Brazilian during these years. The outlook then was positive; pettiness made no sense. Even the inhabitants of the *favellas* displayed the patience of saints whose suffering and vision were going to be rewarded by a social and economic order thought to be in the process of shedding its past evils and deprivations. Everyone from the youngest to the oldest, from the richest to the poorest, felt he was on a winning team and willingly put aside whatever grievances he might have harbored as trivial and unworthy. The eyes of the world were on Brazil as the portent and harbinger of a new age of plenty. This incipient elation found expression in the titles of new Brazilian business enterprises, and even in the renaming of old ones with company names that almost without regard to the nature of the business activity in question proudly bore the word "Tecnologia" as a symbol of participation and identification with the miracle to come.

It is hard to say exactly when the bubble burst and disillusionment and depression began to set in. But by the 1980s the atmosphere in Brazil had completely changed. Civil disorder and rioting, unheard of during the preceding period, became commonplace. Understanding why and how this situation deteriorated is less crucial than recognizing the all-important and all-pervading effect that hope, or its lack, can have on people everywhere.

— Chapter 5 —

5-10. The popular discussion on whether insects, animals or machines display intelligence steers us away from the crucial issue of what kind of intelligence is involved. That such intelligence sometimes seems to come uncomfortably close to rivaling that which we commonly take to be human intelligence should serve as a caution.

Also, we often fantasize about disconcertingly man-like machines displaying "artificial intelligence." Ironically, the concrete realization of these fantasies is inevitable. When our machines end up aping us, we will finally be confronted with the mechanicality we ourselves display. For the thought men normally exhibit — the reflective thought of distracted intelligence — is merely mechanistic, regardless of what fantasies it realizes for us.

The difference between insect and animal intelligence is considerable, but it is more a difference of degree than of kind. This is not to say that there are not qualitative aspects of even a striking nature — for instance, the emotions plainly discernible in some animals. Yet even these "qualitative" differences can be shown to derive from the hierarchical synthesis of behavioral building blocks of a lower order, as perhaps animal emotions can be shown to be an elaboration of the insect's instinctive sense of itself in its "fight or flight" mode.

It sometimes frightens people to think that what we call human intelligence, along with all the invention, art and knowledge this intelligence has produced, could be the result of nothing more than a massive buildup of soulless on-off switches that we share in common with insects, animals and computers. Yet when one thinks about it, simple common sense dictates that however divine human nature may be, and whatever its potential, in the material world some physical mechanism must be required to render possible the expression of that divine nature and that potential.

Thus, in spirituality our physical body is often considered a "temple" or "receptacle" that houses the spirit. Similarly, concepts and ideas — the forms of our thought that accommodate the various inputs we get from the world around us — are the forms our minds assume in seeking to meld with the highest realities we can conceive. In this way, a "spiritual" or at least non-physical entity is spawned by a physical mold. A physical "essence" has given birth to a being of materiality finer than that conventionally recognized as such — matter of the subtlety of which thought is made. This "spiritual" entity (of very fine materiality and thus of inherently higher intelligence than its mold) has the added virtue of being able to acquire an existence independent of its physical mold through the acquisition of its own structural and functional integrity. This state of maturity allows it, in its turn, to act as the mold through which a new spiritual entity of a still finer materiality can be conceived, and so on.

In the beginning, it may have seemed as though the physical nature of the essence/seed/mold would have a determining influence in the formation of the spiritual entity it would spawn — giving due respect to environmental aspects which themselves have a major role in deciding what aspects of our potential will find expression. The spiritual entity serves, in its turn, as a receptacle, for "substances" even more subtle. This suggests that not only does "environment" have a determining influence, but that just as there are levels of matter, the subtlety of which is beyond us, so the environmental realities that act on these substances are finer and more subtle still, suggesting a hierarchy of environments or "worlds."

We should further recognize that the finer the realm or world in question, the more precise and determinate that environmental influence will be. The less opportunity for deviance that is left to the receptacle, the less that is left to chance. It stands to reason that an entity with a constitution of finer materiality also has perceptions, feelings and thoughts of correspondingly higher finesse and intelligence.

5-21. Truly creative breakthroughs seldom involve more than one event, while the earmark of an "establishment" breakthrough is its more or less simultaneous discovery by different researchers in different places. For a time, at least, these radical discoveries are usually met by controversy and/or incomprehension. When realized, they tend to cause dislocations to an even greater extent than does conventional breakthrough.

Dislocation is a function of the importance of the discovery's implications concerning how we understand the material organization of our world. Such dislocation hints at the material transformations foreshadowed by discovery. Each new revelation and invention poses its own challenge to society by the new habits and social patterns it induces.

The major advances in civilization are processes that all but wreck the societies in which they occur. (Alfred North Whitehead)

5-23. In the broadest sense, it could be said that the goal, mission and destiny of the human mind is to penetrate the veil of ignorance occluding it, and arrive at a comprehensive knowledge of all the forces that operate in the knowable cosmos: in short, to master every facet of knowable reality. Sooner or later, we discover that the ability to enlarge our perspective and broaden our understanding requires more than simply collecting and collating information. A certain level of feeling or energy must be present in us to render all or even part of that information operative in our lives.

Discovery, and more specifically creative discovery, lifts our spirit by releasing us from the bonds that exist either in the outside physical world (bonds that require technical solutions for their resolution) or strictly in our own minds. We must release ourselves from these bonds from within. The dynamics of this creative process show how the limitations we encounter outside of ourselves and those we recognize as coming from within are intimately linked.

The process of creative discovery ultimately can lead to Accelerated Thought. Along with the energy that is thereby released, we ourselves may be liberated from restriction. Latent resources and potentials become actualized, bringing us ever closer to reaching the total mastery of knowledge and matter. Roger characterizes this process of self-actualization:

The mainspring of creativity appears to be the same tendency which we discover so deeply as the curative force in psychotherapy—man's tendency to actualize himself, to become his potentialities. By this I mean the directional trend which is evident in all organic and human life — the urge to expand, extend, develop, mature, the tendency to express and activate all the capacities of the organism, to the extent that such activation enhances the organism or the self. This tendency may become deeply buried under layer after layer of encrusted psychological defenses; it may be hidden behind elaborate facades which deny its existence; it is my belief however, based on my experience, that it exists in every individual and awaits only the proper conditions to be released and expressed. It is this tendency which is the primary motivation for creativity as the organism forms new relationships to the environment in its endeavor most fully to be itself. (Rogers, "Toward a theory of creativity," 11:252.)

Nonetheless, while self-actualization may be nature's goal for man, man, to be actualized, must pursue goals of his own. These goals must be relevant to his terrestrial existence and the challenge posed to his spirit by matter, temporality and mortality.

5-24. Without dwelling too much on the process of reflection and its inherent limitations as a tool for penetrating closer to the heart of reality, it would be worthwhile even at this early stage to raise the question of self-reflection. A significant part of the time our reflection — our everyday thought — is directed back towards ourselves and our immediate, often petty, concerns.

We reflect upon ourselves as discrete, independent agents, rather than recognizing ourselves as integral parts of a mysterious continuum which is the larger reality to which we rightfully belong, and in which we should aspire to participate. Organic self-observation permits such participation and will be shown later to be one of the noble effects of Accelerated Thought. Meanwhile we separate ourselves from this continuum, creating our own restricted reality which is a fiction belying the total unity and integrity of existence.

The principal consequence of reflective thought is that in perceiving ourselves as separate entities — "egos" independent of that higher reality of which coarse matter is only an expression or projection — we perceive ourselves (in a measure corresponding to that separation) as being of that same coarse matter. Yet we are potentially integrated parcels of awareness in a sentient universe — concentrations of pure conscious intelligence.

The fundamental vanity of the tendency to separation that derives from reflection, particularly self-reflection, shows up best in ego-phenomena. Self-importance, pride, arrogance and all the other forms of pettiness are simply emotional crystallizations, the intellectual equivalents of which are personal opinion and conventional knowledge.

All that we do is touched with the ocean, yet we remain on the shore of what we know. (Richard Wilbur)

5-25. Not only is there a whole literature on the subject of creativity, there are even university courses that attempt to deal with the subject, all the way from theoretical research to attempting to enhance the creative powers of students.

Less well known are businesses based on creativity-related disciplines and ideologies. These enterprises vary from the one-person business to small organizations, sometimes contained within larger corporate entities and consulting companies. Participants are usually middle and, less often, high-level executives in such organizations as industrial or commercial companies, institutes, associations, utilities, government ministries, etc.

While their activities and objectives are far from those of Accelerated Thought, their intent does point in a roughly similar direction. Creative bull sessions can include mental and physical limbering up exercises, exercises for reducing inhibition, and exercises for maximizing the subjects' associational involvement with practical or hypothetical problems. One thing almost all schools of creativity have in common, besides a batch-processing view of creativity, is the group concept of the process. It is as though the sharpening of creative vision requires constant associational and motivational stimulation from others.

After encouraging members to suspend judgment about ideas generated by the group, they are asked to offer their uninhibited input toward the solution of some problem or the creation of some new possibility. The opportunity to exhibit one's prowess before others and the prospects that one's ideas, sheltered from judgmentalism, will be appreciated and used suggests work conditions that could be considered ideal when compared with the discouraging ones we most often encounter. Such conditions, to the extent that practitioners succeed in producing them, are severely isolated in time and space. Any creative sparks that happen to coalesce from such a sheltered, inspirational pool will, against the wet blanket of everyday distracted, labyrinthine reality, have little more chance of implementation than the proverbial "snowball in hell." Furthermore, environments designed to shield participants from distraction have all lacked one principal feature — prepared individuals. In the absence of individuals relatively untainted by convention, who manifest true sparks of individuality, there will be no true affinity between participants and environments meant to awaken their latent creativity.

Unfortunately, despite the claims of certain particularly aggressive practitioners, these systems and seminars have found little more than marginal usefulness or acceptance. After all, even a small but consistent increase in creativity would necessarily lead to substantial improvements in efficiency and profitability. The news of such impact would spread like wildfire and transform the industrial and economic landscape before our very eyes. We'd all be clamoring to participate.

This inherently noble profession, while it has its supporters and adherents in management, tends to be reduced to entertaining and distracting executives more as a perk than anything else. Management's justification for its cost may simulate agreement with the ideological line of the creativity firm chosen, but it is a rare boss who will genuinely invite proposals that contradict his own mind set — even if such proposals do claim to be "creative." To the general chagrin of those who are professionally, intellectually or in any way committed to the promotion and encouragement of creativity, those in authority rarely pay more than lip-service to this discipline and the importance of its aspirations.

While these comments may condemn tendencies of the established creativity field, their purpose is to recognize the existence of this field and to acknowledge the wisdom accumulated in its literature. The glaring discrepancy between the material and spiritual expectations of the field compared with its inconsequential practical effects needs to be underscored. If there was ever a mouse that roared, this is it. Still, the fault perhaps lies less with shortcomings of the field and its practitioners and more with the enormous conventional forces of conservatism that express our abiding faith in the ascendancy of form and matter, and throttle our creative capacity. Even creativity specialists can be forgiven for underestimating the almost inconceivable virulence of man's attachment to the given, the banal and the status quo.

5-26. Even a modest number of successes could transform life as we know it. Ouspensky saw the implications:

Imagine that there are two or three people who are awake in the midst of a multitude of sleeping people. They will certainly know each other. But those who are asleep cannot know them. How many are they? We do not know and we cannot know until we become like them. It has been clearly said before that each man can only see on the level of his own being. But two hundred conscious people, if they existed and if they found it necessary and legitimate, could change the whole of life on earth. (Ouspensky, *In Search of the Miraculous*, 310.)

5-36. Subjectivity and cultural values plainly carry some weight in determining choices, even choices concerning utility. Nevertheless, we are all able to acknowledge the validity of an appliance having a function that is foreign to us, even if personally we have no use for such an appliance. Disagreements of this kind, when they do occur, arise mostly around inventions of marginal importance. None of us would have much trouble itemizing dozens of indispensable home objects used internationally, even if we might have trouble recognizing many of their functional components out of context. The point is that inventions responding to real human needs become universally compelling once they are introduced. Technical breakthroughs that take new account of fundamental natural phenomena bestow power upon those who command them, obliging the rest of us to master the new art in question or find ourselves at the mercy of those who are stronger by virtue of their having done so.

5-37. One occasionally hears the comment, "there's no accounting for tastes." This is often taken to mean that art and aesthetics are inherently subjective, even irrational phenomena and that no objective, quantifiable criteria for evaluation are conceivable. Yet we tend to forget that mankind still has a long way to go in technical, aesthetic and human development. Just as we aspire to attain some day to scientific theory that will account for all the phenomena of the natural world, we should also recognize that a unified theory of man, including his capacity for aesthetic appreciation, makes up an inseparable part of the knowledge we crave. But the capacity to understand directly and intuitively the precise significance of aesthetics and how they influence us, will have to wait until our inner development catches up with our external ambitions.

5-38. Lacking a rigorous and widely accepted definition of art, we are free to speculate not only on what guides artists of all kinds during the process of creating (much of which is inevitably subjective), but also on what might be the fundamental purpose of art with respect to human appreciation and inner response. Jung envisioned art as belonging to a reality more universal than our habitual, petty concerns:

> The secret of artistic creation and of the effectiveness of art is to be found in a return to the state of participation mystique — to that level of experience at which it is man who lives, and not the individual, and at which the weal or woe of the single human being does not count, but only human existence. This is why every great work of art is objective and impersonal, but none the less profoundly moves us each and all. And this is also why the personal life of the poet cannot be held essential to his art — but at most a help or a hindrance to his creative task. (Jung, Modern Man, 172.)

Could we not say that a true master of any art form should be able through his art to evoke any unequivocal response he desires from his audience, regardless of individual differences? And does not the mastery of art which attempts to evoke a response in humanity imply a profound understanding of that humanity?

5-40. Religious and spiritual disciplines suffer from much the same matter-free paradox but find it an even greater embarrassment. Let us take for granted, for argument's sake, that some such systems do possess total truth, even though this truth may be couched in terms, images and languages varying from one system to another. And let us note that this truth concerns the nature of the cosmos and of man: the how and why of Creation, and of our destiny. Let us further assume that this truth has the power to transform those who adapt to it. Let us also, for the sake of argument, grant the efficacy of this influence in those who make the necessary sacrifices and leaps of faith and assume that they do gain admittance to the kingdom of heaven.

We can still ask why so few reach this prescribed goal, and why the proponents of these doctrines are so helpless in the face of matter that all their material support must come through the mundane strivings and contributions of the faithful rather than through the practical application of divine knowledge itself — the working of miracles — as reported in legend. What religion commands through its wisdom and knowledge the means for directly influencing matter? Why must religion defer to science when it comes to the manipulation of matter and the accomplishment of even such banal feats as transportation and communication? Isn't matter also part of G-d's domain?

In pursuit of our salvation, however we manage to understand it, we will have to come to terms with the coarse world of matter as an integral part of whatever higher reality we choose to explore. Concerning the few who do manage to enter higher worlds without mastering the substance of this lower one, their reward may be worth the risk of their endeavor. But how about the millions of faithful who fail to make the grade? For them might the longer road of truly intensive engagement with matter ultimately prove to be the shortest route to liberty and paradise? Remember the tortoise and the hare?

Putting aside for a moment the reasonable claim that religion does not contradict or detract from science, it could be said without exaggeration that the whole field of practical knowledge pertaining to matter has been left forfeit to the unbelievers and the impious. Indeed, religion does not detract from the scientist's effort. To the contrary, it most often gives him strength. But this is only as regards science as we know it — conventional science.

"Breakthrough" science, with Accelerated Thought as its motor, demands that all our inner resources, all our energy, all our attention, be withdrawn from normal everyday interests and be concentrated on the problem at hand. For it is here that the belief in mind over matter can bring tangible results. As a bonus, in transforming the world we transform ourselves. The scope of that transformation is limited only to the scope of our own vision and daring. Thoreau acknowledges the discrepancy between what man credits himself with having done and what remains for him to do:

> *The whole ground of human life seems to some to have been gone over by their predecessors, both the heights and the valleys, and all things to have been cared for. Hippocrates has even left directions how we should cut our nails; that is, even with the ends of our fingers, neither shorter nor longer. Undoubtedly the very tedium and ennui which presume to have exhausted the variety and joys of life are as old as Adam. But man's capacities have never been measured; nor are we to judge of what he can do by any precedents, so little has been tried.* (Thoreau, "Walden," 112.)

While Thoreau feels that we haven't begun to scratch the surface of our potential, Berg goes a step further and suggests to what extent mind was meant to prevail over matter:

> *The possibility, for instance, that consciousness might play a role in the process of celestial activity remains well beyond the realm of comprehension of all but a few of the most radical metaphysical thinkers. The vast majority of traditional*

scientists, clergy and laymen would not entertain for a moment the idea that the human mind could influence the phenomena of physical reality. Yet, the Scripture asks us to accept without question that consciousness can enable certain individuals to transcend the laws of physics. Who, or what, are we to believe? (Berg, *Power of Aleph Beth*, 1:154.)

5-41. Buckminster Fuller believed that man's salvation lay in what he called "the design revolution." The design he had in mind involved the external molding of existing matter in radical, unconventional ways to respond to man's needs. He had an unbounded faith in the potential of intelligence and in breakthrough thinking. He shared Frank Lloyd Wright's admiration for the new materials that made new designs possible, and like Wright he put his faith mainly in the genius of externally forming matter. Neither he nor Wright foresaw the full importance of the transformation of matter itself (i.e., of form inherent in matter).

5-43. Paradoxically, abstractions enjoying no clearly established grounding in reality can be singularly useful in trying to deduce the form and function of macro-level phenomena, from the birth and death of celestial bodies to the "shape" of higher dimensions and parallel worlds. In fact, inferences of this kind based on the slimmest of empirical observations, but enjoying a forceful boost from intuition, can turn out to be powerful inductive tools for solving problems involving the matter of our immediate world. In other words:

Those who refuse to go beyond fact rarely get as far as fact; and anyone who has studied the history of science knows that almost every step therein has been made by . . . the invention of a hypothesis which, though verifiable, often had little foundation to start with. (T.H.Huxley)

Without the relational tools of abstraction, we would be completely hobbled in our ability to speculate and extrapolate, to deduce and induce. Yet the psychological phenomenon of certainty, so crucial to the energy-releasing process of Accelerated Thought, and so germane even to the Eureka experience, presupposes that we come into direct sensory contact with the phenomena under study. As does McClintock:

Since her days as a graduate student, she had always carried out the most laborious parts of her investigations herself, leaving none of the labor, however onerous or routine, to others. In this she did as almost all beginning scientists do. But most scientists, as they mature, learn to delegate more and more of the routine work to others. There are, of course, exceptions, and Emerson, who, according to Harriet Creighton, "didn't regard anything as routine," was one. He prided himself on doing his own work. For McClintock, more than pride was involved. Her virtuosity resided in her capacity to observe, and to process and interpret what she observed. As she grew older, it became less and less possible to delegate any part of her work; she was developing skills that she could hardly identify herself, much less impart to others.

Perhaps the answer, once again, depends on the intimate and total knowledge she sought about each and every plant. A colleague once remarked that she

*could write the "autobiography" of each plant she worked with. Her respect for
the unfathomable workings of the mind was matched by her regard for the
complex workings of the plant, but she was confident that with due attentive-
ness, she could trust the intuitions the one produced of the other. In the years
to come, that confidence would become a source of vital sustenance.* (Keller,
A Feeling for the Organism, 103-5; reprinted with permission.)

It is only the incredibly fine-grained nature of physical reality that
provides us with the immediate, vital and true impressions that, framed and
conditioned by our conceptual matrices (for no amount of observation will
help us if we have no notion of what we are looking at) can awaken the
essential, subliminal recognition of reality of which we as human beings are
"instinctively" capable. The closer our perceptions (guided by abstract
concepts) correspond to one another and to reality, the more likely this
instinctive-intuitive recognition is likely to be evoked from the evolutionary
record of existence impressed upon the subconscious memory within essence.

We tend to think in terms of animal life whenever "instinctive" knowledge is mentioned. Natural science is full of the lore of how plants and animals
adapt remarkably to their environments, often displaying a mastery of
engineering, architecture and physics that man can envy. But instinct in man
and in animals means more than we normally realize:

*A high regard for the unconscious psyche as a source of knowledge is by no
means such a delusion as our Western rationalism likes to suppose. We are
inclined to assume that, in the last resort, all knowledge comes from without.
Yet today we know for certain that the unconscious contains contents which
would mean an immeasurable increase of knowledge if they could only be made
conscious. Modern investigation of animal instinct, as for example in insects,
has brought together a rich fund of empirical findings which show that if a man
acted as certain insects do he would possess a higher intelligence than at
present. It cannot, of course, be proved that insects have conscious knowledge,
but common-sense cannot doubt that their unconscious action-patterns are
psychic functions. Man's unconscious likewise contains all the patterns of life
and behaviour inherited from his ancestors, so that every human child, prior to
consciousness, is possessed of a potential system of adapted psychic functioning.* (Jung, *Modern Man*, 185.)

As life goes by, we tend to lose sight of the existence of the amazingly
complex unconscious knowledge that enables plants, animals and humans to
digest their food, circulate their blood, resist disease and survive. These life
processes and the physiological structures that accomplish them are themselves embodiments of the cosmic law that shaped them and shapes all reality.
These we are reluctant to acknowledge:

*It would be positively grotesque for us to call this immense system of the
experience of the unconscious psyche an illusion, for our visible and tangible*

body itself is just such a system. It still carries within it the discernible traces of primeval evolution, and it is certainly a whole that functions purposively — for otherwise we could not live. (Ibid., 187.)

Human instinct includes an aeons-old record of how to survive not only through the plant and animal aspects of our makeup, but also as human beings. And so our humanness also can be said to be largely hidden in the subconscious, essential form of survival-related knowledge that has herein informally and perhaps somewhat irreverently been called "instinct." But in our development as a species, if it can be said that we have realized most of our plant and animal potential (by virtue of the ascendancy over the vegetable and animal worlds that nature has bestowed upon us), the human component of our potential — the "intelligence" mentioned earlier — is still mostly hidden. In this connection, Koestler makes deprecating reference to Kohler's theory of "psycho-physical isomorphism," which comes very close to this essence theory of intelligence, yet unknowingly does so in a way that almost validates isomorphism. (Koestler, *The Act of Creation*, 592-93.)

Owing to his ignorance of the principle of "distraction" that governs conventional consciousness, Koestler, in his skepticism, passes over a major key to the understanding of creativity. He overlooks the fact that without direct conscious contact with the realities around us, we are thrown back on the limitation of reflective thought. This includes many faculties that he mentions — including "scanning," "coding," "abstraction," etc. — and some that he doesn't. While these lower thought faculties are indispensable to us in the struggle to free ourselves of the tyranny of distracted consciousness, they are nothing more than evolutionary precursors of Accelerated Thought that springs from the subconscious.

Undoubtedly, there is nothing in the world more underestimated than the richness and potential of this dimension of the human subconscious. Nothing is more worth awakening to and rendering manifest. Nor is anything more natural than the process whereby impressions of environmental reality awaken within us this unconscious record, nor anything more human than our use of ideation and intuition to interpret conceptually and amplify these impressions to accelerate this awakening.

The mind of man is capable of anything, because everything is in it, all the past as well as the future. (Joseph Conrad)

While the idea that certain universal symbols are latent within us and resonate into awareness when we encounter corresponding forms in life and in art supports this notion of essence, in a way it also contradicts it. Aspects of the cultural world can awaken forms dormant within us — just as living forms are made to emerge from a seed when aroused from inertness by a corresponding external fertilizing agent. Mirrored in this we see the larger pattern whereby impressions coming in from the environment push our essence towards self-realization. Man the essence — the sleeping seed — is prodded into cosmic consciousness by the fertilizing agent of cosmic energy that mates with essence in all its facets. We are called upon to awaken to ourselves — to become ourselves. The troubling aspect of the universal symbols we call "archetypes" is that they are colored by conditioning that compromises their "universality." Analysis can filter for cultural and individual bias, but this is more art than science. Yet it should not surprise us that symbols emerging from deep within essence should impact so strongly on the carapace of our sleep — our "collective unconscious" — arousing us to a feeling of urgency of awakening to cosmic reality. After all, the sleep of our daily distracted consciousness is analogous to death, while the total waking experience of cosmic consciousness, evoked by archetypes, is analogous to life — the real life for which man is destined and that has been calling to him from myth and tradition of every ilk.

In the coming world they will not ask me, "Why were you not Moses?" They will ask me, "Why were you not Zusya?" (Zusya, Talmud)

5-45. The word "mineral" must seem odd in a list of life forms, even a list of broad classifications. Yet if we think of life as a state of Being and the different life forms as representing levels of Being, this usage begins to make sense if "mineral" is taken as the lowest rung in a continuum within the animated cosmic hierarchy.

The level of activity or inertness of an "inanimate" object, such as a rock, is an indication of the level of its Being. Just as some human beings can be seen to have more Being than others (some might call it vitality, presence or substance) some minerals seem more active, more "alive" than others. We know from chemistry that some elements are immensely more reactive than others and still others more conductive of electricity. Minerals are a major item in the diet of plants, and different levels of plant life require different minerals in varying proportions. Ouspensky recognizes that the hierarchy of materiality is a hierarchy of intelligence, consciousness and life itself:

We must now realize that the density of vibrations and the density of matter express many other properties of matter. For instance, till now we have said nothing about the intelligence or consciousness of matter. Meanwhile the speed of vibrations of a matter shows there is nothing dead or inanimate in nature. Everything in its own way is intelligent and conscious. Only this consciousness and intelligence is expressed in a different way on different levels of being — that is, on different scales. But you must understand once and for all that nothing is dead or inanimate in nature, there are simply different degrees of animation and different scales. (Ouspensky, In Search of the Miraculous, 317.)

5-46. Wonder is something we experience only rarely. It represents a momentary change in the way we feel about life and about ourselves. Accordingly, it is much more difficult to evoke than other classes of feeling. Epithets such as "oceanic feeling," "awe," "astonishment," "euphoria," "elation" and "reverence" are sometimes used to express wonder. Some aspects are:

• a sense of harmony, beauty, at-oneness and peace • a sense of belonging to a larger, merciful, all-embracing reality • a sense of being totally loved and cared for • a sense of loving all existence, the bad along with the good • a sense of intimate connection with everything • a sense of total freedom and well-being • a sense of certainty about one's existence and destiny • a sense of imminent divinity.

Wonder is triggered by different things at different times for different individuals, but most often quoted are the witnessing of birth, falling in love, a beautiful sunset, awesome scenery, viewing the earth from space, music, being "reborn" to religion, a "near death" experience, jogging, meditation, etc.

What most characterizes wonder is the unusually deep sense of appreciation — the emotional-aesthetic aspect — of a total, if brief, involvement in a peak or Eureka experience. Such an experience implies a high degree of integration of all our sensibilities and faculties so that all our energy and attention (everything we see, hear, feel, think and sense) participate, at least momentarily, in one single, direct, experiential event that changes our emotional perspective. It is as though momentarily we become a monolithic receptacle for a single, all-embracing, all-inclusive taste of some aspect of higher existence from which we are ordinarily cut off and yet to which we feel we belong.

A residue lingers for a time and leaves us with only filaments of our connection with that higher reality. As we return slowly to our ordinary state of segmented perception, we still savor, reflect and "wonder" at the experience.

Mihaly Csikszentmihalyi, in *FLOW* (New York: Harper Perennial, 1991) and in other works, refers to "optimal experience" as "autotelic" (activity for its own sake) and recommends it as the path to happiness and development. "Flow" derives from activities that are totally engrossing because they seem to be a near-perfect match for our current interests and abilities. A feeling of well-being is generated from our complete sense of competence and appropriateness. But optimizing experience implies more than Csikszentmihalyi seems to realize, for our potential for negative entropy and development is infinite. Likewise, the traps of distraction surpass anything men have envisioned. "Flow," like the residue of wonder, can lead up many false trails and to situations that are less than optimal. Even the satisfying flow of efficaciously moving forward largely begs the question of what activity one should be pursuing and whether or not, in joyful innocence, one is heading for a dead end.

5-47. Many psychological theories see pleasure, and erotic pleasure in particular, as the life-blood of human existence. Other theories of a more esoteric nature equate certain fine cosmic energies with sexual energy, or at least see affinities between the two. Few people would deny that it is usually pleasure (desire fulfillment) that drives us, while few pleasures are so powerful as to overwhelm us and cause us temporarily to lose our sense of identity.

This kind of self-transcendence, in contrast with the transcendence that constitutes the cornerstone of most spiritual activity, is rarely entered into as a discipline. It happens more or less fortuitously when, thanks to circumstances, there is an unusual buildup of surplus energy. As concerns sexual climax, "circumstances" are firmly backed by nature's imperatives. But we should not forget other, less biologically determined forms of pleasurable, climactic release and their transcendent aspects.

Elation can be seen as an emotional climax with fading wonder as its denouement. Unquestionably, we can lose ourselves in euphoria. Less common is the mental ecstasy of sudden, overdue discovery in which many pieces of a puzzle fall into place after much effort. For a moment we forget ourselves before the elegance of the higher order that is revealed. Depending upon our personal involvement and the implications of the discovery, this can trigger an emotional high. Combined, this characterizes the "quality" of the Eureka experience.

That we can lose ourselves in pleasure (physical, emotional and intellectual) and that, when we are not lost in it, we are pursuing and competing for it, suggests that the key to overcoming separation and conflict between people and nations lies in gaining continuing access to higher energy and the separation-annulling ecstasy it brings. The activity that generates the capacity for continuously receiving this energy is Accelerated Thought.

A climax — a sudden, pleasurable discharge of energy — is the planting of a seed aimed at producing the fruit that bears new seeds. In science, these plantings are the insights that lead to discoveries (fruit) and new hypotheses (seeds). The sustained connection with a higher reality — Accelerated Thought — rather than producing momentary discharges (short-circuits) leads to ongoing energizing, transformation and self-realization. This is the difference between a brief taste of paradise and paradise itself. The holistic science to emerge from Project Mind, in piercing all of nature's secrets — in conquering matter — will complete science's mission, breaking the endless cycle of "seed-fruit-seed."

5-48. An aspect of the idea of transformation comes disguised in the notion of "sublimation." Freud, extending his idea that "libido" is the motive behind our actions, suggests that our more refined modes of expression — creativity and spirituality in particular — are substitutions for repressed sexual energies.

As valid as it is conceptually to connect vital energy, sex and the various ways we seek fulfillment, we tend to take things the wrong way. The commonly accepted notion of sublimation assumes that sexual fulfillment is the most elemental and ideal (if not always the socially most desirable) expression of our energy, and that higher expressions represent the frustration of our more natural drives. This perspective presupposes that we are, first and foremost, animals, and supports the exclusively "bottom-up," Darwinian view of evolution. It denies the idea that we have a higher origin. It negates the idea of a divinely created essence and of a higher calling. It asserts that whatever meaning we may discover belongs exclusively to the external universe and that no corresponding inner truth lies buried within us to be awakened — that nothing new we discover can have any inborn correspondence allowing us the possibility of recognizing truth when we encounter it.

In short, the term "sublimation," in its conventional, psychological use, reduces us to something much less than creatures conceived in the image of G-d. Behold how a popular theory can empower a simple word to help enslave our spirits and deflect us from our destiny. How many such words embedded in a culture does it take to weave an ironclad force-field inhibiting the inspiration that might otherwise lead our species to restriction-free salvation?

— Chapter 6 —

6-4. Following is an intriguing comment on intuition:

He said that the feeling everyone knows as 'intuition' is the activation of our link with intent. And since sorcerers deliberately pursue the understanding and strengthening of that link, it could be said that they intuit everything unerringly and accurately. Reading omens is commonplace for sorcerers — mistakes happen only when personal feelings intervene and cloud the sorcerers' connecting link with intent. Otherwise their direct knowledge is totally accurate and functional. (Carlos Castaneda, *Power of Silence* [United Kingdom: Black Swan Books, 1988], 31.)

A related passage from the same work reveals the core of intuition with which "intent" can connect us:

Don Juan asserted that the reason for man's cynicism and despair is the bit of silent knowledge left in him, which does two things: one, it gives man an inkling of his ancient connection with the source of everything; and two, it makes man feel that without this connection, he has no hope of peace, of satisfaction, of attainment. (Ibid., 157.)

Castaneda also comments on convention as that which cuts us off from intuition and direct perception:

He said that possibly every human being under normal living conditions had had at one time or another the opportunity to break away from the bindings of convention. He stressed that he did not mean social convention, but the conventions binding our perception. A moment of elation would suffice to move our assemblage points and break our conventions. So, too, a moment of fright, ill health, anger, or grief. But ordinarily, whenever we had a chance to move our assemblage points we became frightened. Our religious, academic, social backgrounds would come into play. They would assure our safe return to the flock; the return of our assemblage points to the prescribed position of normal living.

He told me that all the mystics and spiritual teachers I knew of had done just that: their assemblage points moved, either through discipline or accident, to a certain point; and then they returned to normalcy carrying a memory that lasted them a lifetime. (Ibid., 215.)

The key opportunity to "break away from the bindings of convention" is that moment when one child in a million, facing the prospect of disillusionment (more correctly, illusionment), refuses the imposition of convention, affirms the validity of paradise from which he came and declares that it's a lie — "the emperor is naked."

It is useful to think of intuition as the resulting narrow track of inner awareness — a vein in our psyche that has survived the debilitating effects of socialization — which permits the restricted yet direct exercise of consciousness. It is that remnant of consciousness that allows furtive glimpses of reality to touch those aspects of existence where we have somehow remained uncompromised. When it functions, it acts as a channel joining this still operative part of our essence — that "bit of silent knowledge" — with some external reality, thereby connecting us to that reality, to ourselves, and to what Castaneda calls "intent:" the focus of the experience.

6-6. As regards meaning and what is possible to mankind or even to an individual man, society leads us to believe that what is considered reasonable and possible by social convention corresponds to reality, and that we are pathetically limited beings who, regardless of social or political system, must submit to "the will of the people" as incarnated in the "mind set" of the current social paradigm.

About the limitations that society would have us believe about ourselves, Harman and Rheingold have composed a list of "implicit premises" that have "gone unchallenged until recently." These include the notion that mind is only a function of the brain, that knowledge can be acquired only through the senses, that quality can always be reduced to quantity, that there is a clear distinction between objective fact and subjective experience, that freedom of choice is an illusion, that genius is rare and IQ is a fair measure of native intelligence, and that extrasensory type phenomena have no basis in reality. (Harman and Rheingold, *Higher Creativity*, 60-61.)

6-12. *A study using 62 characteristics as measuring factors was made by Torrance (1965) to obtain teachers' concepts of the ideal pupil. The study indicated that the teachers had a great deal of ambivalence toward the kind of pupil who could be described as highly creative. Among the 62 characteristics, the teachers rated independence in thinking second, independence in judgment 19th and courage 29th. It was far more important to teachers that children be courteous than that they be courageous. It was also more important that children do their work on time, be industrious, be obedient, be popular among their peers and have other traits of this kind than that they be courageous. Because of a limited concept of giftedness and an emphasis on academic prowess, it is quite natural that the child who answers questions correctly,* *produces what he is told and knows what the textbook says is considered by teachers to be superior. The creative child often fails to fit this model.* (T. A. Razik, *Explorations in Creativity* [New York: Harper & Row, 1967], 305.)

6-13. *Numerous precautions are taken, beginning in nursery school (itself hardly an individualizing institution), to avoid elaboration of personal discernment and to instill fear of separation from the group. Group acceptance is stressed through formal and informal popularity contests, teamwork and polling. Education altogether stresses group instruction. For instance, the size of his classes and the class average, not the qualities of individual pupils, are often considered the measure of the teacher. The student himself is so much treated as a part of the group that, except in higher education (which is only partly immune), he may be automatically promoted with his group regardless of individual achievement or variation.* (Ernest van den Haag, "Of Happiness and Despair We Have No Measure," in *Mass Culture*, Bernard Rosenberg and David White, eds. [The Free Press of Glencoe, 1957].)

6-15. According to certain traditions, smell is the only sense left somewhat intact after our expulsion from the Garden of Eden, which helps explain the widespread ceremonial use of incense and our often extreme susceptibility to fragrance. Robbins offers intimations of this:

Fragrance is a conduit for our earliest memories, on the one hand; on the other, it may accompany us as we enter the next life. In between, it creates mood, stimulates fantasy, shapes thought and modifies behavior. It is our strongest link to the past, our closest fellow traveler to the future. Prehistory, history and the afterworld, all are its domain. Fragrance may well be the signature of eternity. (Robbins, *Jitterbug Perfume*, 257.)

6-17. Creativity and genius are often associated with mental and emotional disorder. It should be obvious that in some people the inclination to create stems in part from some serious maladjustment that, along with a constellation of factors, drives them to try to "change things." Fieve comments:

Creative people are inclined to be individualists, and there is a tendency for others to interpret their unusual behavioral patterns as emotional disturbances rather than as unique behavior of people of potential genius. Their single-mindedness of endeavor is also characteristic of many psychiatric conditions. However in the emotionally disturbed neurotic or psychotic, these endeavors are usually unintelligible and disorganized. A well-organized artistic production does not result. In contrast, the extraordinarily talented person, no matter how bizarre his ideas usually finds someone who can understand the thrust and genius of his work.

Of course, there have been geniuses who were psychotic. It does not follow, however, that because some artists develop psychosis or neurosis all others have this same potential. The offbeat nature of the artist's thinking, his unrelatedness to conventional thought or achievement, and quite often the disturbing elements in his work combine to sustain the myth that a genius is also mad. (Ronald R. Fieve, Moodswing, *[New York: Bantam Books, 1981], 37.)*

In many creative people, psychological disturbances derive more from the stresses stemming from the redeployment of psychic energy during the creative process than anything in their own nature or background. In addition, the purity of motive behind a given creative urge is always of interest because this has important implications for the results of the urge. Ulterior or neurotic motives do not lead very far in the direction of truth, even if the exceptional circumstance of reasonably favorable terrain for creativity should occur and permit expression of this kind of drive.

The touchstone of authentic creativity is the quality of awareness involved. To be driven to create without knowledge of where or why augurs poorly for one's inner development in spite of apparent results. For those rare few with spectacular natural gifts, nothing is more important than the need to understand the meaning and purpose of those gifts. Otherwise, instead of becoming a tool for realizing their destiny, these gifts risk enslaving them through the vanity, greed and weakness that have led to the derangement and downfall of many a genius.

— Chapter 7 —

7-12. Conditions of life being what they are, we are allowed to develop any given capacity only to a limited extent. If we concentrate in one direction we necessarily neglect others. It is virtually impossible to be consistently diligent in all things. Popular wisdom, recognizing this, encourages us to choose and pursue a personal life aim — putting all our eggs into one "vocational" basket in the hope that we pick the one "basket" that most suits the "eggs" destiny has seen fit to grant us.

But to excel in that which means the most to us signifies much more than the judicious use of our resources. It implies the realization of our potential — the purpose for which we were created. If man's most profound nature is deemed in the vast scale of life to be little more than trivial, then whatever goals he can conceive and in rare cases realize must be deemed correspondingly trivial, since his possibilities (or rather the limits thereof), are defined by his nature.

Our dilemma is that when we specialize, our perspective narrows — and thus we ourselves become narrow. If the choice of an aim does not mean substantially sacrificing all the other sides of ourselves, how much "overallness" can be retained without sacrificing the aim itself?

Yet, can a person truly be considered narrow if he resolutely pursues that which means most to him? Will not the depth of character and of perception that naturally develop out of heroic self-application to lifetime endeavors (however narrow they may appear at first) far outweigh in value very much more "rounded" but correspondingly more shallow personalities? And in the single-minded pursuit of his aim, narrow as it may seem to others, will a person not be forced to take account of many of the fundamentals of existence which, by the very nature of our interconnected world, bring him to broaden his perspective?

7-13. Even the best dissembler or self-deceiver can muster only limited commitment for a task his heart just isn't into. Even the strongest artificial motive is not sufficient for the inner effort necessary for generating the energy required for creative thought, let alone Accelerated Thought.

At first glance this seems like nothing more than one of nature's safeguard mechanisms to prevent the theft of cosmic energy. But when we consider that any discovery is rooted in self-discovery, we realize that we cannot discover that with which we have no affinity. In other words, we cannot possibly generate a powerful nostalgia for something that doesn't already in some real, if mysterious, way pertain to our essence.

Energy can be "stolen," or at least "borrowed" for a time, through the intensive abuse of imagination. We see this in cases of manic-depression where injudicious borrowing of energy through unrealistically anticipated rewards is repaid with interest in the coin of depression. Just as we receive the bonus of hope and a newly gained confidence in our efficaciousness when making a discovery, we pay the penalty of despair when, following failure, we lose faith in our capacities.

An extreme example of energy theft would be the wholesale abuse of such power as the imposition of one's demonic designs on others, as in the case of the Nazis. A discussion of the penalty for this level of abuse is beyond the scope of this book. Abuses of energy on any level involve the borrowing of energy from one domain and its exploitation in another. In a kind of downward transcendence often called "identification," in a short-sighted and usually unconscious strategy of survival adaptation we allow ourselves to be carried away or lost in such things as crowd delirium, drugs and sex — even coarse emotional faith in G-d can fall into this category. This usually means using modicums of energy pumped out of the domain of the spirit and invested in the mundane world of the ego. Unlike modern economies, spirit is too noble to permit deficits in its realm, and extracts what is due from those who abuse the uniquely human, spiritual option of free choice.

7-15. For most people, "self-awareness" has a conventional connotation that risks leading us astray at this point of the discussion. Self-awareness here is not meant to denote self-image or opinions we may have of ourselves which help define ourselves to ourselves and to others in the process of getting through life. Nor is the usage meant to connote a form of nervousness or embarrassment.

Self-awareness is used here to express a sense of ourselves participating in our general presence by pervading our whole body with meaning. It accompanies us with each thought and action, bestowing a coherent sense of ourselves and our mission to each moment of our life. It means that our acts are authentically conscious ones and not merely reactions to our environment — as appropriate as these reactions may sometimes be. Behind our behavior and supporting it is an awareness of the larger context of our life and purpose, that there is a conscious observer within us (behind our eyes, as it were) and throughout our body. Some thinkers attribute this capacity to every living cell in our body.

7-17. These authors claim that, early on, researchers had a vested interest in positivism which made it particularly difficult to recognize questions about consciousness that might have arisen in the development of such disciplines as psychology and anthropology. They also surmise that, with the problems inherent in the study of consciousness such as subjectivity, the private nature of conscious phenomena, replicability, social appropriateness, etc., the first scientists naturally preferred to concentrate on subjects which lent themselves more readily to empirical study. (Harman & Rheingold, *Higher Creativity*, 68-69.)

— Chapter 8 —

8-1. Time is strictly a function of the level of materiality man is able to experience. This is recognized by many traditions, including Buddhism:

Buddhist cosmology claims that some humans experience multi-dimensional consciousness where, by contrast to three-dimension Cartesian consciousness, it's possible to convert time into space. If you stand back far enough, then instead of seeing time and the arrow of time with its flow, you perceive them simultaneously as conscious, present experience. Time is transformed into space. (Renée Weber, *Dialogues with Scientists and Sages: The Search for Unity.* [London & New York: Routledge & Kegan Paul, 1986], 196.)

The quality of that experience is limited to the superficial level of conventional consciousness that characterizes our age with its very particular brand of shallow materialism. How we experience time is a function of the quality of our presence. Time is the medium by which causes are separated from effects. The more encumbered by matter our minds, the coarser the level of materiality we experience and the more complex the world seems. We find ourselves caught up in a bewilderingly entwined multiplicity of causes and effects. Conversely, the finer the level of consciousness at which we operate the less separation there seems to be between causes and their effects, and the simpler and more comprehensible the world in which we find ourselves.

In the future, when competition for scarce and valuable commodities becomes increasingly unnecessary (owing to universal abundance), each new convenience will be seen more objectively as the means of releasing our spirit from its captivity in mechanical functions that add no intrinsic value to our lives. Step by step, as our relationship to matter changes, we will be freed to rise towards the realization of higher and richer forms of experience.

As our mastery of matter frees our mind to function at higher levels, our grasp of time changes. Although the objective rate of our bodily functions and all things that depend on our body will remain the same, their rhythms will seem subjectively much slower, just as when we deeply concentrate on our heartbeat or breathing, the slower they seem (even after discounting the objective slowing down due to the relaxation inherent to such observation). Drudgery will be progressively eliminated from life and from the mind.

Not only will we become immeasurably more active, but our experience of life will be correspondingly richer. We will have more "time" at our disposal. Far more life (i.e., awareness) will be packed into each moment. Thus our lives will be experienced as more leisurely and filled with content, for it is the density of experience that constitutes the true inner measure of our lives.

Meanwhile, each time we are confronted with an invention (which is just one form of matter transformed by one person's mind into another form), something escapes our notice. Innovation is really the difference in materiality between the old object and the new one. It is the measure of matter that has actually disappeared, like magic, and been replaced by intelligence. In our torpor, we remain blind to this phenomenon — numb and jaded to the point that we fail to notice the miraculous disappearance of matter before our very eyes. We are too engrossed in competing and too busy greedily exploiting the results of innovation to stop and wonder at its true significance.

The old forms consisting of displaced, obsolete, defunct objects fade into past time just as men do in death. Except for a few token objects — collector's items — frozen in time on the shelves of museums, these forms fade away, lost to us in past time. We quickly forget the time saved by new inventions in the form of appliances, gadgets, conveniences, etc. Life has a way of discounting these savings and taxing us for them. What once was a time-saving luxury soon becomes an indispensable necessity, the lack of which would leave us swamped and unable to cope or compete.

We simply do not see what is happening any more than a sleeper follows waking events. The sleeper reacts to extremes of heat and cold, noise and silence, comfort and discomfort. But he is absent from the scene of the action. He sees neither causes nor effects nor process.

Accordingly, whenever some new invention comes into our life it might shock us into a momentary awareness akin to a state of wonder at the greatness and mystery of the unknown. At least it might awaken in us an appreciation for the advantages and new possibilities the invention could open up. Very soon, however, like the sleeper who translates real impressions of heat and cold, sound and pressure into the fanciful details of his dreams, we bring the phenomenon down to our own level.

We quickly forget that an invention is the living evidence of a miracle, a miracle of creation. We end up cynically and greedily exploiting it, first incorporating it into whatever modalities we find functionally expedient and then into the comfort of our invariably banal and often comatose routines. In this we have very little choice. The society in which we live has a vested interest in keeping us preoccupied and our consciousness entangled in routine. Personal routines articulate with family routines and they, in turn, with institutional routines, and so on in ever-widening collars of captivity.

A change of consciousness immediately invokes changes of routine, and to some extent *vice-versa*. A sleeper interacts with the world very differently when he awakens; he becomes animated in a completely new way. If very many people were to awaken suddenly to a higher awareness and thereby to the possibilities open to them through the process of Accelerated Thought, society would have to reorganize itself according to different principles and priorities: in short, according to some new level of awareness of time and materiality.

But time is a dimension into which higher principles and potentials are rendered manifest through innovative forms. On the merciful side it is also a medium in which deviations from rigid, unforgiving, eternal truth are tolerated. Free choice — the possibility of nonconformity with strict cosmic law — provides the flexibility that makes for space, matter and time a realm of restriction, limitation, accident and death. Thus the freedom to deviate from the spiritual norm makes possible not only the existence of this temporal world of coarse materiality, but also the merciful medium of time that gives us the leeway through our own initiative to rediscover our higher origins.

Time is nature's way of preventing everything from happening at once. (Anonymous)

8-2. The question could be raised: What in this new world of security and plenty will prevent deviates from ignoring social guidelines, mores and standards just as they do in today's world?

It is usually conceded that drunkenness, drug addiction and vice are almost always related to environmental and developmental conditions of stress and deprivation — mental, emotional and physical. Almost all, if not all remaining instances, including the unbecoming manifestations of the wealthy and privileged, can be attributed to the boredom, frustration and anomie of being unable to find satisfying personal meaning in life. This condition itself breeds stress and deprivation.

In a world where everyone is free to realize his potential in a supportive atmosphere free of arbitrary danger, obstructions and humiliations, men will be able to accept and live with themselves and one another. Essential distinctions among individuals and groups will transform into factors of mutual assistance and sources of mutual respect rather than jealousy, rancor and strife. This will happen because people's eyes will have been opened to the divine greatness in each of us that transcends differences, and to the essential and beneficial complementarity of such differences.

8-3. Those readers in any way informed on the subject of spiritual growth cannot be blamed at balking at the suggestion that anything like total self-realization can be attained this readily. After all, is not the inner potential of each of us virtually infinite?

The answer is: "yes" on the objective level, and "no" on the subjective level. Almost all our cosmic potential is buried in what we commonly call the "matter" of our bodies, not in our personalities, thoughts, or any other of our manifest features or capabilities — not even in our spirits. It is true these are all expressions of our essential, carnal matter, but only superficially so. These expressions of essence are less than trivial when compared with our true, hidden potential locked deeply inside that same matter.

Piercing this essential veil of materially-imposed obscurity to redeem increment after increment of consciousness is the shared objective of all forms of effort aimed at spiritual awakening. Yet the effort extracted from us in the daily process of surviving and maturing also necessarily releases some of the intelligence hidden within the essential form the human body represents (although this amount is only a minuscule proportion of the intelligence latent within us). This intelligence is expressed on many levels and through many skills through functions broadly classified as "motor," "emotional" and "intellectual."

Before their corruption, these functions were meant to operate as a single organic unit. They do tend towards organic integration when, through the purification of inner striving, they become less impeded by the false or foreign elements in the personality. Instead of passing the buck to one another as totally separate entities (more or less efficiently), they begin to function as they should. Bathed in the awareness of what they are collectively, they gain a regard for their interdependence. In the moral sphere, this is the difference between someone who merely has "his act together" and someone who has true integrity. A change from one to the other is a change from inorganic to organic functioning. In consciousness, "false" personality is transformed into "true" personality.

When our subject's inorganic integration becomes as organic as it can become (as defined by the extent to which the elements in his true personality are compatible with his ambient reality), he reaches the limits of his "subjective consciousness." A more propitious environment can be expected to somewhat favor improved inner integration. But without utopian conditions of existence, significant progress can only come from confronting the great unknown — the unilluminated and as yet inanimate forms sequestered in the materiality of his world and of his body.

8-4. Influences of various kinds (notably those belonging to different levels of Being) vary in their ability to compel us to recognize their existence and conform to the requirements implied by this recognition. They also vary in the ways they make their demands of us. For instance, a physical reality affects us in one way while a political reality affects us in another.

All influences, if we fail to recognize them in their finer embodiments, ultimately find a way of reaching us on the most fundamental, physical level, by which means they force us to note their claim upon us. Having impinged upon our awareness, cosmic truth transmits its message to us simultaneously on all levels including, most significantly, the level just above our current awareness. It then invites us to take notice of it in its next finer, more subtle manifestation. Following this progression, perhaps in some future life we may finally assume the primordial, essential awareness for a complete perception of its truth — truth perceived through the very act of conformity it demands of us.

By analogy, if we neglect to pay our debts a reminder notice is sent, then perhaps a phone call or registered letter. Eventually we may find our home without vital services or, under certain circumstances, have a representative of the law call at our door. If our behavior still fails to conform to established norms, the law officer may feel obliged to draw our attention to the firearm on his hip. Finally, we could find ourselves in confinement or worse.

8-5. In the portion "Jethro" of Exodus is a passage (Chapters 19-21) describing G-d's descent upon Mount Sinai. It covers Israel's "close encounter" with the most concentrated reality ever to confront mankind, and the preparations and purifications that mobilized their capacity to embrace the energy of such a confrontation. Fluctuations in the experience of this sacred force field of reality, which included visual and aural manifestations of divinity, caused people to approach and withdraw from the mountain like a human tide. G-d warned that proximity might cause many people to be overcome and die (from overexposure to reality).

In everyday life, not to mention the intense engagement with life on the part of someone intensively pursuing truth, we also experience fluctuations in the degree to which we are challenged by our ambient reality. We can prepare ourselves by marshalling our wits by whatever methods we have at our disposal, and mustering the best within us by self-purification. Such fluctuations can be a function in changing conditions within our psyche or within the environment or both, always keeping in mind that "environment" can mean anything from our immediate conditions to political, geological, astronomical and cosmic influences. Sanitariums are full of those who have overdosed on reality.

8-6. In the process of developing our "Being," the illumination of essence, as in the genetic expression of a seed, is contingent upon its differentiation. In childhood, before our free spirit and basic faith in existence become almost hopelessly compromised, our desires and aspirations stemming from essence can be very powerful. But these desires are an inner, inchoate, expression of our potential of what in essence we are. Kabbalah sees what we are in terms of "desire:"

> *Desire has two faces. One, the Desire to Receive for the Sake of Sharing, is an attribute of the Circle. The second, the Desire to Receive for Oneself Alone, is*

a characteristic of the Line. Desire is humanity's most important asset in the struggle for physical survival, but it is also the largest obstacle on the path toward personal and planetary redemption. It is our most negative trait, but also our greatest opportunity for correction. By Restricting the negative side of Desire we create a circular concept (an affinity or similarity of form between the Light and the Vessel) and thereby convert the negative aspect of Desire into the positive aspect.

The Sefirot of Circles provide the impetus for all activity in the World of Restriction. They initiate all of our unconscious yearnings to return to our original Infinite condition. Were it not for those vague, primal memories of our past fulfillment being indelibly etched in our circular vessels we would be totally devoid of all longing and desire — which would greatly hasten the extinction of the human race. (Berg, *Kabbalah for the Layman*, 2:46-47.)

Concerning the two "faces of desire" of which the Kabbalah of Rabbi Yehuda L. Ashlag speaks, there are four basic orientations possible to man:

1. We can desire to receive for ourselves alone. This is the attitude of greed, the taste of which we all know, at least in its coarser manifestations. An excess of this kind of desire leads us to vice, and eventually, to crime.

2. The desire to give in order to receive is the principle upon which civilization is founded. We work for gain — to feed ourselves and our families. Most of us consider this attitude, as long as it doesn't lead to excess and degrade into bold-faced greed, to represent virtue itself. Those of us in this class who believe in G-d, tend to negotiate with heaven, promising to do good, give charity or abstain from vice in return for some form of help.

3. The desire to give purely for the sake of giving (i.e., pure charity) is more common as an ideal than as an act, and for good reason. To give fully can be done only once. Since it leaves us totally depleted it constitutes an act of self-sacrifice — annihilation. While this ultimate sacrifice negates our very existence, to sacrifice our subjective way of seeing things — our sense of self or ego — is analogous; but it allows us to go on living, purified and transformed. Yet the most important lesson to be learned from the exercise of selfless charity is that in reality we have nothing to give. Everything that we have, we receive "from above" or (in more empirical terms) from the constant, life-sustaining influx of sensory input, originating in higher dimensions.

4. This brings us to the final modality of existence — receiving in order to give. The more we open to new impressions, the more bounty is transmitted through us. The larger the conduit we represent, the richer we become. This derives not from what we capture, which would render us as limited and static in our receiving as do

the first two modalities, but from being the site through which increasingly large volumes of energy flow.

The logic is simple and the consequences unavoidable. Our essential desire (as defined by the "image of G-d" within us) is to give, and for this we have no other recourse than to receive. When we fill our *raison d'être* through the effective transmission of influence — each according to his unique individuality — we necessarily receive the required energy. Our purpose is giving, and the means, receiving — not the other way around, as illusion would have it. Personal transformation is likewise the result of this dynamic — not our purpose. Those who take transformation as their aim are caught in the same tangle as those who believe that man's true nature is the desire to receive for himself alone. Spiritual greed — lusting after spiritual purity — is material greed's refined twin.

Giving and receiving are the two fundamental and indivisible aspects of our individuality, analogous to inhalation and exhalation, ingestion and excretion. The desire to receive for the sake of sharing is the mechanism whereby a person can act as a channel to reveal and transmit into this world that aspect of higher reality to which his essence especially pertains. This divine form of receiving bestows the gift of giving that, given the right conditions, can be ours, making benefactors of us all. In the words of Johnston:

Logically, to receive is to take. Yet in practice, nothing lies closer to the essence of giving. Authentic receptivity empowers all who come near it. (Charles M. Johnston, *The Creative Imperative* [Berkeley: Celestial Arts, 1986], 238.)

But in the illusory daily life of self-seeking behavior, even our "altruistic" impulses are deeply conditioned by the desire to receive. At the very least we insist on receiving that gratifying "thank you" that gives us a social edge over the recipient. The beneficiaries of our patronage are, all too often, victims of our patronizing. With our essential desire fragmented into thousands of petty, selfish impulses by the prism of distraction, we are prevented from acting as a coherent channel of blessing.

Although in principle each small desire has its own particular flavor, the driving desires in the experience of the child remain mostly incipient and undifferentiated. Denied the conditions of nurturing demanded by its nature, and largely lacking the means of interpreting and giving adequate outer expression to its inner desires and impulses, the child turns to infantile daydreams of conquest and accolade. To a much lesser degree, he also turns to the somewhat more externalized outlets of interpersonal relationships and acting out, which permit little latitude for grandiose gestures or achievements. When an adult reverts to escapist reverie and fantasizing, we immediately recognize the symptoms of frustrated desires. Only anarchy and war provide arenas where, through heroic antics, we can give ample if brief physical expression to our most frustrated daydreams. Jung reminds us that these fantasies, neurotic as they are, emanate from deep within:

Since the normal fantasies of a child are nothing other, at bottom, than the imagination born of the instinctive impulses, and may thus be regarded as preliminary exercises in the use of future conscious activities, it follows that the fantasies of the neurotic, even though pathologically altered and perhaps perverted by the regression of energy, contain a core of normal instinct, the hallmark of which is adaptedness. (Jung, *The Undiscovered Self,* 80.)

Unfortunately, the expression of a fantasy, even fantasy issuing from essence-emanated "instinct," is very far from a rectified, conscious expression of essence-desire. One is as far from the other as a fried egg is from a living chicken. Why then, do we so cherish our fondest aspirations as expressed in fantasy, and why is fantasy such a coveted capacity?

Conventional beings that we are, we tend to demand a schematic vision of what we desire before we are prepared to give ourselves entirely to the holistic experience of that desire. It is as if an acorn required a photograph of the oak sequestered within it before allowing itself to be fertilized and nurtured by nature. We fail to realize that, like the acorn, we ourselves are essentially the image or photograph of what we are meant to be.

The photograph is in coded form to be sure. But like the interference pattern that produces a hologram, it contains all the instructions for the full elaboration of its own potential. All that lacks is proper exposure to germane, kindred inputs from outside that, to us, would represent the coherent light revealing a three-dimensional hologram from a two-dimensional holographic interference pattern. But in distraction, we remain impregnably closed off from the influence of these cosmic inputs, preferring, with the help of the odd intuitive spark, to dream our development in a pathetic bid to engender the stirring of something real within us.

As a rule — a rule we mostly fail to recognize — the full and elaborated experience of desire is the prerequisite for its physical expression and fulfillment. Given the holistic experience of desire, we cannot resist saying or doing that which, in the moment, we perceive with certainty to be totally necessary and appropriate. Thus it would seem that despite the apparent dearth of such realizations, essential desires and their rectified expression were inexorably ordained by destiny. Otherwise the very existence of seeds and essences would be pointless.

As it happens, very few successfully established adults ever even fantasize seriously about the meaning of their uniqueness or the special role they were meant to fill in the cosmos. Having found their workaday niche in the machine of society, they are smugly content to live their plastic lives rather than even try to dream real ones. In this regard, conventional wisdom always prefers a bird in the hand, regardless of how paltry the bird, to two in the bush.

All the same, there are certain vital, life-bestowing urges that for very seminal and primeval reasons take precedence over others — urges that cannot be so easily tamed. It is in this realm and concerning these urges that fantasizing is most universally rampant. If an individual is not afforded a reasonable opportunity to express his essence, what are the chances he'll be able to find and win over his soul mate — that person of the opposite sex whose essence most perfectly matches and complements his own? The frustration of an urge that coincides with a natural imperative as powerful as that of reproduction — an urge that refuses to be totally ignored, denied or subdued to convention — must inevitably express itself in fantasy or wreak havoc on the psyche of the individual.

8-8. Pascal comments on this distraction-inspired confusion:

Hence it comes that almost all philosophers have confused ideas of things, and speak of material things in spiritual terms, and of spiritual things in material terms. For they say boldly that bodies have a tendency to fall, that they seek after their centre, that they fly from destruction, that they fear the void, that they have inclinations, sympathies, antipathies, all of which attributes pertain only to mind. And in speaking of minds, they consider them as in a place, and attribute to them movement from one place to another; and these are qualities that belong only to bodies.

Instead of receiving the ideas of these things in their purity, we colour them with our own qualities, and stamp with our composite being all the simple things which we contemplate.

Who would not think, seeing us compose all things of mind and body, but that this mixture would be quite intelligible to us? Yet it is the very thing we least understand. Man is to himself the most wonderful object in nature; for he cannot conceive what the body is, still less what the mind is, and least of all how a body should be united to a mind. This is the consummation of his difficulties, and yet it is his very being. (Blaise Pascal, "Pensees," *Man and Spirit, The Speculative Philosophers*, Saxe Commins and Robert N. Linscott, eds. [New York: Washington Square Press, 1966], 204-5).

8-9. Low-octane gasoline is coarser and burns hotter than does high-octane. Diesel fuel is heavier again and burns still hotter. We use fine, high-octane type fuels mainly because they burn more readily, more easily. For this reason they are more dangerous to have around. On the cosmic level, the same principle applies to stellar, thermonuclear or fusion transformation.

Certain spiritual disciplines emphasize that the greatest quantity of light is released from the darkest obscurity and that the worst criminals are potentially the greatest saints. Clearly, great potentials of this kind are the hardest to realize, just as the heaviest fuels are the hardest to ignite.

Refined fuels are in a sense pre-digested and easy to ignite. Devices that consume them need be less robust. Certain aircraft and racing cars require refined, high-octane fuels sometimes called "white gasoline." These high performance engines are delicate and built to fine tolerances. Diesel engines, used in heavy vehicles and in some railway locomotives, require less pampering and provide the heavy-duty combustion chambers capable of extracting the high energy bound within heavy diesel fuels.

To start a log fire we begin with light, easy-to-ignite materials such as paper, wood shavings, twigs and other forms of kindling until the energy level reaches the point at which the log can begin to support combustion unaided. Analogically, an atom bomb, based on an unstable uranium isotope, is used as a trigger to set off a hydrogen bomb (based on hydrogen, which is stable). Atomic bombs are rated in kilotons of T.N.T.; hydrogen bombs in megatons.

I should not want to change eras, for I also know and respect the greatness of this one. I have always thought that the maximum danger implied the maximum hope. (Albert Camus, *The Rebel.*)

8-10. Such social sciences as psychology and sociology have established their own standards of validity for results they consider "statistically significant," a phrase often erroneously taken to mean "significantly related." However, since virtually no concept within these fields has been defined with anything like the precision required in the "hard" sciences, concepts can only be speculatively compared and related to one another, leaving room for little more than conjecture.

Most tragic for these "sciences" is that underlying virtually all their enquiry lies deeply buried the assumption that the humans under study are conscious and acting more or less rationally. Such a misapprehension has virtually no impact on the physical sciences (except to delay discovery), as matter is impervious to man's nature. To sciences that take man as the object of their study, the effects are catastrophic since they haven't even the most elementary notion concerning the true nature of their subject matter.

8-12. There is an attitude prevalent in our society that frowns upon the pronouncements of affirmations as if they were fact. Accordingly, members "in good standing" of our society take it upon themselves to chasten the authors of such assertions, bidding them to preface their remarks with "in my opinion."

It does us no good to retort that uttering any speculative statement about the nature of reality presupposes that an opinion is being stated. It does no good "in my opinion" because the very ring of conviction and self-assurance clangs uncomfortably in the ears of all who have abdicated their faculty of critical thought and their vibrant sense of individuality in favor of a self-effacing, ostrich-like refuge in their social affiliation.

The ring of independence of someone who, with guileless "arrogance" declares his position in the cosmos without feeling the need to invoke the meekness of being a mere "opinion holder," somehow reminds "members in good standing" of their treason towards themselves. This renders their introverted side momentarily apprehensive for the condition of their souls, and their extroverted side resentful of the affront to the collective in which they have sold those same souls.

8-17. Our social consciousness tends to rebel at the suggestion that the various forms of "security" society provides are illusory. After all, it does provide us with police and municipal services, military defense and a framework within which to seek the means of our sustenance.

We forget all too easily that in our scale of values, these socially mediated benefits assume totally distorted proportions which are promoted, dignified and perpetuated by social convention. The distortion of values in question is not simply a matter of relative emphasis. It is more of a short circuit that prevents us from generating any more energy of awareness than is consistent with social stability.

In a moment of lucidity we discover to our dismay that over the course of time our priorities have been reversed. Instead of eating in order to have the strength to work, explore life and create as we tended to do in early childhood, we find we have barely enough energy to maintain the physical plant of our body and satisfy our matter-based appetites. Everything around us is structured to keep it that way and to prevent us from seeing this situation for what it is. This is the kind of "security" that betrays us and renders us vulnerable.

8-23. We must keep separate certain concepts. The term "subjective" is used in the sense of our self-indulgent, non-objective, limited view of life that cuts us off from our own essence. "Conscious subjectivity," unlike the distracted variety, is a dynamic (if incomplete) manifestation of essence itself. It puts all personal knowledge in objective perspective, simultaneously releasing a measure of conscious energy in proportion to the amount of personal knowledge that can be transformed and incorporated within this new consciousness.

Here "subjectivity" is given an objective dimension, and the energy of awareness thereby released belies our former subjective pretensions to both individuality and consciousness. Nonetheless we are forced to use the word "subjective" in describing even this elevated form of consciousness, since limitation still remains. Limitation is still operative, in that subjective consciousness is restricted to those aspects of the world associated with the subject's life and limited personal perspective. It is true that in the light of consciousness these aspects take on vastly enhanced meaning, some small part of our essential individuality having been activated. Nevertheless, the bulk of this essence, and the objective knowledge it incarnates, if only in "seed" form, remain for the moment beyond reach, like data recorded on a computer disk but, for some reason, inaccessible.

This appearance of conscious energy gives the lie not only to old ideas about ourselves and our capacities, but also to many notions and opinions about the world to which we cling. The absurdity of these notions and opinions becomes apparent only in the light of conscious truth. It is thanks to the relative richness and gratification of this new state of awareness that we are willing to repudiate opinions that have only now lost all meaning by being excluded from our dynamic new thought system.

8-24. Although we seldom think in such terms, what defines who we are and reveals the significance of our life activities (after we are momentarily relieved of our illusions and vanities following some death-related shock, or with finality on our own deathbed) — is the seriousness with which we take the question of life. This means more than just the preservation of our biological functions.

By "illusions" and "vanities" is meant all those activities, involvements and distractions that captivate us by being sanctioned and even prescribed by society. But society is an amorphous, inanimate entity acting as the agent of matter in providing an ordered medium to accommodate and promote man's matter-induced aberrations.

What life asks of us is authentic involvement — real, responsible, individual involvement — not the distracted abandon of a spectator captivated by a sports match. This means a commitment to the preservation of life. In turn, this implies the absolute imperative of a rational, concerted, all-out assault upon matter which, through the aspect of the physical matter of our bodies, holds us in abject psychological and spiritual subjugation throughout our lifetimes and at the end destroys us.

All striving is in some way connected to the drive to survive. Yet through the havoc and confusion that matter has sown, we perceive this connection all too dimly and become easily distracted from the urgency of our predicament. Whether passive (derived from the external demands of what we call "life") — or active (fostered through the connivance and abdication of self-induced inner repression), through the ages this distraction has become fixed in us as a form of consciousness which is the unconsciousness or waking sleep of distracted consciousness.

8-25. One of the strongest and most perverse paradoxes characterizing our age is the striking contradiction between the spectacular achievements of science and technology over the past 100 years and the spreading skepticism and even pessimism concerning the efficacy of the mind — as though as a species we lacked the intelligence to think our way out of a paper bag. Much of this growing disillusionment derives from the threat of mounting stresses to domestic and world systems (economy, ecology, politics, justice, etc.). Things seem to be getting out of hand in spite of — and in the view of many, because of — our prowess.

Our predicament stems from a confusion between means and ends which tend to remain irreconcilable as long as thought remains divorced from consciousness. Such thought is little more than a mechanical, disembodied, dispirited function from which the larger context of reality is missing. Accordingly, thought is considered just a tool — a means to an end. But our ends are restricted in the scope of the vision they embody. In their turn, they become the means to other limited ends in a mechanistic chain of cause and effect preventing thought and its results from being guided by any kind of objective overview. Only a mind integrating thought within consciousness is able to unite ends and means within one coherent whole.

The fault is not with the function of thought itself, which is virtually unlimited in its possibilities, but with the conditions of existence that drain thought of the energy it needs to function consciously. The results of unconscious thought cannot reasonably be expected to meet the real needs of our individual and collective well-being and development. For example, when a person's career corresponds less with his purpose in life (if indeed he sees his life as having a purpose) and more with less essential, less encompassing aims, how can the results of his work reasonably be expected to answer to his or anyone else's real fundamental needs?

— Chapter 9 —

9-1. In the early days of man, before rationality as we know it took hold of man's mind and led him down the primrose, greed-driven path of conventional science and technology, man was much more in touch with his essence. He had a sense of existence that was more harmonious than ours today. This sense of existence included a sense of the sacred — a sense of the different dimensions of existence and levels of materiality reaching all the way to divine unity.

What he lacked was the ability to derive physical and temporal benefits and comforts from this state of harmony. Although connected with higher realities, man was nonetheless subject to accident, disease, violence, suffering and death. Through mundane cunning, any brute could overwhelm him. He felt constrained to become preoccupied with temporality, to the detriment of his spirit and inner harmony. Wonder became a luxury. Like a fetus ejected from the womb, man was forced out of "Eden" — his state of oneness with nature — and was made to fend for himself. In this lower world matter lends itself to manipulation, and the delicate organization of matter that sustains life's fragile balances is easily disrupted.

To preserve bodily integrity, man had to begin compromising his spiritual integrity — integrity maintained by the "glue" of awareness. Awareness grew ever thinner until eventually his obsession with physical security left room for little else than a restricted consciousness. In relentlessly pursuing the "how" of life he managed to lose track of the "what" and "why." Of all the generations that have preceded us, ours is by far the most factually knowledgeable and the most competent to deal with matter. Ours is also, undoubtedly, the most confused in terms of our place in life's general scheme and the most in doubt about our future, our fate and the meaning of life.

No other generation has been able to manipulate matter to the extent we have, yet none has been occupied with trivia and self-indulgence, violence and destruction on so vast a scale. There has never been evidence of such discrepancy between man's inventive capacity and his wisdom in the application of that capacity. This grotesque combination of power and helplessness, strength and weakness, intelligence and stupidity, information and ignorance — in a nutshell, light and obscurity — is unique to our age.

The more information we gather — that is, information not integrated within our consciousness — the more pressure of potential integration builds up in our psyche. The larger this discrepancy, the larger our potential for approaching consciousness — provided that the information corresponds in some degree to reality (i.e., that it is fit in principle for integration). For while linear, reflective thought is capable of accepting virtually any absurdity (each of us has his own brand), consciousness is inherently too noble to encompass anything but reality.

Only a discrepancy/potential on this unprecedented scale, both in our minds and as expressed by present world conditions, could call out for measures as potent as Accelerated Thought. The greater the accumulation of combustibles, the greater the blaze. The more mass that collects in a star, the more brightly it will burn. The greater the obscurity, the greater the light that will be revealed. What process other than Accelerated Thought could generate the heat and light necessary to integrate such massive contradictions into one coherent, dynamically integrated whole?

9-2. Inevitably, as the veils of coarse materiality are lifted and matter loses its nefarious hold on our minds, we will begin to better comprehend the relative nature of materiality. As our minds are gradually released from the bondage of distracted, socially dominated conventional thought and, as consciousness begins to organize itself and shine within us, we will begin to realize that ideas and constructs from the subjective realm — ideas corresponding to reality — have, from the viewpoint of consciousness, objective validity, meaning and function every bit as precise and unforgiving as we now (owing to the materiality of our physical bodies) find the physical world to be.

9-3. As creatures having a physical dimension, we find the nonphysical considerably more forgiving than the physical. Some would say we can "get away with murder;" others, that the proverbial "free lunch" does exist.

It is difficult to provide useful examples from finer levels of materiality. However, an analogy from the sphere of morality could illustrate the question of justice and mercy. If, for instance, reward and punishment were as rigorous and immediate in ethics and morality as in the physical realm, and if moral laws were as hard and fast as the laws of physics, an act of theft would cause our hand to fall off, profanity would cost us our tongue, bearing false witness would delete our eyes or ears, etc. In other words, the slightest nonconformity would be incompatible with life.

Yet somewhere, deep inside, most of us realize we pay a price for allowing any contradiction into our thoughts and feelings, whether this concerns our relationship with ourselves, with others, or just in general. Such contradictions can be likened to electrical short circuits. Somewhere within ourselves, there are moments when we know we would do well to open ourselves to some new idea or feeling, to face some challenge, or accept the consequences for a given act.

When we take the easy way out and allow ourselves to disregard what we know to be right, we allow our energy to follow the easier, shorter pathway and do less work than would be done otherwise. Having granted ourselves the luxury of this shorter circuit, something is compromised and a precedent set for the next time. Included in the decision to make a "longer" or "shorter" circuit — to make more or less effort — is whether we will be more, or less, aware of ourselves and the challenge confronting us. Thus the immediate effect of a foreshortened circuit is that our consciousness is deprived of the difference. A secondary consequence is that a shorter circuit, requiring less energy, leaves less of a trace — less of an impression — on our psychic apparatus, and this incapacitates us to some degree the next time a similar effort is needed.

The necessity of making efforts of one kind or another is usually brought to our attention by outside circumstances that press upon us. We are able to meet such circumstances only to the extent that we have a corresponding awareness of the nature of the effort required. Thus we cannot possibly throw a perfect vessel the first time we sit down at a potter's wheel, regardless of how much we'd like to or how easy it may at first appear. We are said to lack the necessary experience, which simply means we haven't experienced the efforts that lay down the traces or impressions allowing us an awareness of the precise flow of energy needed to guide our senses and limbs to do the job.

Accordingly, when we indulge ourselves in dishonesty on any level other than that of physical materiality, we rarely see immediate consequences. Yet payment is extracted inexorably, as night follows day. We pay for each such "sin" in terms of the awareness we sacrifice to comfort and the illusion we embrace regarding our security. The traces of our experience weaken without reinforcement. We barely notice our dimming awareness, just as we fail to notice ourselves falling asleep.

While falling asleep at the wheel of a car can quickly become fatal (since this concerns the world of physical matter), closing our eyes to the requirements of personal or social standards of thought, feeling and action brings disaster in subtler form. It causes those standards and the awareness that maintains them to erode and disappear over time, leaving us morally and ethically bereft. If these standards fall low enough, we can end up intellectually, emotionally and, in the end, physically incapacitated. Since traces or impressions weaken with time, if we do not make efforts to rise in awareness we inevitably slip into sleep.

This is where mercy comes in. We are spared instant, irrevocable punishment for any given weakness or mistake. Instead, we are allowed to pay piecemeal in the coin of our life — the energy of consciousness. Yet we are given time and the pressures of existence in order to take notice of our decline and make compensatory efforts.

Thus, paradoxically, absolute, merciless justice does determine the disposition of our energy. It limits the quality of our life and the richness of our experience on whatever level we are, and the restriction corresponds precisely to the extent of our offense. Mercy, on the other hand, is made possible by the very existence of levels of awareness through which we rise and fall. We pay for this mercy (or forbearance, as it is sometimes called), through the dimming of awareness. We are forced to submit because the dynamics of this whole process are largely hidden from us.

Expecting life to treat you well because you are a good person is like expecting an angry bull not to charge because you are a vegetarian. (Shari R. Barr)

9-4. Objective knowledge implies not only a comprehensive awareness of all the aspects of an object, substance, or phenomenon, but also where the object, substance or phenomenon belongs in the total cosmic context. Comprehensive knowledge of the part implies knowledge of the whole, since the part derives its meaning from its place within the whole. As this cosmic whole includes various levels of materiality, sometimes referred to as different "worlds," only an awareness that embodies these different levels, or worlds, could possibly encompass the cosmic totality enabling us to see the parts in their proper perspective. Lacking this perspective, we have only an incomplete idea of the role, structure and properties of the parts themselves.

9-5. Lately, at least, the laws overlooked by science turn out to pertain to phenomena on exceedingly small or grand scales. This concerns subatomic particles on the one hand, and objects or distances of stellar and even intergalactic proportions, on the other. The effects of these laws cannot be noticed on our scale. Yet they are here all around us in the sense that our world depends completely on what goes on both on the macro and micro levels. Eventually the discovery of such new laws and phenomena lead to their embodiment in new devices for manipulating and studying matter, some of which help us detect still more unknown laws and phenomena. Despite the progress being made, science still appears to have some way to go before it comes to grips with laws that account for the level of materiality to which psychic phenomena and, in particular, consciousness belong.

9-7. This is to say that the materiality of our bodies (i.e., the level or world of physical reality) is the hardest level to comprehend. Nonetheless, it is commonly believed that it is just the higher realities — the finer levels of materiality — that are most difficult to grasp.

Both statements are true in that the realization of higher levels depends on the lower and vice-versa. The fine energy of attention with which subjective consciousness is initiated is retrieved and redeemed from common, distracted consciousness. This is a process of energy conservation, not one of material transformation. However, the plasma-like flame of subjective consciousness feeds and grows on the forms and meanings constituting the materiality of subjective reality. As we are beginning to see, the still hotter, brighter and finer fire of objective consciousness is supported, through the process of Accelerated Thought, by the coarsest of matters derived from our world of physical reality.

One point that should not be overlooked is that as objective reality is revealed, different levels of materiality are discovered to be merely different aspects or phases of one single objective reality. In other words, these levels continue to exist, but in the mind of the individual who touches objective reality they form one complete functional unity. This whole gives sense and meaning to its parts, just as the gradual deciphering of these parts and their redemption from the obscurity of confusion and uncertainty, step by step and stage by stage, reveal the radiant existence of the whole in all its glory. Matter and energy are finally reconciled.

9-8. Rand says:

There is only one fundamental alternative in the universe: existence or non-existence — and it pertains to a single class of entities: to living organisms. It is only a living organism that faces a constant alternative: the issue of life and death. It is only the concept of "Life" that makes the concept of "Value" possible. It is only to a living entity that things can be good or evil. (Rand, *Atlas Shrugged*, 939.)

Implied in these words, although not stated explicitly, is that the "self-sustaining" and "self-generating" action necessary for supporting life pertains to action *vis à vis* the "inanimate" matter that is the vehicle, receptacle or cocoon within which (and at the mercy of which) life finds itself.

In her books, including *Atlas Shrugged*, Ayn Rand deals with the spirit, values and epistemology necessary for the sustenance and enhancement of life. Project Mind addresses itself to the actual method and means — physical, psychological and spiritual — for the realization of life's greatest potentialities, including objective consciousness and immortality.

9-9. According to many spiritual disciplines, immortality becomes an attribute of intelligence when the fine materiality commensurate with this level of consciousness elaborates into a dynamic form having sufficient structural and functional integrity to exist independently of the physical body. When complete, this intelligence is sometimes called the "spirit," sometimes the "soul" or "soul body," and sometimes the "astral body." It is considered to have functions analogous to those of the physical body, including the attribute of consciousness that can evolve in its turn into a body (e.g., "causal body" or "mental body") belonging to a plane of still finer materiality.

The number of these higher bodies, believed to evolve from one another depends on the system in question. However, any recognized doctrine conceding the possibility of immortality of the physical body or even the transmutation of physical substance, except through miracles, would be rare. Even the medieval science of alchemy that made open reference to the transmutation of physical matter is said to have done so only by way of analogy in order to protect itself from the violently aggressive superstition of the Middle Ages, and that alchemical terms referred symbolically to inner, spiritual processes.

It is not that all systems of spiritual or "inner" work are mistaken in their intent. On the contrary, the truths such systems contain undoubtedly provide the basis for any hope we do have. But in ignoring aspects of the world around them, they have fallen short in generating the level of psychic energies necessary for the realization of these truths in most of even that minuscule portion of humanity that actually engages in such efforts. Brunton comments:

I perceived how I had over-idealized mystics in the past and wrongly thought them to be sages, how I had mistaken their attainment of Yogic peace for true self-realization, and how inevitable was their preoccupation with themselves when the knowledge of universal truth alone could give the wider interest in the welfare of others. (Paul Brunton, *Reflections on My Life and Writings* [New York: Larson Publications, 1987], 8:115.)

Theon is even more explicit:

While the mystics exhaust themselves in crying aloud for the help of the invisible, the, by them, much despised scientific student will, in his laboratory, manifest and utilize the knowledge for the reception of which his earnest desire for knowledge and for truth, and his increasing labour to attain it, have fitted his mentality. And by visible, tangible and logical means he will find a way by which the now mortal, that is the body, can attain, first longevity and then immortality. (Max Theon, *La Tradition Cosmique*, [Paris: Bibliothéque Chacornac, 1904], 2:361.)

Paradoxically, in wishing to rid themselves of the psychic impediment of matter, and in attempting to transcend matter and rise to higher levels of awareness, mystics and spiritual adepts forget that the coarse levels of materiality from which they most justifiably wish to flee also contain, tightly bound within them the very energies that are the means to their aim. In their tendency to fall into contempt for science's short-sightedness, those seeking to follow the Ways tend to forget that the proper function of the higher functions they seek — higher thought in particular — is the penetration of the veil of matter and the liberation of the energy necessary for total, simultaneous transformation of the world and of themselves.

9-10. As a rule, efforts leading to inner freedom and growth in the sense of development of consciousness, especially in the sense of self-knowledge, belong to the domain of spiritual discipline. In most if not all such disciplines, the goal of reaching consciousness through self-knowledge is more or less explicit from the start. Using various terminologies, these disciplines (some may qualify as traditions) speak of higher and lower worlds, finer and coarser degrees of materiality, and often of the possibility of developing higher "soul bodies" bearing the attribute of immortality.

An individual attempting to mobilize his mind with the revolutionary intent of imposing new realities (the results of innovation) upon society does so normally without the guidance of a guru or spiritual system, for his goal is not inner development, or at least not explicitly so. His objective is to change outer reality. He benefits personally only subsequently from the changed and presumably improved environment, and from whatever material compensation comes from the commercialization of his invention. Inner changes, including changes in the way he experiences himself, usually take him by surprise. Even if, owing to prior experience, reading or hearsay he expects some change, the change itself, however welcome, is not the object of his efforts.

To further draw a contrast between these two classes of endeavor, one should notice that inventors engage in "doing," spiritual adepts in "non-doing." Inventors are achievement oriented; adepts pursue "non-desire." Inventors identify with their objectives; adepts seek freedom from identification. Above all, the inventor aspires to change the world through a daring act of intellectual adventure leading to social intervention, while the spiritual adept quietly propagates his influence in the world primarily through silence and the transformation of his own inner Being, perhaps somewhat through "good works." Friedman's comments on Kafka dramatize this point:

> Both the judgment and the call come to man through the absurd. His task, therefore, is not to escape from the absurd into inward contemplation but to stand and withstand, to hear and contend . . . Kafka fights against the Transience of the world, not by leaving the world for some immutable, metaphysical realm but through perceiving and creating, hoping and despairing. It is in existence—his own and that which comes to meet him—that Kafka glimpses the indestructible and the eternal. (Maurice Friedman, Problematic Rebel: An Image of Modern Man [New York: Random House, 1963], 430.)

This having been said, there is no reason why these two approaches cannot be reconciled:

> Some beings shorten their time out of total union with the Divine by working consciously upon themselves. This does not exempt them from the particular task from which they were called, created, formed and made, but obligates and equips them all the more to help in the Work of unification. (Z'ev Ben Shimon Halevi, The Work of the Kabbalist [USA: Samuel Weiser Inc., 1985], 3.)

9-15. Because man contains substances and energies corresponding to virtually all levels of materiality existing in the cosmos, from the most ethereal of vibrations constituting consciousness to the heaviest, most inanimate of minerals often found only in trace amounts in the body, nothing in the universe can ultimately be irrelevant to him. If the search for meaning expands, much more of what goes on in the world takes on "personal" significance and becomes relevant. For an individual intent on realizing and rendering conscious all the potential implied by the entire range of materiality represented within him, virtually all existence must become significant to him.

An awareness of the finest levels of materiality in the cosmos implies the sympathetic vibration of corresponding energies in our psyche. Without this correspondence we cannot commune with phenomena belonging to these levels, and their significance will remain hidden from us. Furthermore, unless the distribution of materiality in our own makeup becomes proportional to that of the total structure of cosmic reality, this correspondence and the sought-for resonance cannot be achieved. The quest for this quality of awareness implies the need for us to redeploy our attention and accumulate objective self-knowledge.

Considerable psychological courage is required to relinquish the imaginary form of self-knowledge characteristic of distracted consciousness and reflective thought. This "knowledge," acting as an inner agent and embodiment of the distracting influence of outside stimulation, surreptitiously obliterates whatever fledgling sense of genuine self circumstances may have mercifully spared us. The first major step towards subjective consciousness and authentic self-knowledge occurs when those aspects of our thoughts and feelings about ourselves that correspond in some way to reality become more or less permanently present in us as a sense of self (making due allowance for inevitable fluctuations and lapses into distraction). Instead of being overwhelmed by external input, this conscious impression of self is continually sustained by undistorted impressions coming in from the real world. These impressions are now processed in a real way through the integrative process that consciously reconciles energy and matter.

We seem to be afraid of acknowledging to what extreme degree we depend on our environment for sustenance. We readily enough admit our need for food and shelter. With the growing dilemma of environmental pollution, we are also becoming somewhat more aware of how dependent we are on the air we breathe. However, only someone having undergone a sensory deprivation experiment in an isolation tank could have even an inkling of our colossal instant-by-instant craving for sensory input that provides us with impressions of reality essential for our survival and well-being. It doesn't take very long for such deprivation to cause outright hallucinations. Even the tiniest fraction of a second of total deprivation — implying gross cessation of electrical activity in the nervous system — would mean instant death.

Science does not know very much about this need or its true parameters. Physics is continually discovering new sub-atomic particles from the electromagnetic phenomena that impinge upon us. For the most part, these pass right through us as through a coarse sieve since in the insensitivity of distraction we remain oblivious to any but the lowest of cosmic emanations. We lack a sentient net fine enough to detect any but the least subtle cosmic nuance.

It is the impressions which these sensory inputs awaken in us from the "engrams" — impressions latent in essence — that permit us to envisage reality either indirectly through the coarse fragmentation of distracted consciousness, or directly through the fine grain of subjective consciousness. Even here, the process includes only superficial layers of our essence. In his own way, each of us is striving to resolve the mind-matter (or, put differently, the spirit-matter) paradox. This striving is the basis of our very nature in its encounter with reality. Even when we take the easy, self-indulgent approach to life, our acts, however futile, are still attempts to solve this paradox. When we are gluttonous, we are trying to fill an emptiness in ourselves. Quite apart from the mechanical and physiological reasons for feeling hunger, there remains the experience itself. Between the most depraved and the most saintly of us, the attitude towards hunger, and thus the experience of hunger, differs considerably.

The saint approaches the matter we call "food" as a sacrament. He enters as pure an inner state as he can, in which his body participates in a luminous awareness — integrated, unified and attentive — as if it had become a single coherent intelligence. In this state, he savors his food with great attention. Through direct experience, he tastes, to a most uncommon depth, the essence, reality and source of that food. In experiencing the higher, normally invisible "spiritual" aspects (noumena) of food (those subtleties of taste that most of us are too coarse and distracted to appreciate), the saint reveals the particular quality of divinity at the root of the existence of any particular food. The physical aspect of that same food is digested to fuel the mechanisms that support such higher perceptions. In serving this higher purpose, and in participating in the transformation of the individual through the generation of higher modalities of experience, the food itself is processed — transmuted — to become the substrate of that higher experience. This gives another perspective on the common expression "you are what you eat," and is a corollary derived from the less common truism "you are what you experience."

The glutton, on the other hand, takes his habitual level of experience and appreciation, and the quality of what he himself is, as fixed. He believes that any fluctuations in his appreciation of food come not from any effort of attention on his part, but strictly from the nature and quality of what he eats. There is just enough truth in this to prevent him from discovering his own latent capacities of transformation and transmutation and keep him locked into distraction. Yet his experience of hunger for the pleasure of foods more and more pleasing to his palate is real and organically integrated with sensations of emptiness that come from the stomach. For him, the act of eating is not one of participating in something higher wherein he is a "part" and the food a link to something more complete. As a prisoner of distraction, he sees himself as the "whole" that can be completed only through the assimilation of elements (food) outside himself, into himself.

With luck, there comes a point when our hunger for reality is aroused sufficiently for us to alter our orientation towards sensory input. Having largely let go of the water-wings of illusory distraction for the solid stabilizing purchase of a limited personal reality (and bolstered by sensory impressions that illuminate our first really conscious experience of reality), we find ourselves faced for the first time with the possibility of letting go of all artificial and exterior buttresses to our awareness. We are invited to permit the lawful influence of cosmic energies to penetrate and animate our essence directly. We are ready to renounce further benefit of our faithless recourse to intellectual theorizing, one of the chief earmarks of distracted consciousness.

We are invited to recognize through direct experience that the essential mold that we are in every way mirrors the cosmos in which we find ourselves. By allowing the cosmic energetic complement of sensory input to mate with the corresponding forms of our essence, we can consciously experience all the undreamed wonders of multi-layered cosmic reality and thus realize the potential for which we were created.

— Chapter 10—

10-2. Paradoxically, in principle if not in fact, physical immortality is not strictly necessary for us to become free of the nefarious influences and illusions that bring about our perverse attitude towards matter, the world and ourselves.

Were we able to believe in the possibility of an integrity of intelligence as functionally and structurally complete as that of our biological body, and had we a faith that allowed us to experience the intelligence buried within us as vividly and convincingly as we "believe" in the physical aspect of our body, we would find ourselves in a much better position to exercise and develop that intelligence. Would that this were possible without the "childish" need for unequivocal, concrete proof of salvation in order to put things in perspective and secure the release of our spirit from the paralyzing illusions stemming from matter's tyrannical rule.

Is this, in fact, not the role of faith in everyday life? Would we be able to get anything done at all if we required conclusive proof before expending energy or assuming any kind of risk? When we flick on a light switch or take a step, we do so in the faith that things will function as they should and that disaster is not lurking around every corner. Faith in the everyday, and courage to experiment with the new and unknown, are built upon the certainty that experience brings. Faith and courage are called for anew each time we experiment in a bid to expand the scope and depth of our experience.

Furthermore, the faith in question here primarily involves risks of a non-physical nature. In principle, all we need to do is redirect our attention from everything that engenders our idolatry of the visible (especially the material aspect of our own body) towards that in us which is most fine, most alive. The risks here are real, but threaten little more than our complacent image of ourselves and the comfort of old ruts — dysfunctional habits of body, feeling and thought. This calls for an extended course of adjustment consisting of endless cycles of experimentation and discovery based on faith and the certainty that comes of comprehension until, little by little, we become detoxified of the effects of a most abnormal existence.

Most faith in evidence today, rather than leading to inner experimentation and discovery, assumes the conventionally intellectual and sentimental forms that characterize most modern religion. Modern religion tends to promote the prejudice and self-serving kind of faith that abdicates the responsibility of critical thought in favor of whatever culturally acceptable external representations of divinity most successfully solicit the submission of the faithful. Hoffer acknowledges this state of affairs:

> All mass movements rank obedience with the highest virtues and put it on a level with faith: "union of minds requires not only a perfect accord in the one Faith, but complete submission and obedience of will to the Church and the Roman Pontiff as to God Himself." Obedience is not only the first law of God, but also the first tenet of a revolutionary party and of fervent nationalism. "Not to reason why" is considered by all mass movements the mark of a strong and generous spirit. (Hoffer, *The True Believer*, 108.)

In this enfeebled state so typical of humanity today, what remains of genuine faith lacks the force to guide us unerringly toward a sense of what is authentic. In our private lives we end up requiring concrete proof before we dare take any step away from our habitual, conventional mode of experiencing — what we ordinarily call reality. Our inner convictions are those of the herd. Jung comments:

> It is, unfortunately, only too clear that if the individual is not truly regenerated in spirit, society cannot be either, for society is the sum total of individuals in need of redemption. I can therefore see it only as a delusion when the Churches try — as they apparently do — to rope the individual into a social organization and reduce him to a condition of diminished responsibility, instead of raising him out of the torpid, mindless mass and making clear to him that the salvation of the world consists in the salvation of the individual soul. (Jung, *The Undiscovered Self*, 68-69).

The problem is that our confusion is accelerating even faster than our scientific knowledge of the cosmos. Yet modern civilization hopes this knowledge will enlighten us about the structure and meaning of reality. Unfortunately, at our present rate of spiritual deterioration, even if global disaster could be delayed by conventional means the hoped-for enlightenment would arrive too late to save us from ourselves. By that time we would be too far gone to be susceptible to the influence of objective truth, just as we are already now mostly beyond the influence of religious truth. Barrett recognizes this problem:

> In losing religion, man lost the concrete connection with a transcendent realm of being; he was set free to deal with this world in all its brute objectivity. But he was bound to feel homeless in such a world, which no longer answered the needs of his spirit. A home is the accepted framework which habitually contains our life. To lose one's psychic container is to be cast adrift, to become a wanderer on the face of the earth. (William Barrett, *Irrational Man: A Study in Existential Philosophy* [Doubleday & Co., Inc., 1958].)

Having already lost much of our capacity to appreciate truth through the now almost extinct faculties of refined feeling and religious sensibility, we are well on our way to losing the keenness of our mental faculties of discernment and deductive logic that have begun to atrophy from disuse. Just as the proliferation of laws and the growing complexity of our social affiliations rob us of initiative and individuality, thereby weakening our aptitudes for sensation and feeling, so our growing reliance on the media, calculators and computers render increasingly passive and effortless our learning, reckoning and decision making. Instead of enhancing our creativity as they were meant to do, they tend to deprive us of our powers of discrimination and what little is left of our common sense. Our thinking becomes more and more mechanical as, in the process of becoming technicians, we replace quality with quantity and adapt to serving a vast machine whose depravity we cannot see.

What will remain of man's inner resources, meant to bring him to an appreciation of the full cosmic significance of multi-layered reality, if his thought, feeling and sensation of individuality (three faculties that must cooperate in harmony to produce manifestations of conscious intelligence) become so badly crippled?

It is likely we still retain enough of our wits so that the stimulation of repeated spectacular revelations of Accelerated Thought will convince us of the possibilities lying hidden within each of us, and thus reanimate and galvanize us out of our depressive stupor. It appears that only an influence of such intensity could succeed in making hope and faith once again operative in our search for meaning, and reinstate the inner freedom that is the mainstay of human dignity. As our functions begin to regenerate, we will better appreciate the full measure of our fall and the abuse that brought it about, very much like a victim of acute heart disease during recovery who realizes he must learn to live differently.

Then not only will machines eliminate the tedium of what we now call "work," but computers will quickly take over most of those automatic functions we include in our idea of "thought." By peeling away the mechanical from the requirements of everyday life and assuming the functions of technicians, the products of Accelerated Thought will reveal our creative potential even to those who consider themselves (or are considered by others) pedestrian.

10-3. Receiving the illumination of wisdom inherent in new awareness is a most edifying experience and gives us a foretaste of good things to come. But true realization and conscious participation in a world of finer materiality is untainted by pleasure or any other particularist sensation. The vision that bestows wisdom and its complement — pleasure — is only a function of Being, albeit a higher function. It is the vision of a higher body.

10-6. Of all nature's creations, only man is capable of disrupting nature's balances, but the range of this destructive capacity is considerable. What is the aspect of nature and the cosmic laws underlying nature that render possible its destruction by one of its own creations? Does nature have a "death wish," a kind of built-in self-destruct mechanism based upon man's immense destructive capacity?

Yet man has within himself the potential for raising the level of his own inner integration and for finding harmony within himself, with others, with nature and with the cosmos. To the contrary, this, along with his potential for mastering the matter of the cosmos at virtually all levels of materiality, strongly suggests that mankind has some constructive, integrative role to play. It further suggests that the initial, non-harmonious, incomplete and apparently unnatural condition from which he must emerge is but a springboard created for this very purpose.

10-7. To the extent that the combustive process is not clean and imminent awareness is sacrificed to the pleasure of an emotional "high," it will resemble the manic phase of manic-depressive syndrome (bipolar disorder). Some physicians recognize the possible existential and spiritual dimensions of the disorder:

> *I have emphasized that manic depression is a spectacular disease because of its bizarre, excruciating, and at times beneficial and even ecstatic symptoms. It is spectacular because people who suffer from the illness in its milder forms of moodswing tend to be magnificent performers, magnetic personalities and true achievers. Many forms of manic elation seem to be a genetic endowment of the same order as perfect pitch, a photographic memory, great intelligence, or artistic talent of any sort. Manics not only have fabulous energy when they're not too manic, but a qualitatively different, quicker, more perceptive grasp of their surroundings.* (Fieve, *Moodswing*, 222.)

To the extent that clarity of vision is absent, the borrowing of energy through the mechanism of anticipation will approximate the act of reckless gambling characteristic of mania. When we allow ourselves the luxury of expecting too much too soon from a vision that presents but a fuzzy outline to us, we reveal the lack of inner discipline and restraint central to this condition.

In the more extreme manifestations of his weakness and lack of responsibility for his own psychological hygiene, the manic individual loses sight of the cause of his exalted mood and naively considers it an integral and permanent feature of his nature. He tends to undertake plans and commitments that presuppose the permanence of this intense flow of vital energy until he crashes into the depleted state called depression.

There is a school of thought that holds that extreme cases of mood swing usually suggest an inherited, genetically determined, neuro-biochemically mediated imbalance. Practitioners who follow this line tend to lean on chemical means (e.g., lithium carbonate) in treating manic depression. This treatment, depending on dosage, impedes the affected individual from borrowing quite as liberally as before from his reservoir of psychic energy. It is as though he is made to forget the secret inner code for arousing the anticipation needed to tap directly into his emotional fountainhead.

In "normal" people this energy reservoir is guarded by what some call "balance" and others "common sense." Society conditions us to keep our expectations within conventional bounds which makes for restricted prospects. We come to accept that what is normative is good for us. We opt for the safety of a stagnant balance. But unwittingly we do it at the expense of authentic inner development that could be ours by assuming the risk of the unavoidable temporary chaos and imbalance on the way to a higher-level, high-energy state of equilibrium. Banal expectations make for banal people and the illusory safety of a banal world. How ironic the term "social security" when looked at from this angle.

Society frightens us with the prospect of danger. Admittedly, the dangers of inner development are real. Society provides sociological and pharmaceutical prophylaxis to shelter us from this danger and to keep us docile. Society does not speak to us of inner or higher knowledge, of the possibilities hidden within man or of the worthwhileness of competently guided psychological adventure. It sanctions only treatments that lead to "normality" (i.e., the socially normative).

No recognized social purpose is served by individual development or evolution. So in addition to the many institutionalized sources of intimidation, we are dissuaded from exploring such pathways by the personal tragedies of those such as "manic-depressives" who try through their lone intuitive efforts without direction or supervision to break out of the psychological and emotional straight-jacket to which the rest of us have grown so accustomed.

10-8. The subject quite unwittingly brings this upon himself. To his peers he seems to be making some pretentious identity claim. But he is only trying to share a new discovery — to help others join him in perceiving a new possibility. To him, the satisfactions of the discovery and the elevation of spirit that accompany it are enough to swamp and render insignificant any ego-satisfactions that might otherwise be derived at the expense of his listeners. In their state of conventional distraction, they cannot fathom such motivation and instead interpret things according to conventional standards. If they are not won over, they make their influence felt through verbal resistance, censure and other channels of social sanction.

Naively, our subject does not anticipate meeting resistance to his new "truth" any more than he would if he were offering a friend some important news or a tip on the stock market. The painful shock of such an encounter tends to reactivate his old sense of ego-separateness.

10-11. There exists a whole range of non-physical "bodily" activity. Meditation is a case in point. In a wide variety of meditative techniques and systems, the awareness of bodily energies is often prescribed.

Meditation does not usually include movement except in cases of conscious walking, sacred dances and movements. However, various grades of sensing the body are allowed to blend with thought and feeling in stillness and silence. The purpose is not so much to integrate with outer reality, but to seek the experience of harmonious inner integration under conditions of minimum stress and distraction.

This could be thought of as a kind of recalibration to counter the destabilizing effects of distraction and to neutralize the psychic drain of repetitive, reflective thought. After benefiting from the shelter of this temporary retreat, one is more "centered," present to oneself and better prepared to handle life.

One who hasn't learned to seek this balanced state under turbulent conditions is at a disadvantage. In the everyday world he is soon engulfed in distraction. That is not to deny that some benefit must accumulate with daily persistence in such efforts. But how many lifetimes would it take to accumulate sufficient virtue in this way to meet life head-on, consciously?

Any kind of intense effort temporarily deprives reflective thought, emotional agitation and bodily unrest of the energy that animates them. For example, sufficiently strenuous and prolonged hard physical labor rechannels these energies from reverie to the practical task immediately at hand *via* the circuitry of our Being. It is this Being that represents our capacity for directly engaging reality. As a result it makes us more real. Even purely mental effort, if sufficiently disciplined, can pull us out of our mental and emotional meandering. The effort of memorization or calculation can channel the energy normally invested in reverie into useful, waking contact with the world.

The main difficulty we usually attribute to these kinds of efforts is not so much in the activities themselves, which are normal, healthy and even enjoyable once we get into them. It is in the irksome discomfort and distress of having to forfeit the illusion that our chronically distracted state is one of consciousness — or that our reflection is true thought, or that our emotional torpor and reactivity represent states of true feeling.

This is not to say that such efforts render us conscious or initiate Accelerated Thought. Distraction's hold on us is more deeply rooted than that. These efforts do, however, accord us some increased measure of therapeutic interaction with outer and inner reality. Once we become accustomed to an effort and it begins to be routine, our attention is once again freed to flow into reverie unless we renew and intensify the effort at the right moment — something we almost never do. To do this sufficiently to break out of distraction, tremendous motivation would be required — the kind briefly found in confrontations with death and, more particularly, the kind that animates the hearts and spirits of the pioneers of Accelerated Thought.

Man was not meant to be immobile, not even consciously immobile. We have been given thought to assimilate meaning from our environment. We have been given feeling to integrate that meaning in our conscious Being. We have been given physical movement to carry out the intentions that emanate from our Being.

— Chapter 11 —

11-1. That heightened awareness can be developed using various methods, some of which have existed from time immemorial, has already been touched upon in this work. In terms of the effort required for this kind of undertaking, there are different ways of taking hold of the "beast."

Accelerated Thought and the possibility of transforming matter are aims from which other systems generally steer away. They are more directly concerned with the transformation and realization of "self." The exceptions (those systems that do recognize the imperative of addressing the issue of transforming matter) tend to believe that when it happens it will be directly metaphysical — "mind over matter" in the most literal sense. Berg illustrates:

According to both the Zohar and to the quantum physicist the human consciousness has the unique ability to influence and even radically alter the physical nature of the universe.

Most traditional scientists, clergy and laymen would not entertain for a moment the idea that the human mind could influence the phenomena of physical reality. Yet, the Scripture asks us to accept without question that consciousness can enable certain individuals to transcend the laws of physics. Who, or what, are we to believe? (Berg, *Power of Aleph Beth*, 1:119-54.)

The following excerpt from Castaneda suggests similar possibilities in an entirely different register:

The second attention is unavoidably drawn to focus on our total being as a field of energy, and transforms that energy into anything suitable. The easiest thing is of course the image of the physical body, with which we are already thoroughly familiar from our daily lives and the use of our first attention. What channels the energy of our total being to produce anything that might be within the boundaries of possibility is known as will. Don Juan would not say what those boundaries were, except that at the level of luminous beings the range is so broad that it is futile to try to establish limits—thus, the energy of a luminous being can be transformed through will into anything. (Carlos Castaneda, *The Eagle's Gift* [New York: Penguin Books, 1982], 25.)

That in our time mind will attain this degree of potency remains to be seen. In the meanwhile, sadly, "matter over mind" is very much the state of things.

Most spiritual disciplines redirect the attention of the apprentice back towards himself (meaning his body) under the assumption — hidden or not — that the outside physical world already has more than enough of our attention, and that it is incumbent on us to withdraw some of it and reinvest it in an awareness of our own existence. We are meant to discover that we "are" (or, in the case of religious esoterism, that we "are created") in the image of G-d. Just how attention is redeployed to this end and using what techniques (e.g., trance, dance, prayer, fasting, self-denial, drugs, precepts, meditation, relaxation, division of attention, etc.) varies from system to system. But most seek a special form of inner balance among the thinking, feeling and motor functions, and all strive for transformation.

This tends to ignore that the attainment of the highest levels of consciousness, involving the finest degrees of materiality, depends upon parallel attainment concerning the lowest and the coarsest. Consider Berg's comment on this subject:

> The natural law of the metaphysical realm is that the first vessels—the energy-intelligence that makes manifest the Force after restriction—are those with a higher degree of purity and, consequently, a lesser degree of the desire to receive. The opposite is true of the lights, the energy-intelligence of the Force. Here the first lights to emerge are those with smaller amounts of energy.
>
> The upper, more powerful level lights, which appear at a later stage of emanation, cannot descend to their appropriate vessel until the appearance of the lower or more intense energy-intelligences of the desire to receive. The paradox we find in this process, is that the supreme level of the Force, Yehida, must wait and cannot be expressed, until the lowest, most intense energy-intelligence of the desire to receive makes it manifest. (Berg, *Power of Aleph Beth*, 1:182-83.)

One possible knee-jerk reaction to this point of view is the argument that one might do well first to accomplish the more modest and yet still very ambitious task of redeeming attention from the unruly appetites and passions pertaining to the bodily senses. Indeed, all sincere inner effort, including acts of preparation (e.g., self-purification), bring us forward. But we must go beyond preparation. We must not overlook the fundamental principle that the higher we aim, the closer we are likely to come to tapping into the primordial, motive force of our essence.

11-2. It is with this free and fickle function of the "higher," "geographically" outer layers of the intellect that I associate the common and often justified idea that intellectuals tend to be superficial. Intellectuals referred to in this way are probably those for whom feeling and bodily sensation are divorced from thought. They live mostly in layers of mind furthest removed from feeling and action. By residing in these layers, such people largely avoid the commitment of applying their ideas and subjecting them to the acid test of reality. They are the very antithesis of men of action who typically "do" a lot, but without much reflection. According to Simmel:

> The intellect ... has its locus in the transparent, conscious, higher layers of the psyche; it is the most adaptable of our inner forces. In order to accommodate to change and to the contrast of phenomena, the intellect does not require any shocks and inner upheavals; it is only through such upheavals that the more conservative mind could accommodate to the metropolitan rhythm of events.

(Georg Simmel, *The Sociology of Georg Simmel* [The Free Press of Glencoe, Inc., 1950].)

Ram Dass puts it more poetically:

The intellect is a beautiful servant, but a terrible master. Intellect is the power tool of our separateness. The intuitive, compassionate heart is the doorway to our unity. (Ram Dass, "Promises and Pitfalls of the Spiritual Path," *Spiritual Emergency*, 186).

11-9. The reader might very well feel that certain liberties have been taken here with the term "food." It also should be clear that man is nourished on several levels — "not by bread alone." Furthermore, when a person changes his way of being, there are corresponding changes in his patterns of eating and breathing. For example, even a simple state of elation resulting from incipient Accelerated Thought or even from a particularly intense Eureka experience, can cause an individual to lose interest in food and sex. One is carried on a wave of energy that temporarily defuses and occludes normal drives and seeks to establish new, cosmic rhythms.

The inner aspects of changes such as these remain invisible to the casual observer, but have profound implications for how the body assimilates the elements it requires for the new psychic needs of the transformed individual. Campbell offers his vision of the hierarchy of foods:

The effect of the successful adventure of the hero is the unlocking and release again of the flow of life into the body of the world. The miracle of this flow may be represented in physical terms as a circulation of food substance, dynamically as a streaming of energy, or spiritually as a manifestation of grace. Such varieties of image alternate easily, representing three degrees of condensation of the life force. An abundant harvest is the sign of God's grace; God's grace is the food of the soul; the lightning bolt is the harbinger of fertilizing rain, and at the same time the manifestation of the released energy of God. Grace, food substance, energy: these pour into the living world, and wherever they fail, life decomposes into death. (Joseph Campbell, *The Hero with a Thousand Faces* [Princeton, 1949], 15.)

11-10. More in the past than today, certain religious and spiritual practices required the abstention from all but the most basic of life's needs. Such suffering was undertaken in the hope of accustoming the body to live according to its essential needs — as opposed to superfluous "animal" desires and appetites. This was meant to bring the body into conformity with the "sacred" — an exalted form of functioning — and thus, with the help of prayer, induce transformation to a higher, more efficient plane of existence where desire is pure and excess has no place. We must not forget that:

The source of all appetition, whether in men or in animals, is the hunger for the Immortal, the Good, the One. (W. T. Stace, *Mysticism and Philosophy* [Los Angeles: Tarcher, 1987], 328.)

The gross material nature of the body was seen as a kind of prism that fractionates, distorts and debases our higher, more essential desires. Abstention and self-denial were the instruments to subdue animal urges and reveal their source. Self-knowledge was seen as a corrective. To recognize the origin and exalted nature of desire was to become free of its more ignoble expressions. Harman and Rheingold offer:

> *According to the mystics, when one comes to truly know oneself, the pull of the material body and ego personality become greatly decreased and one finds that the deepest motivation is to participate fully, with conscious awareness, in the evolutionary process and the fulfillment of humankind. To put it another way, one becomes aware that what appeared to be driving motivations were mainly illusory ego needs and that the desires of the true Self are one's real needs.* (Harman and Rheingold, *Higher Creativity*, 135).

The inspiration for the effort that could support the suffering of self-denial was mainly religious faith and suited the age during which it was practiced. It is questionable whether today there are men with the force of faith equal to the task of transformation through this avenue, or whether, indeed, they were fully up to it even back then.

Modern man is called upon to complete this task, begun by our forebears, in a modality that suits our modern age. Faith here is no less operative, for as already explained, Accelerated Thought is generated through faith in our ability to pierce the veil of matter through scientific breakthrough. More precisely, faith is redirected to the fundamental aspect of our plight. It is for us to remove the root cause of all that is sordid (i.e., lack and restriction) by scientifically transforming matter, including that of our body, so that the sublime nature of our essential desire can be revealed fully and without needless suffering.

Interestingly enough, according to Jewish tradition the "Messiah son of David" will appear riding on a white donkey to usher in the Millennium — the seventh period of one thousand years. The year 2000 A.D. corresponds on the Jewish calendar, to 5760 — only 240 years shy of the latest possible date for the beginning of the Millennium. In Hebrew, the word "donkey" is virtually identical with the word "matter." According to the Holy Zohar — probably the most important Jewish esoteric Scripture (credited to the sage Shimon Bar — Yohai of the 2nd century A.D.), "donkey" is the Old Testament's code word for matter. It is the whiteness of the donkey that is significant here. Whiteness, which normally signifies purity, in the donkey indicates transformation — the transformation of matter.

11-11. According to tradition, the ultimate "will" and extension of influence is, of course, G-d's, whose very thought flawlessly creates worlds and cosmic laws, including the laws of lack, restriction and distraction. He foresees all contingencies and conseqences, and only He knows with total certainty that all is, was and forever will be in mercy and perfection. Thus, inevitably, the striving for success of any kind is, within the limits of our wisdom and understanding, an attempt to emulate Him.

11-13. In some readers, this reference to connectedness may evoke the experiential wealth of psychedelic experience. The big difference is that in Accelerated Thought the nodes of connectedness are a concrete part of the individual's everyday world. Instead of leaving one world to sojourn in another, the subject's vision encompasses two worlds at once. In actualizing that vision in the world of matter, he binds these worlds ever more closely, relieving others of the slavery and distraction induced by this separation.

• • •

GLOSSARY

Accelerated Thought. A process driven by essential desire whereby the infinite intelligence latent in man finds expression through the rapid revelation of natural and cosmic secrets.

Addiction. Acquired need that abuses essence by inducing satisfaction of desires violating the sequence demanded by cosmic design which calls for work to be done in proportion to energy drawn. In extreme forms depletes the system and mortgages the soul. The mechanism of egoism.

Aim (or Purpose). The imagined or perceived path of one striving towards a desired result. The validity of the selected aim for a given person is measured by the degree of self-realization resulting from the attainment of the aim, the successful attainment of which depends most fundamentally upon the depth of contact a person establishes with the essence-desire which defines his individuality.

Appreciation. The process whereby one's emotional perspective is enlarged and accompanied by a feeling of enhanced harmony with one's surroundings.

Attention. Energy mobilized to form a receptacle (or vessel) for an act of perception.

Attachment (or "Cleaving"). An act or state through which voluntarily or involuntarily, intentionally or unintentionally, the energy of attention flows towards or encompasses some phenomenon.

Attraction. The force of affinity realized when a receptacle, in the process of rectification, approaches a similarity of form with the light of reality it was meant to accommodate. Receptacles attract one another when they express affinities for similar realities. Opposites attract only through their similarities.

Awareness. An attitude that defines the disposition and quality of attention. Awareness can range from quasi-unconsciousness to total consciousness.

Body. A vessel (or receptacle) which, owing to the correspondence between its matter and form and, to the degree it gives expression to the "image of G-d," can accommodate energy and realize intelligence starting from the faintest glimmer of awareness up to the infinite light of total consciousness. "Body" is the essence of mind.

Being. The awareness of existence that includes self-awareness, the degree of which is determined, in any given layer of essence, by the accommodation of energy and, consequently, through the expression of the intelligence for which essence was created.

Breakthrough. Radical progress in understanding, leading to personal and material transformation.

Certainty. A particularly pure and complete state of Being in which one's faith in and love of life are experientially confirmed, temporarily expunging all doubt.

Channel. A pathway of energy linking levels of essence and mind.

Chaos. Temporary absence of structure inherent in the process of purification and self-effacement. A phase in the transition from one state to another.

Circuit. A pathway of energy executing or defining a thought, feeling, movement, perception, or experience.

Cleaving. See "attachment."

Commitment. Attachment to aims and principles which orient the modulation of one's energy.

Communion. A state of Being involving intimate attachment facilitated by similarity or compatibility of essences.

Comprehension. All connections possible concerning a percept or concept for a given level of Being, producing understanding.

Concentration. The effort to orient attention selectively so as to exclude all but certain phenomena.

Condition. Constraints in the inner or outer environment that impose limits on perception and manifestation.

Conditioning. Internalized constraints in perception and manifestation that become part of one's nature and exercise control as if imposed from without.

Confrontation. Intense meeting of conflicting inner and outer realities that demands resolution through inner or outer accommodation.

Conscience. The strongest, most intimate, most deeply hidden connection to life and truth. It derives from uniqueness of individuality and defines the specific reason for one's existence.

Consciousness. A state with many possible subjective and objective ramifications and permutations graded by the extent to which the potential of essence is expressed through Being.

Convention. Norms and prescriptions for perception, thought and behavior that make up human conditioning.

Core (of Essence). One's innermost, most individuating part.

Cosmic Consciousness. Direct vision of the integrated wholeness of Creation.

Cosmology. Theory of the structure and function of cosmic reality including cosmic law.

Creativity. The divinely inspired process of participating actively and through one's essential individuality in the realization of the cosmic plan.

Death. Systemic cessation of energy circulation and subsequent dissolution of substance caused by the disruption of essential circuits that, on any given level, form the receptacle of life. Spiritual death comes with the incapacity to deploy attention so as to form a receptacle for spiritual energy.

Desire. The prime attribute of all created entities which, through lack and longing, reflects both separation from the source of all life and essential affinity with and attraction to that source, depending on how close the entity's origin is to that source. That which motivates everything.

Destiny. One's cosmic destination or assignation as defined by one's essence which, when fully expressed through Being, has filled its potential and attained its cosmic purpose.

Distraction. A state in which the energy of attention is attracted and engaged in diverse and conflicting directions according to the dictates of convention.

Divinity. The energy that animates individuality. Benevolence in all forms.

Effort. Voluntary movement of energy.

Ego. Identifying with an image of oneself as opposed to experiencing oneself through Being. Ego is increased by the identificatory pleasure of the enhancement of that image.

Egoism. The pursuit of pleasure.

Elation (Euphoria). Massive, systemic infusion of energy, attended by a heightened and generalized sense of well-being or exaltation.

Emotion. A reaction that consists of an evaluation of one's circumstances.

Energy. A grade of materiality finer than one's level of Being which produces experience through its movement within Being. Energy, inherently formless and still, becomes "force" when it gains vectors channeled by desire or external conditions.

Essence. Seed, germ or nucleus of a human, animal, vegetable, or inanimate entity having highly integrated form and substance and bearing the unexpressed potential of that entity. A potential influence.

Essence-desire. Objective need or lack as motivating impulse inherent in essence.

Essence-friend. A person with whom one shares commonalities or perceived complementarities in the deeper, more individuating layers of essence.

Essence-struggle. The pursuit of real aim rooted in essence.

Essence-trait. A fundamental characteristic.

Euphoria. See "Elation."

Eureka. The experience of sudden revelation usually accompanied by elation.

Existence. The cosmos. That which is.

Experience. Actively or passively receiving energy. Imprints of past experiential events.

Experiment. The effort to deploy energy to form a vessel permitting new perceptions, experiences or outer results.

Faith. Confidence in the benevolence of existence, reinforced by moments of certainty, disposing one to undertake experiments.

False personality. An expression of selfhood grounded in emotion that is acquired through imitation and that does not derive from essence.

Family. Entities or beings sharing essence-traits.

Fate. What actually happens owing to chance as opposed to destiny.

Feeling. The center of gravity of one's Being at any given moment, connecting thought and action and providing an ongoing evaluation of one's situation.

Focus. The point of concentration of one's energy. The precise orientation of one's energy.

Form. That which enables matter to accommodate light. The intelligence imprinted upon any given matter defining its nature and potential. The second component of essence (matter being the first).

Force. Energy with a vector. Directed energy.

Genius. Precocious display of higher intelligence. The latent capacity of all human intelligence.

Giving. The act of emulating G-d.

G-d. The unknowable source of everything including endless infinity.

G-d manifest. All of Creation that is, in principle, knowable to man.

Greed. Acquired, non-essential desire characteristic of egoism and marked by excess.

Habit. Movement of energy through a well-established circuit or family of circuits.

Harmony. Coordinated functioning of one's various constituents in accordance with essence and cosmic flow.

Higher function. Incommensurately increased efficiency in modulating energy and processing reality, attributable to harmony and consistent with the evolving of a higher body.

Hope. Intuition that arouses a spark of faith as to the benevolence of existence.

Hypnosis. A trance based on suggestibility and submission.

Identification [objective]. Intentional attachment to a phenomenon connected with essence.

Identification [subjective]. Usually unconscious attachment to a phenomenon of thought, feeling or sensation such that one doesn't distinguish the phenomenon from one's sense of self.

Impartiality. An attribute of Being that permits one to see things substantially as they are.

Impression. Cosmic design or a fragment of cosmic design impressed upon essence, comprising a potential vessel (or receptacle) awakened and activated as Being in the process of realization. This term is often confused with sensory stimulus that awakens impressions.

Impulse. A surge of energy originating from inside, deriving from the establishment of connections in the unconscious. An impulse or urge, as a transitory event, is to be distinguished from desire which is more organic and pertains to essence.

Inclination. Bias or affinity determined by essence or convention.

Individuality. That which, rooted in the deeper layers of essence, makes one unique.

Intelligence. The prime attribute of mind signaling the degree to which one adapts to cosmic reality.

Intention. The disposition to act. Voluntary mobilization of energy to produce an inner or outer act.

Interest. The capture of attention through essential or artificial desire often deriving from, or producing, attachment and identification.

Intuition. A precocious channel of awareness of relatively deep layers of essence, revealing desires connected with individuality.

Layers [of essence]. Levels of potential Being which, according to the "onion" metaphor, increasingly express individuality as one approaches the center. The integral experience of any given layer from the periphery inwards provides the illusion of Being in the whole of oneself. Precocious contact with deeper layers accounts for giftedness, intuition, creativity, prophesy, "genius," and other psychic phenomena.

Level. A degree of potential or of realization.

Life. Intelligence tending to consciousness, including increasing degrees of autonomous action, adaptation and development, deriving from an almost perfect correspondence of form and matter.

Light. Energy; The energy of life. That aspect of reality a vessel (or receptacle) is meant to receive.

Love. Benevolence deriving from deep essential contact with life providing conviction concerning its supreme value.

Materiality. The measure of cosmic restriction.

Matter. The substrate of all things created. The first component of essence (form being the second). Physical matter is the ultimate crystallization and expression of cosmic restriction.

Meaning. The experience of intelligence forming as new connections lend coherence and richness to precepts and concepts.

Mechanicality (Mechanicity). A mode of manifestation requiring minimum effort and which repeats experience.

Meditation. The act of saturating oneself with aspects of a percept or concept to enhance Being.

Mind. A living receptacle (or vessel) capable of containing, expressing and expanding intelligence.

Need. Imperative desire. Desire the fulfillment of which is determining for a given state of Being.

Non-essential. Pertaining to needs, desires and experiences that do not respect the sequence of energy flow of receiving in order to give demanded by cosmic law and inherent to essential form.

Objective consciousness. The highest function of mind; state of Being encompassing objective knowledge.

Objective knowledge. Full conscious grasp of cosmic phenomena.

Objectivity. Attitude or quality of Being that gives expression to truth.

Obscurity. Obfuscation of mind, difficulty of understanding or lack of consciousness stemming from the restricting aspect of the matter.

Onion. Metaphor for essence. See "layers."

Openness. Attitude permitting new inputs and perspectives, often deriving from self-purifying efforts of detachment and disidentification such as renouncement, self-effacement and submission, collectively known as "non doing."

Paradigm. Frame of reference. Matrix of meaning.

Peak experience. Elevation of spirit or state of inspiration deriving from an experience of cosmic harmony. (Term coined by Laslow)

Personality. A complex of traits characterizing an individual.

Pleasure. The experience of desire, need or lack being satisfied. A vessel (or receptacle) receiving the energy or "light" destined for it.

Potential. The degree of reality destined for a being or entity. The highest light or finest energy that can possibly be received. Maximum or highest utility for a tool or instrument.

Purification. The process of abandoning a closed, distracted state, thereby creating openness and a new state more closely conforming to Being, as demanded by essence. Often induced through ritual and other acts of renouncement, submission and self-effacement. Preparation for real doing - the extension of influence.

Purpose. See "Aim."

Question. Attitude or state of Being-insufficiency expressing awareness that all is not known.

Race. Those with shared traits stemming from moderately deep, individuating layers of essence.

Reality. Essence and that which complements and completes essence.

Realization. The rectified expression of essence or potential.

Receptacle (or Vessel). An existing organ or the disposition of energy (e.g., the energy of attention) within a living entity to become organized in emulation of an organ, so as to be able to vibrate with and thus contain still finer energy.

Rectification. The process of becoming free of distraction; arriving at the expression of essence through Being. The aim of purification.

Reflection. Low-grade, preliminary effort of thought laboring under distraction.

Reflectivity. Quality of thought conditioned by distraction.

Resistance. The impedance of realization by restriction or distraction.

Restriction. The quality whereby all created materiality resists realization.

Science. Methodology for revealing knowledge.

Self. The center of gravity of one's being which gives the particular flavor of one's existence.

Self-effacement. The dissolution or suspension of one's sense of self, preferably in the form of openness or creative chaos.

Self-realization. The acquisition of a new degree of Being through purification or essence-struggle; the fulfillment of one's individual potential.

Self-reflection. A distraction-conditioned mode of thought that takes the self as an object rather than as process.

Shell. That aspect of self including personality and false personality crystallized under the influence of distraction that most resists the assimilation of reality. Crystallized restriction.

Shock. Sensory or conceptual input that awakens impressions connecting one to reality through Being, at least momentarily.

Short-circuit. Non-essential pathways of energy (discharges) constituting one's shell including such distraction-inspired phenomena as greed, negativity, passion, and identification.

Sleep. Lack of self-awareness.

Soul. Generic name for the innermost part. Technical name for the level of Being immediately above the spirit. Soul is the highest level of Being that does not include eternal life or the full realization of individuality.

Soul mate. A person of the opposite sex whose essence is closest and most complementary to one's own. (See essence-friend.)

Spirit. Generic name for the energy that animates the different levels of Being. Technical name for the level of Being immediately below the soul.

Spirituality. Philosophies and efforts aimed at generating Being. Term expressing the belief that existence includes more than just physical reality.

Struggle. See "Essence-struggle."

Subconscious. Unexpressed essence. That part of essence unexpressed through Being or personality.

Subjectivity. The bias given to anything, especially awareness, by the action of restriction upon one's essence or personality.

Submission. The relinquishing of one's willfulness.

Superficial. Pertaining to one's shell. Pertaining to the "higher" or "external" layers of intellect. Pertaining to the outer layers of essence. Unencompassing.

Talent. Exceptional motor, aesthetic, emotional, and/or intellectual abilities deriving from preferential contact (normally inherited) with aspects of essence. Prodigy and genius are limit cases.

Thought. The effort to assimilate reality on any level, but usually restricted by distraction to the intellect.

Thought compression. A form of concentration whereby the field of effort is narrowed to and maintained upon the object or phenomenon of contemplation longer than distraction would normally allow or convention would demand. The result of confrontative reflection.

Trace. See "Impression."

Trance. A temporary, non-banal, quasi-stable disposition of attention accompanied by a marked change in the way one experiences oneself and one's surroundings, usually beyond the control or understanding of the person so affected. Self-absorption.

Transformation. A change of Being leaving one incommensurably different in the way one experiences and processes reality. A step in the evolution of intelligence.

Unconsciousness. Everything not integrated within or illuminated by the light of awareness, including one's repertoire of knowledge, feelings, skills, habits, etc., including the subconscious. Everything not included in awareness. Everything not included in Being.

Understanding. The energy of comprehension that maintains faith and animates the soul.

Utopia. Ideal conditions of existence favoring self-realization and the development of Being through the pursuit of essence-desire.

Vessel. See "Receptacle."

Vision. Higher Being-function using the energy of wisdom and allowing the direct acquisition of objective knowledge.

Will. The full, organic, conscious expression of a given level of essence-desire.

Willfulness. The tendency to accord to an impulse the status of will.

Wisdom. The energy of certainty and eternal life.

• • •

REFERENCES

Abell, Arthur. *Talks with the Great Composers*. Garmisch-Partenkirchen, Germany: G.E. Schroeder-Verlag, 1964.

Barrett, William. *Irrational Man: A Study in Existential Philosophy*. Doubleday & Co., Inc., 1958.

Bassis, Edward M. Unpublished paper.

Berg, Philip S. *Power of Aleph Beth*. Jerusalem - New York: Research Centre of Kabbalah Press, 1988.

— *Kabbalah for the Layman*. New York: Research Centre of Kabbalah Press, 1988.

— Translator, compiler and editor of *The Zohar Parshat Pinhas*. Jerusalem - New York: Research Center of Kabbalah Press, 1987.

Bernanos, Georges. *Diary of a Country Priest*. Translated by Pamela Morris. New York: The Macmillan Co., 1937.

Bohm, David. "The implicate order and the super-implicate order." In *Dialogues With Scientists and Sages: The Search for Unity* by Renée Weber. London & New York: Routledge & Kegan Paul, 1986.

— *Wholeness and the Implicate Order* (London: Routledge & Kegan Paul, 1980).

Branden, Nathaniel. *The Psychology of Self-Esteem*. New York: Bantam Books, March 1971.

Breton, Denise and Christopher Largent. *The Soul of Economies*. Wilmington: Idea House, 1991.

Briggs, John. *Fire in the Crucible*. Los Angeles: Tarcher, 1990.

Bronowski, J. *The Common Sense of Science*. Harvard University Press, 1953.

Brunton, Paul. *Reflections on My Life and Writings*. New York: Larson Publications, 1987.

Brussel, James A. and George La Fond Cantzlaar. *The Layman's Dictionary of Psychiatry*. New York: Barnes and Noble, 1968.

Buber, Martin. *Between Man and Man*. Translated by Ronald Gregor Smith. New York: Macmillan Paperbacks, 1965.

Campbell, Joseph. *The Hero with a Thousand Faces*. Princeton, 1949. Princeton University Press.

Castaneda, Carlos. *Power of Silence*. United Kingdon: Black Swan Books, 1988.

— *The Eagle's Gift*. New York: Penguin Books, 1982.

Cattell, R.B. and H. J. Butcher. *The Prediction of Achievement and Creativity*. Bobbs-Merill, 1968.

Csikszentmihalyi, Mihaly. *FLOW*. New York: Harper Perennial, 1991.

The Creative Process. Edited by Brewster Ghiselin. New York: Mentor Books, 1964.

— Spender, Stephen. "The making of a poem."

Dass, Ram. "Promises and Pitfalls of the Spiritual Path." In *Spiritual Emergency*.

Drexler, K. Eric. *Engines of Creation*. New York: Anchor Books, 1990.

Emerson, Ralph Waldo. *Essays: First and Second Series*. New York: Vintage Books, 1990.

Fieve, Ronald R. *Moodswing*. New York: Bantam Books, 1981.

Frankl, Viktor E. *The Will to Meaning*. New York: NAL Penguin, 1988.

Friedman, Maurice. *Problematic Rebel: An image of modern man*. New York: Random House, 1963.

Gasset, Jose Ortega y. "In Search of Goethe from Within." Translated by Willard Trask. Edited by William Phillips and Philip Rahv. *The New Partisan Reader, 1945-1953*. New York: Andre Deutsch, 1953.

Ghiselin, Brewster, editor. *The Creative Process*. New York: Mentor Books, 1964.

Grof, Stanislav and Christina Grof. *Spiritual Emergency*. Los Angeles: Tarcher, 1990.

Gurdjieff, G. I. *All and Everything*. United Kingdom: Routledge and Kegan Paul, 1973.

Haddon, F.A. and H. Lytton, "Teaching approach and the development of divergent thinking abilities in primary schools." In *British Journal of Educational Psychology*, 38 (1968):171.

Halevi, Z'ev Ben Shimon. *The Work of the Kabbalist*. United States: Samuel Weiser, Inc., 1985.

Harman, Willis and Howard Rheingold. *Higher Creativity*. Los Angeles: Tarcher 1984.

Hesse, Hermann. *Siddhartha*. Translated by Hilda Rosner. New York: New Directions Paperback, 1951.

Hoffer, Eric. *The True Believer*. New York: Harper & Row, 1951.

Hofstadter, Douglas R. *Metamagical Themas: Questing for the Essence of Mind and Pattern*. United Kingdom: Penguin, 1985.

Hudson, L. "The question of creativity." In *Contrary Imaginations*. Methuen, 1966; Penguin books edition, 1967.

Janov, Arthur. *The Primal Scream*. New York: Dell, 1975.

Jeffrey and Lilly. *John Lilly so far . . .* Los Angeles: Jeremy P. Tarcher, 1990.

Johnston, Charles M. *The Creative Imperative*. Berkeley, California: Celestial Arts, 1986.

Man Alone: Alienation in Modern Society. Edited with an introduction by Eric and Mary Josephson. New York: Dell, 1969.

Jung, Carl Gustav. *The Undiscovered Self*. Translated by R. F. C. Hull. New York: Mentor, Nal Penguin Inc., 1958.

— *Modern Man in Search of a Soul*. Translated by W. S. Dell and C. F. Baynes. New York: Harcourt Brace and Jovanovich, 1933.

Keller, Evelyn Fox. *A Feeling for the Organism: The Life and Work of Barbara McClintock*. W. H. Freeman and Company, 1983.

Kierkegaard, Sören. *The Present Age*. Translated by Alexander Dru. New York: Harper Torchbooks, 1962.

Koestler, Arthur. *The Act of Creation*. London: Pan Books, 1966.

Laing, R.D. "Transcendental Experience in Relation to Religion and Psychosis." In *Spiritual Emergency*. Edited by Stanislav Grof and Christina Grof. Los Angeles: Tarcher, 1990.

Leary, Timothy. *Flashbacks*. Los Angeles: Tarcher, 1990.

Leonard, George B. *The Transformation*. Los Angeles: Jeremy P. Tarcher, 1981.

Lyman, Stanford M. and Arvin B. Scott. *A Sociology of the Absurd*. New York: Meredith Corporation, 1970.

More, Sir Thomas. *Utopia*. Translated by Peter K. Marshall. New York: Washington Square Press, 1966.

Munk, Rabbi Elie. *The Call of the Torah*. Translated from the French by E.S. Maser. Jerusalem - New York: Feldheim Publishers, 1980.

Needleman, Jacob. *Money and the Meaning of Life*. New York: Doubleday, 1991.

Ouspensky, P.D. *The Psychology of Man's Possible Evolution*. New York: Vintage Books, 1973.

— *In Search of the Miraculous*. New York: Harcourt, Brace & World, 1949.

Pascal, Blaise. "Pensees." In *Man and Spirit: The Speculative Philosophers*. Edited by Saxe Commins and Robert N. Linscott. New York: Washington Square Press, 1966.

Peat, David F. *Synchronicity: The Bridge Between Matter and Mind*. New York: Bantam New Age Books, 1988.

Perry, John Weir. "Spiritual Emergency and Renewal." In *Spiritual Emergency*. Edited by Grof and Grof. Los Angeles: Jeremy P. Tarcher, 1990.

Poincaré, H. *The Foundations of Science*. Science Press, 1924.

Rand, Ayn. *Atlas Shrugged*. New York: Signet Books, 1960.

— *The Romantic Manifesto*. New York: Signet Books, 1975.

Razik, T. A. *Explorations in Creativity*. New York: Harper & Row, 1967.

Robbins, Tom. *Jitterbug Perfume*. New York: Bantam Books, 1985.

Rogers, C. R. "Toward a theory of creativity." *ETC: A Review of General Semantics*, 11, 1954.

Rushdie, Salman. *The Satanic Verses*. United Kingdom: Viking Penguin, 1988.

Russell, Peter. *The Global Brain*. Los Angeles: Tarcher, 1983.

Schachtel, Ernest G. "On Alienated Concepts of Identity." *The American Journal of Psychoanalysis*. November 1961.

Simmel, Georg. *The Sociology of Georg Simmel*. The Free Press of Glencoe, Inc., 1950.

Spender, Stephen. "The making of a poem." *The Creative Process*. Edited by Brewster Ghiselin. New York: Mentor Books, 1964.

Stace, W.T. *Mysticism and Philosophy*. Los Angeles: Tarcher, 1987.

Stanford, M. Lyman and Arvin B. Scott. *A Sociology of the Absurd*. New York: Meredith Corporation, 1970.

Tart, Charles T. *Waking Up — Overcoming the Obstacles to Human Potential*. Boston: New Science Library, 1986.

Tesla, Nikola. "My Inventions." *Electrical Experimenter*, 1919.

— *My Inventions*. Zagreb: Skolsa Kjiga, 1977.

Theon, Max. *Visions of the Eternal Present*. Jerusalem: Argaman, 1991.

— *La Tradition Cosmique*. Paris: Bibliothèque Chacornac, 1904.

Thoreau, Henry David. "The Journal." *Walden and Other Writings*. Edited by Joseph W. Krutch. New York: Bantam Books, 1982.

— "Life Without Principle." *Walden and Other Writings*.

— "Walden." *Walden and Other Writings*.

— "The Maine Woods." *Walden and Other Writings*.

Van den Haag, Ernest. "Of Happiness and Despair We Have No Measure." In *Mass Culture*. Edited by Bernard Rosenberg and David White. The Free Press of Glencoe, 1957.

Weber, Renée. *Dialogues With Scientists and Sages: The Search for Unity*. London & New York: Routledge & Kegan Paul, 1986.

Weil, Simone. *Waiting for God*. Translated by Emma Craufurd. New York: G.P. Putnam Sons, 1959.

Whitfield, P.R. *Creativity in Industry*. United Kingdom: Penguin Books, 1975.

• • •

Index

abstractions 215
abundance
anesthetizing quality
of 25
effect of 27
envisioned by Project
Mind 25
freeing power of 28
of wealth and
power 25
universal 28
Accelerated Thought
19, 34, 38, 53,
55, 60
advantage over me-
chanical
thought 157
and "breakthrough"
science 214
and energy 70
and feelings of cer-
tainty 119
and psychic en-
ergy 70
and the practical im-
plications of dis-
covery 66
as a molder of cultural
environment 81
as a route to shar-
ing 121
benefitting man-
kind 54
candidates
for 42, 55, 74
creative discovery as a
means to 209
definition of 54
depleted attention
blocks access
to 125
energy is acquired
through extrapola-
tion 154
insights in the second

phase of 108
keeping on track dur-
ing 109
leads to objective con-
sciousness and im-
mortality 182
pleasure as a motive
for 133
power to overcome
distraction 19
process freed from the
usual bounds of
experimenta-
tion 155
produces clarity of
thought 119
rationale for 6
reasons for avoidance
of 71
relationship
to Eureka experi-
ence 54
with Project Mind 19
second stage of 150
self-induced bouts
of 55
self-observation as an
effect of 210
two determinants of
the capacity
for 144
visions that give it im-
petus 135
addiction
mass 26
to closure 4
addictive
needs of others 28
power
as the foundation
of evils 25
adventure 72, 75, 76
path of 5
aim
achieved through sat-

isfying channels
xiii
according to popular
wisdom 224
aimless routine 74
author's father's wis-
dom concerning 20
caring about 95
choice of 224
compass of 109
death as release for
aimlessness 187
difficulty in remem-
bering 18
efficient expression of
153
energies as means to
243
esoterism not compat-
ible with 17
full force of "self"
must be harnessed
for pursuit of xiii
half-way point 110
impossibility of at-
taining 199
materials necessary to
accomplish 17
of individuality 193
of suspending obses-
sion with matter
of this book and
project xvi
pleasure binds subject
to 133
sacrificing 224
single-minded pursuit
of 224
take stock of 6
transformation taken
as 232
transforming matter
253
worthy of the author's
full potential 15

alchemy 244, 195
alienation 51
    and distraction 197
    and success 197
    definition of 22
    expressed in estrange-
        ment from es-
        sence 117
    from ourselves 51
    produced by restric-
        tion 19
    promoted by greed 22
altruism
    as man's most distin-
        guishing fea-
        ture 12
anesthetizing
    effect of abundance
        25
    influence of matter 19
anomie
    produced by restric-
        tion 19
    promoted by greed 22
    trigger for 204
anticipation 69
    mechanism for releas-
        ing energy 139
anxiety
    from the threat of glo-
        bal holocaust 25
    increasing level of in
        the world 21
art
    and creativity 62
artificial intelligence
    208
Ashlag, Rabbi Yehuda
    L. 231
assignation See calling
    and mission
attention 50, 57, 124
    absorbed by associa-
        tive reflection 45
    distracted from seri-
        ous matters 26
    distraction's effect
        on 46
    energy of 44
    leading to immortal-
        ity 17
    quality of, related to
        Being 125
    related to effi-
        ciency 48

    use of 45
    usually insufficient
        for Accelerated
        Thought 124
    wavering 1
autism
    irrelevancy of
        cause 49
    offering immunity
        from distrac-
        tion 52
    relation to creativ-
        ity 48
    simulation of 49
awaken
    appetite for reality 25
    from reverie 3
    to adventure 7
awakening 46
    to states of higher
        consciousness 6
    subjective plus objec-
        tive dimensions in
        Accelerated
        Thought 132

Being 52, 107, 114
    determined by the
        quality of our at-
        tention 125
    related to essence 116
Being-obligation, begin-
    ning sense of 183
belonging
    as a vice 113
biology
    as a new science 29
body 80
    as a nervous cir-
        cuit 45
    energy and good will
        in 13
    materiality of 29
body-essence 143
body-mind 46, 108
    key to understanding
        the "larger real-
        ity" 46
brain   52, 68, 79
    as a catalytic agent 44
    as a nervous circuit 45
    head-brain 46
brain washing 78
breakthrough 47
    ability to produce sci-

        entific and techni-
        cal 42
    as hit-and-miss af-
        fairs 52
    bringing about de-
        mocratization of
        physical material-
        ity 38
    creative vs. establish-
        ment 209
    effect of increasing
        the frequency
        of 103
    effects of a "freed"
        mind upon 135
    establishment type 44
    few and far between
        27
    generating 103
    into true realization of
        our family-
        hood 33
    leading to prosperity
        and well-being 6
    making up for lost
        time 42
    necessity of frequency
        and high qual-
        ity 42
    passive 69
    producing a general
        awareness 33
    proposed development
        of 191
    providing a sense of
        forward move-
        ment 52
    rare ability to produce
        conceptual
        ones 43
    reason for rarity 44
    revealed through cre-
        ativity 33
    usage of, in Project
        Mind 190
Brunton, Paul ix, 21,
    41, 105, 202, 243

calling
    and conventional am-
        bition 184
    certainty of 183
    Darwinism denies 221
    investment of faith in
        89

pursuit of xv
cause and effect
as a universal
law 198
certainty 125, 129
experience of 118
intuitive
renunciation
of 143
related to Accelerated
Thought
121
change
results of the chal-
lenge of 204
complementarity 173,
185
as a connection 185
of differences 228
concepts
with images, leads to
awareness 69
conformity 145
dangers of 117
connectedness 157, 158
of the intellect and
other functions,
difficulty of 158
restrictions of 159
**connectedness-to-ideas
ratio** 157
connection
as meaning 158
as the secret to im-
mortality 158
basic motor and sen-
sory ones easily es-
tablished 158
conscience
operative in the aver-
age man 32
conscious dimension
116
consciousness
distracted 153
flame of 133
growth of 129
questions about 226
subjective 153
cosmic environment
energy of 175
cosmic law
related to mind 158
cosmic pattern
understanding of 48

cosmic reality 61
man related to 108
cosmic truth 230
of mind-body 118
cosmology
definition of 206
cosmos
as a conscious en-
tity 159
contains many levels
of energy 139
creativity inherent
in 48
creative discovery
as a means to Acceler-
ated Thought 209
creative genius
conditions for promot-
ing 62
creative thought
recognizing the crys-
tallized results
of 17
creative vision
development of 50
creativity 210
and art 62
and genius 223
and unified intelli-
gence 59
as a continuing state
of Being 59
computer "whiz-kids"
and 63
core function of 60
discouraged by dis-
traction 72
motivation for 72
price paid for a lack
of 34
process of 59
related to break-
through 33
related to the subcon-
scious 61
suffers when
blocked 56
theory of 34
Torrance's study of, in
children 222
touchstone of 224

death
and funerals 204
as the ultimate

shock 204
coming to terms
with 132
physical
as the ultimate re-
linquishing of par-
ticularity 187
produced by restric-
tion 19
root of 20
systemic 200
depletion
produced by restric-
tion 19
deprivation
with lack, inherent to
cosmic reality 201
desire 231
as a tool for eliminat-
ing distraction 178
beneficial *vs.* harmful
force 5
experience of 233
Kabbalah's two faces
of 231
destiny
actualization of 136
and true calling xv
as master 88
connection to 116
contact with others
190
conviction of being
destined for some-
thing better 73
deflected by popular
theory 221
desires ordained by
233
destined reality 75
destined to receive
154
feeling of 73
freedom to pursue 161
how and why of 213
inevitability 154
investment of faith in
89
knows requirements
of 100
mankind's ix
most salient aspect of
20
of human mind 209
pursuit of 81, 163

real life 218
realizing 224
seeking soulmate 178
discontinuity
state of 106
dissonance
dealing with 143
distraction 1, 4, 5, 6,
17, 19, 26, 178
adverse effect on at-
tention 124
breaking through the
barrier of 34
consequences of 51
discourages creativity
72
distracted awareness
inhibiting vision 61
related to reflective
thought 46
distracted state 1
distracted thought 5
final elimination
of 153
forces of 47
induced by matter 48
masks creative intelli-
gence 48
meditation as an anti-
dote to 252
problems of 4
Project Mind's com-
pensation for 180
psychological aspects
of 6
relating to suggestibil-
ity 4
Drexler, K. Eric 38

effort
Accelerated Thought
not object of xiii
and elation 220
as circuit 240
artificial effort not
sufficient 225
by-product of 136
change not object of
244
concerning autism 48
concerted x
doomed to failure 19
domain of most 243
effect of 252
extent of 20

fate of 198
for breakthrough 105
for theory's assimila-
tion 57
fortified by certainty
122
greed for effortless
existence 21
hazardous 168
inspiration for 256
intensifying 252
intuitive 251
mature 9
mental 252
modification of 139
more fulfilling 35
motor behind 149
of assimilation 144
of attention 17, 246
of childhood 158
of comprehension and
ego adaptation 57
of focusing 45
of meditation 180
of non-desire 180
of self-observation 1
of stilling the mind
179
one becomes deterred
from x
outwardly directed
xiii
releases intelligence
229
rendered unlikely 124
repeatedly 126
renewing routine 252
see Chapter 7
shared objective of
229
sincere inner 254
succeed in fulfilling
23
superhuman 177
therapeutic 252
to initiate Accelerated
Thought 74
to maintain preten-
tious aims 163
to make sense of con-
tradictions 190
to sacrifice stability
22
energy
ability to tap cosmic

reservoirs of 139
contained in the cos-
mos 139
level differs according
to the form of mat-
ter 67
of our cosmic envi-
ronment 175
reconciled with mat-
ter 243
released by anticipa-
tion 139
released from a higher
dimension 142
results of abuse
of 225
trapped 72
with matter, two sides
of a coin 125
with matter and form,
three aspects of
one thing 66
essence
alienation and 117
as a recorder of in-
stinct 60
clarity of thought
related to 119
complete contact
with 108
double nature of 176
expressed through the
growth of Being
116
link with intu-
ition 108
related to clarity of
thought 119
related to the soul and
the subconscious
59
source of feeling of
destiny 73
essence-desire 233, 181
as our personal
truth 5
found in all man-
kind 188
essence-mind 108
essence-truth 108
essential aim 153
**Eureka experi-
ence** 53, 55
Archimedes 53
leading to Accelerated

Thought 54
quality of a 220
relation to Acceler-
ated Thought 54
vs. peak experience
181
**expanding conscious-
ness**
other ways of "know-
ing" 146
extrapolation 155
as a source of energy
for Accelerated
Thought 154
extrapolative thought
155

fairy tales
need for 75
feeling
and reality 184
as ordinary feel-
ing 153
need for new pros-
pects for sur-
vival 151
of wonder 218
related to outer trans-
formation 143
requirements of 144
usefulness of 142
"flow" 220
forces of destruction 33
form
with matter and en-
ergy, three forms
of one thing 66
Frankl, Viktor E. xiii
Fuller, Buckminster
21, 89
**functional complex-
ity** 39
future shock 26

genius
and the status quo 43
constrained 44
difficulty in recogniz-
ing 58
isolated instances
of 52
manifestation of 43
trademark of 54
with creativity, often
associated with

mental and emo-
tional disorders
223
goal
anticipation of 185
as trap 175
choosing 111
conventional 87
forgetting 109
goal-defined intelli-
gence 170
influenced 198
likelihood of mistrust 5
nature's and man's 210
"never be deterred in"
(author's father's
wisdom concern-
ing) 20
of reaching conscious-
ness 243
of the human mind
209
predestined 188
process of realizing 5
selecting 78
socially sanctioned
189
take stock of 6
"to physically over-
come death" (Rob-
ins quotation) 160
greed
epidemic proportions
of 21
for material advance-
ment 21
modern consequences
of 22
predicted results of its
irrelevancy 23
promoted by media 21
satisfaction will not
extinguish human
failings 25
Gurdjieff, G. I. 202

higher thought
empowerment of 153
hypnosis 180, 59

idea-universe 156, 157
idiots savant 49
immortality 243
as an attribute of intel-
ligence 244

aspirations to 17
connection as the se-
cret of 158
physical and spiri-
tual 160
realization of 243
stems from Acceler-
ated Thought 182
implicate order 44, 111
inner chatter
as a psychological
crutch 3
produces barriers 4
related to distrac-
tion 2
insight 135, 127
meta-insight 135
inspiration
difficulty of becoming
a breakthrough 47
instinct
in man and animals
216
related to the con-
scious and the un-
conscious 59
underestimated 217
integration
increasing possibility
of 131
intellect
as ordinary mind 153
related to an organ-
ism's internal com-
munication 144
intelligence 39, 40
and immortality 244
artificial intelli-
gence 39
as "astral body" 244
as predictor of suc-
cess 58
checks and balances
with matter 207
innate to our human-
ness 40
insect *vs.* animal 208
living 125
manifested through
creativity 50
of silicon chips 39
replacement for mat-
ter 39
true expression
of 157

intelligence (mind) 118
intuition 221
   essence as the source
      of 73
   intuitive insights 127
   link with essence 108

koan 185
Koestler, Arthur 42,
   43, 44, 217

lack
   with deprivation, in-
      herent to cosmic
      reality 201
Laing, R. D. 41
Leary, Timothy
   rules for pursuing un-
      conventional
      ends 56
life-intelligence 158
limitation
   with restriction, the
      essence of matter
      and the root of
      death 20
   governing our
      lives 33

McLuhan, Marshall
   "global village" 32
material
   abundance, effect of
      104
   needs 32
materialism
   benefits of eliminat-
      ing 25
   material needs repre-
      sent higher needs
      32
   vanity of 25
materiality 38
   nature of 239
   of our bodies 243
   satisfies some
      people 25
matter 23, 34, 35, 36
   accelerating our mas-
      tery of 23
   accessory to real-
      ity 35
   aim of suspending our
      obsession with 23
   and mind 34

   as a form of en-
      ergy 67
   as a prison 29
   as an integral part of a
      higher reality 214
   as form 200
   as mostly empty
      space 35
   attachment to 23, 25
   belief in the primacy
      of 37
   checks and balances
      with intelli-
      gence 207
   compatibility of, with
      form 39
   conquest of 34
   constraints of 39
   conversion into en-
      ergy 36
   curse or boon? 165
   deity at root of 111
   desirable refinement
      and conquering
      of 166
   devaluation of 166
   dual relationship
      with 165
   expressions beyond
      earth 36
   former scope of 35
   illusion of 35
   imposing restriction
      on humanity 19
   liberation from the
      tyranny of 135
   limit case of 200
   making ownership ir-
      relevant 27
   man under the limit-
      ing influence
      of 201
   mastery of 37
   merging with 34
   mind over 34, 38
   neutralization of 23
   of the universe 35
   physical 35
   predicted results of its
      irrelevancy 23
   producer of folly and
      corruption 32
   reconciled with en-
      ergy 243
   refinement and con-

      quering of 166
   relationship with 38
   relationship with
      mind 40
   replaced by mind 38
   replacing with intelli-
      gence 39
   restricting mind 39
   special dispositions
      of 39
   submitting to intelli-
      gence 34
   suspending our obses-
      sion with 23
   technical problems 37
   transformation of 36
   vs. spirit 35
   with energy, two sides
      of a coin 125
   with form and energy,
      three aspects of
      one thing 66
**matter-induced intoxi-
cation** 37
matter-related desires
  27
**matter-related obses-
sions** 34
meaning
   as connection 158
   connection with eter-
      nity 74
   related to intelli-
      gence 157
   revealed through in-
      sight 129
   two principal effects
      of the discovery of
      133
media
   promotes greed 21
mentation 51
mid-life crisis 69
**military-industrial com-
plex** 37
Mind 158
mind
   and matter 34
   encompassing materi-
      ality on its finest
      levels 131
   facilitating our ulti-
      mate merging with
      matter 34
   over matter 40

relationship with matter 40
replacing and restricting matter 39
mind-adventure 73, 76
mind-body 158
distorted 158
experienced as infants 118
its hidden cosmic truths 118
mind-forms 66
mission
according to Frankl xiii
how to discover 183
meaningful xiii
of human mind 209
of our soul 193
of Project Mind 52
of science 220
sense of 87, 225
More, Sir Thomas 27
mortality
bodily vulnerability leads to 125
scientific remedy for 132

Nietzsche, Friedrich 60, 95, 158

objective consciousness 133, 153, 185, 129
and a feeling of certainty 119
and the continuity between outer and inner reality 170
depends on subjective consciousness 132
first stable phenomenon of 135
meaning of 133
realization of 243
second stage of Accelerated Thought 150
stems from Accelerated Thought 182
supported by coarsest matter 243
objective reality 124
objective world phenomena 129

objectivity
term clarified 185
vs. subjectivity 110
Ouspensky, P.D. 1, 29, 212, 218

paradigm shift 32
paradigms
as traps of thought 47
of reflective thought 46
peak experience 52
definition of 68
vs. Eureka experience 181
physical reality 131
power
relation to ownership 28
predictive power 126
Primal Scream 77
Project Mind 19, 25, 29, 32, 34, 52, 54
address for 195
aims to achieve objective consciousness and immortality 243
as a haven for 147
as a supportive, protective environment for participants 147
candidates early 71
qualifications for 161
principal criterion for participation in 163
proposed environment of 164
relationship with Accelerated Thought 19
prosperity 38
effect of 37
purpose
as statement 89
author's ix, 6
correspondence with 238
deflection of 109
easily deflected from 44
force harnessed to 133
forces that dilute 18

forgetting 109
giving is our 232
is to give 174-75
not directed at virtue xiii
of animals 170
of art 213
of becoming free 172
of Creation 187
of creativity 88
of existence 95
of finding integration 87
of gifts 224
of our creation 224
of Project Mind 192
of this incarnation 178
realizing 194
religion and science as keys for understanding 186
take stock of 5
transformation not our 232
unnatural conditions as a springboard for 250
worthy of my full potential 15

reality
as a "foreign body" 143
heightened, developing a sense of 136
inner 154
its role in success 116
new ideas incompatible with 143
outer 154
physical 131
possible attunement to various levels of 141
sense of transformed through thought and feeling 184
reflection
as a two-edged sword 175
reflective thought
and perception of one's life role 174
limitation of 156

principal consequence of 210
related to distracted awareness 46
reincarnation
author's position on 178
restriction
with limitation, the essence of matter and the root of death 20

search for meaning 73
self-awareness 225
self-consciousness
stagnation of 105
self-knowledge
authentic first major step toward 245
self-realization 229, 132
potential effect of the power of 109
subjective satisfaction from 81
self-reflection 210
socialization
and candidates for Accelerated Thought 80
soul
related to our subconscious 59
spirit
freedom of, in absence of matter's oppression 103
subconscious
definition of 59
lack of contact with 60
reason for remaining submerged 61
related to Accelerated Thought 60

subjective
use of the term 236
subjective consciousness 243, 132, 124
first major step toward 245
subjectivity
conscious vs. distracted 236
problems with depending on 111
term clarified 185
vs. objectivity 110
sublimation 221
suggestibility
as an aspect of distraction 4

task
See calling and mission
tension
increasing level of in the world 21
Tesla, Nikola 86, 96, 129
Theon, Max 113, 243
thought
and reality 184
related to outer transformation 143
time
a function of materiality in man 226
alteration of, related to breakthroughs 103
related to the refinement of matter 104
spiritual time 104

transformation 36
achievable by man? 256

and the white donkey 256
changes leading to 143
of industry, predicted 23
of mankind 32
of matter 195, 36
ignored by spiritual schools 195
related to alleviating human suffering 176
prophets of 33
spiritual disciplines commonly strive for 254

unified consciousness
as our birthright 61
universal abundance
prospects of 38
utopia 33

vision
if valid, becomes reality 154
vocation
as alternative to dispersion 69
as statement 89
desire, seed of 5
meaningful xiii
of Project Mind 162
professional 74
selecting 78
worthy of my full potential 15

will
as committed conviction 153

Wright, Frank Lloyd 106

• • •

Quotation Index

Abell, Arthur 41
Allen, Woody 135
Anonymous 228

Barr, Shari R. 241
Barrett, William 248
Barth, John 70
Bassis, Edward M. 76
Berg, Philip S. 31, 75,
  214, 230, 253, 254
Bernanos, Georges 93
Bohm, David 24, 111
Branden, Nathaniel
  85, 114, 137, 203
Breton, Denise and
  Christopher Lar-
  gent 24
Briggs, John 44, 86
Brilliant, Ashleigh
  vii, 89, 107, 150
Bronowski 27
Brunton, Paul ix, 21,
  41, 105, 202, 243
Brussel, James A. and
  George La Fond
  Cantzlaar 43
Buber, Martin 86

Campbell, Joseph 255
Camus, Albert 71,
  235
Casals, Pablo 121
Castaneda, Carlos
  221, 222, 253
Cattell, R. B. and H. J.
  Butcher 52
Connolly, Cyril 73
Conrad, Joseph 217

Csikszentmihalyi,
  Mihaly 219

Dass, Ram 255
Dirac, Paul 66
Drexler, K. Eric 38
Duncan, Isadora 62

Ecclesiastes 31, 103
Einstein, Albert 32,
  37, 125, 154
Eluard, Paul 108
Emerson, Ralph
  Waldo 118, 141,
  159

Fieve, Ronald R. 223,
  250
Frankl, Viktor E. xiii
Freud, Sigmund 62
Friedman, Maurice
  89, 244
Fuller, Buckminster
  21, 89

Gasset, José Ortega y
  65
Ghiselin, Brewster
  57, 71, 87, 88, 109
Golas, Thaddeus xi,
  23, 131
Gurdjieff, G. I. 202

Haddon, F. A. and H.
  Lytton 50
Halevi, Z'ev Ben
  Shimon 244

Harman, Willis and
  Howard Rheingold
  33, 58, 222, 226,
  256
Hesse, Hermann 97
Hoffer, Eric 80, 113,
  138, 248
Hofstadter, Douglas
  R. 45
Hudson , L. 50, 58
Huxley, Aldous 80
Huxley, T.H. 215

Janov, Arthur 61, 79,
  126
Jeffrey and Lilly 126
Jerome, Jerome K.
  147
Johnston, Charles M.
  232
Jung, Carl Gustav
  115, 147, 205,
  213, 216, 233, 248

Keller, Evelyn Fox
  23, 47, 53, 57, 60,
  91, 128, 134, 146,
  150, 215
Kierkegaard, Sören
  72, 74, 199
Koestler, Arthur 42,
  43, 44, 217

Laing, R. D. 51
Leary, Timothy 56
Lee, William Francis
  III 1
Leonard, George B.

44, 46, 203, 204
Lyman, Stanford M.
   and Arvin B. Scott
   93

McClintock, Barbara.
   See Keller, Evelyn
   Fox
Maharishi, Ramana 90
Mann, Thomas 51
Mead, Margaret 54
Miller, Henry 110
More, Sir Thomas 27
Murphy's Law 198
Munk, Rabbi Elie 201

Needleman, Jacob 202
Nietzsche, Friedrich
   60, 95, 158

Orr, Leonard 122
Ortega y Gasset, Jose
   65
Ouspensky, P.D. 1,
   29, 212, 218

Pascal, Blaise 234
Peat, F. David 35, 48,
   50, 131

Perry, John Weir 84
Poincaré, H. 64, 65
Proverbs 61, 133,
   138, 154
Psalms 53, 63, 66, 83,
   127, 140, 156
Puccini, Giacomo 41

Rand, Ayn 99, 116,
   146, 151, 160, 242
Razik, T.A. 222
Robbins, Tom 160,
   202, 223
Rogers, C. R. 33, 209
Rudhyar, Dane 158
Rushdie, Salman xiii

Schachtel, Ernest G.
   134
Shah, Idries 93
Shaw, George Bernard
   145
Simmel, Georg 254
Socrates 93
Spender, Stephen 94,
   199
Stace, W. T. 255

Steiner, Rudolf 95
Strauss, Richard 86
Suzuki, Roshi 109

Tesla, Nikola 86, 96,
   129
Theon, Max 113, 243
Thoreau, Henry David
   21, 26, 58, 75, 76,
   85, 94, 97, 99,
   141, 157, 214

Van den Haag, Ernest
   223
Vonnegut, Kurt Jr.
   150

Weber, Renée 78, 226
Weil, Simone 55
Whitfield, P. R. 84
Whitehead, Alfred
   North 209
Wilbur, Richard 210
Wright, Frank Lloyd
   106

Yeats, W. B. 106
Yoda 85

Zusya 218

• • •